THE FRENCH WELFARE STATE

THE FRENCH WELFARE STATE

Surviving Social
and Ideological Change

Edited by
JOHN S. AMBLER

NEW YORK UNIVERSITY PRESS
NEW YORK AND LONDON

Library of Congress Cataloging-in-Publication Data
The French welfare state : surviving social and ideological change /
edited by John S. Ambler.
    p.   cm.
Includes bibliographical references and index.
ISBN 0-8147-0599-5 (alk. paper)
1. France—Social policy.   2. Welfare state.   I. Ambler, John S.
(John Steward)
HN425.5.F74   1991
361.6'1'0944—dc20   91-9734
                                                              CIP

New York University Press books are printed on acid-free paper,
and their binding materials are chosen for strength and durability.

CONTENTS

PREFACE

Much of the world failed to notice that in the 1960s and 1970s France developed into one of the more generous welfare states in the world, translating an old commitment to "solidarity" into a body of social policies that rescued the elderly from poverty, drew virtually the entire population beneath the tent of health and old-age insurance, dramatically expanded opportunities for secondary and higher education, and increased aid to the handicapped and to single mothers. The purpose of this book is to describe and explain this transformation, as well as to examine some of the new problems that have emerged in its wake. The initial chapter, which places France in comparative and historical perspective, offers an overview of the causes of welfare state development. The third chapter, by David Cameron, presents statistical evidence and analysis of the growth of French social expenditures, while Bruno Jobert's concluding essay measures the French welfare state against the standard of social justice, with particular reference to unemployment. The other chapters are devoted to different fields of social policy— pensions, health, housing, and the family.

These essays present no central thesis, although there are recurring themes. We find that in the case of France partisan ideology has had a very limited impact on social policies. Although the French welfare state was strengthened by the center-left governments of the immediate post–World War II years, conservative governments were primarily responsible both for the creation of a general social insurance plan in 1930 and for the dramatic expansion of social benefits in the 1960s and 1970s. There is essential agreement among the authors that the socialist governments of the 1980s did not fundamentally change the social policies that they inherited. This is not to say that ideas have not been important—particularly the concept of social solidarity, which is considerably older than the welfare state.

A second recurring theme is the institutional complexity of the French social security system, attributable in part to the mutual society *(mutualité)* tradition upon which it was built. Our authors are not wholly agreed on the consequences of that complexity. Douglas Ashford and Nathan Schwartz find that it contributes to flexibility in policymaking, while Bruno Jobert concludes that the "corporatist" elements in the administration of French social security strengthen organized interests and inhibit changes required to meet new social neeeds. The difference among the authors stems in part from the different specific policies that they examine, but also from their different perspectives: Ashford, a careful student of institutions, views the diverse network of plans as an excellent fit between the state and French society; Jobert, judging from the perspective of social justice, sees the present system as a source of inequality. We did not attempt to eliminate such tensions from this collection. Let the reader decide.

This book grew out of a symposium in the fall of 1988 on the impact of partisan ideology on French social policy. The original papers, by Douglas Ashford, David Cameron, and David Wilsford, all have been revised for this collection. In order to complement this set of papers, we were fortunate to be able to commission contributions from three specialists: Nathan Schwartz on housing, Rémi Lenoir on family policy, and, finally, Bruno Jobert, who, in a capstone essay, evaluates the performance of French social policy. I am particularly indebted to Douglas Ashford, who was instrumental in locating our three additional collaborators, and to Martin Schain of New York University, who encouraged us to turn the symposium papers into a book. I am also grateful to the American Philosophical Association for summer research support in France, and to Chris Salmon, who assisted with the translation of the chapter by René Lenoir. I am responsible for the final translation of that chapter and of the one by Bruno Jobert. The Jobert chapter is an enlarged version of an article that appeared in *L'Année Sociologique* in 1990. We thank the editors of that review for permission to reprint it here in translation. All other chapters appear here for the first time.

Houston, Texas   JOHN S. AMBLER

CONTRIBUTORS

John S. Ambler is Professor of Political Science at Rice University in Houston, Texas. His recent work has focused primarily on the politics of education in France and Britain. He is author of *The French Army in Politics, 1945–1962*; *The Government and Politics of France*; and editor and coauthor of *The French Socialist Experiment*.

Douglas E. Ashford is Andrew W. Mellon Professor of Comparative Politics, University of Pittsburgh, Pennsylvania. He has written extensively on policymaking and politics in France, most often in comparison with Britain. His major recent books are *The Emergence of the Welfare States* and the edited study, *Political Discretion: Intergovernmental Social Transfers in Eight Countries*.

David R. Cameron is Professor of Political Science at Yale University. He has contributed articles to a number of journals, including the *American Political Science Review*, *Comparative Political Studies*, *Comparative Politics*, *European Journal of Political Research*, *International Organization*, and *Journal of Politics*, as well as to several edited volumes. His areas of research include comparative political economy and mass politics in Europe, North America, and the Pacific. He is currently writing a book entitled *Essays on the Public Economy* and is coediting a book on *Political Control of the Soviet Economy*.

Bruno Jobert is Director of Research with the National Center for Scientific Research (CNRS). He is associated with the Centre de Recherche sur la

Politique, l'Administration et le Territoire (CERAT), which is affiliated with the Fondation Nationale des Sciences Politiques and with the Institut d'Etudes Politiques of Grenoble within the Université des Sciences Sociales in Grenoble. His extensive writings on French social policy include *Le social en plan* and, with P. Muller, *L'Etat en action*.

Rémi Lenoir is *maître de conférence* at the University of Paris. He is also affiliated with the Centre de Sociologie Européenne in Paris. He is author of numerous publications on French society, many concerning family policy, and coauthor of *Initiation à la pratique sociologique*.

Nathan H. Schwartz, Associate Professor of Political Science at the University of Louisville, has previously written on British and American housing policy. His chapter in this volume is one result of a year of field work in France. A subsequent year and a half of research in Germany under the auspices of the Alexander von Humboldt Foundation provided additional material for his book-in-progress comparing housing policy in France, Germany, the United States, and the United Kingdom.

David Wilsford is Assistant Professor of Political Science in the School of International Affairs, Georgia Institute of Technology. He is author of a number of articles on French policy and politics and of *The Politics of Health in France and the United States*.

1

IDEAS, INTERESTS, AND THE FRENCH
WELFARE STATE

JOHN S. AMBLER

The welfare state commonly is viewed as being a creation and creature of the Left, associated in the United States with the New Deal, in Britain with the postwar Labour government, and in Scandinavia with the political dominance of social democratic parties. This is an image that is nurtured by socialist leaders such as former Prime Minister Pierre Mauroy, who in 1986 prefaced a book by a former member of his staff with these words

Our social protection was constructed by means of a permanent battle against conservatism and liberal dogmas, and it is primarily the Left that deserves the credit, for it was always at the front of the battle. The antagonism between liberals and supporters of progress has known its truces, it has never ended (Johanet 1986, 5; translation mine).

French conservatives did indeed delay a number of social programs in the nineteenth and early twentieth centuries; yet the chapters to follow, and particularly that of David Cameron, suggest that partisan ideology has had little impact on social policy in the Fifth Republic. Indeed, as Cameron clearly demonstrates, it was during the long period of conservative dominance of French government from 1958 to 1981 that France rose to her current posture as one of the world leaders in commitment to social welfare. In 1981, when François Mitterrand became president, France was spending 29.5 percent of its Gross Domestic Product on health, education, retirement, and other social programs. Of the nineteen industrial democracies belonging to the Organization for Economic Cooperation and Development, only five spent more (OECD 1985, 21).

How can one account for this apparent paradox? How and why has France become a leading welfare state, even though its parties of the Left rarely have been in power? How has the French welfare state developed and in what ways is it distinctive? How does its manner of development affect its contemporary effectiveness? These are the questions to which this chapter will seek answers.

CAUSES OF THE WELFARE STATE: INDUSTRIALIZATION,IDEAS, INTERESTS, AND INSTITUTIONS

As Harold Wilensky, among others, has reminded us, all industrial societies are welfare states when compared with poorer societies, even though the form and degree of social protection vary considerably among wealthy countries (Wilensky 1975). Since the welfare state in France shares many common features with welfare states in other countries, it seems appropriate to begin a search for causes with an analysis of the broader phenomenon. The welfare state is primarily the product of three forces: the social effects of industrialization, changing ideas about the proper functions of government, and the constraints of existing institutions. These factors sometimes are viewed as alternative explanations, as in Anthony King's emphasis on ideas (King 1973). They are more properly viewed as complementary explanations, each illuminating a portion of a complex mosaic. Yet another explanation of the continuing spread of the welfare state in the 1960s and 1970s centers on the expansion of benefits to the middle class and on the accompanying attachment of that class to their "entitlements." We will examine each of these explanations, looking first at the experience of other Western democracies, then more carefully at that of France.

Industrialization

The fundamental conditions that made the welfare state both necessary and possible were created by the industrial revolution. In the course of the nineteenth and twentieth centuries, in those countries that are now wealthy democracies, traditional support systems for the care of the sick, the old, and the destitute tended to break down in the process of urbanization. The extended family gradually gave way to the nuclear family. Workers drawn off the farm and into industrial firms found that their jobs were vulnerable to the business cycle. The center of population shifted from the village, where family, friends, and the church usually were available in time of need, to the mass society of the city. The industrialization that created the need for new collective support systems also provided the wealth required to fund them. Wilensky's study of government spending patterns in sixty-four countries in the mid–1960s found that, when the countries were ranked according to per capita Gross National Product, public expenditures for social programs rose regularly from 2.5 percent of GNP in the poorest quartile to 13.8 percent in the wealthiest quartile (Wilensky 1975, 19).

In France, as in Britain, the traditional social welfare system of the eighteenth century is separated from the modern welfare state of the twentieth by an era of laissez-faire liberalism, varying in intensity and consistency, in which all forms of social assistance that might weaken the worker's incentive to work and to save were viewed as harmful to society (Rimlinger 1971, 35–86). (We will use the term *liberalism* in its historical and European sense, rather than in its American meaning.) In prerevolutionary France, the Church was the primary agency responsible for education, heath care, and care for the poor. Its charitable activities were supported indirectly through the state by means of legally mandatory tithing. Beginning in the sixteenth century the state extended supervision over certain of these activities, while leaving their administration essentially in Church hands. The first recorded public assistance agency, the Grand bureau des pauvres de Paris, administered by the Church, was established in 1544 (Jambu-Merlin 1970, 10). The Revolution of 1789 destroyed this ancient welfare system without creating new institutions in its place (Jambu-Merlin 1970, 11). Despite the affirmation in the Declaration of the Rights of Man of "the right to public assistance," for a century and more following the Revolution proponents of liberalism fended off demands for the creation of a national system of state-supported public assistance.

It was the perceived failure of classical liberalism to deal with the harmful social effects of industrialization that led to the demand for national social insurance in the late nineteenth and early twentieth centuries. The liberal solution to social risks—savings and private insurance—worked only for workers who earned wages sufficient to permit saving and only so long as savings banks, insurance companies, mutual societies, and companies with pension funds remained solvent (De Swaan 1988, 143–51).

The logic of industrialization contributed in an important way to the

TABLE 1.1

Social Expenditure in OECD Countries, 1960–1981[a]
(Health, Education, Pensions, Unemployment, Welfare) (in percentages)[a]

	Expenditure Share of GDP		Annual Growth Rate of Real GDP		Annual Growth Rate of Deflated Social Expenditure	
	1960	1981	1960–75	1975–81	1960–75	1975–81
Canada	12.1	21.5	5.1	3.3	9.3	3.1
France	13.4[b]	29.5	5.0	2.8	7.3[b]	6.2
Germany	20.5	31.5	3.8	3.0	7.0	2.4
Italy	16.8	29.1	4.6	3.2	7.7	5.1
Japan	8.0	17.5	8.6	4.7	12.8	8.4
United Kingdom	13.9	23.7	2.6	1.0	5.9	1.8
United States	10.9	20.8	3.4	3.2	8.0	3.2
Average of above countries[e]	13.7	24.8	4.7	3.0	8.3	4.3
Australia	10.2	18.8	5.2	2.4	9.6	2.4
Austria	17.9	27.7	4.5	2.9	6.7	5.0
Belgium	17.4	37.6[c]	4.5	2.2[c]	9.3	7.9[c]
Denmark	—	33.3[d]	3.7	2.2	—	5.4[d]
Finland	15.4	25.9	4.5	2.9	7.5	4.8
Greece	8.5	13.4[c]	6.8	3.5	8.4	9.4[c]
Ireland	11.7	18.4	4.3	3.5	9.1	7.1
Netherlands	16.2	36.1	4.5	2.0	10.4	1.6
New Zealand	13.0	19.6	4.0	0.4	5.5	3.5
Norway	11.7	27.1	4.3	4.1	10.1	4.6
Sweden	15.4	33.4	4.0	1.0	7.9	4.7
Switzerland	7.7	14.9[d]	3.4	1.7	7.6	2.7[d]
OECD average[e]	13.1	25.6	4.6	2.6	8.4	4.8

Source: O.E.C.D. 1985. *Social Expenditure, 1960–1990.* Paris: O.E.C.D., p. 21.
[a]Or latest year available. [b]Excluding education. [c]1980. [d]1979. [e]Unweighted average.

development of the welfare state, yet it is an incomplete explanation, for levels of social expenditure vary substantially among the industrialized democracies. A study for the Organization for Economic Cooperation and Development (OECD) showed that as of approximately 1980, the percentage of Gross Domestic Product consumed by public expenditures on education, health, pensions, unemployment compensation, and other income maintenance programs and welfare services, as shown in table 1.1, ranged among member countries from only 14.9 percent in Switzerland and 17.5 percent in Japan to 36.1 percent in the Netherlands and 37.6 percent in Belgium (OECD 1985, 21). Some exceptional cases are partially explicable within the context of the industrialization argument. In Japan, the extended family has remained more intact than in most urban societies, while the strong social solidarity of traditional Japanese culture somehow has survived in the form of a sense of community within modern firms, a phenomenon that is more rarely found in other countries (Pempel 1982, 136; Maruo 1983). Other differences in the extent of social expenditures (e.g., between the United States and Europe, or between Switzerland and Scandinavia) and in the form of social programs (e.g., tax deductions for health costs in the United States, government health insurance in France, the National Health Service in Britain) call for exploration of other possible causal factors, notably ideas and institutions.

Ideas

The extent to which the development of social programs is linked to the strength of the political Left has been a subject of vigorous academic debate in the past two decades. Although the majority of studies have shown a positive relationship between the strength of the Left within the government and expansion of public social expenditures, research findings vary greatly, depending upon the time period, countries, and measures selected (e.g., Wilensky 1975; Castles 1982; O'Connor 1988; Heidenheimer 1989, 222–29; and Cameron chap. 3 below). As we have already noted, partisan ideology does not offer a good explanation for trends in social policy in the French Fifth Republic. Yet, if the welfare state is not simply the creation of socialist reformers, clearly it was built with the assistance of political leaders who believed that the state should tend to the needs of the sick, the elderly, and the destitute. Who were they and why did they press the state into new functions?

Early leadership in the development of the welfare state did not come from the most democratic countries, but rather from countries in which suffrage was comparatively limited and parliament still played a subordinate role (Flora and Albers 1981, 70). The pioneer, of course, was Otto von Bismarck. Under his leadership as chancellor, the German Empire in the 1880s became the leader in social insurance with the establishment of mandatory programs for the protection of workers from loss of income through industrial accidents, disability, and illness. Against the opposition of the trade unions and the outlawed Socialist party, but with the support of segments of big business, Bismarck sought to strengthen the loyalty of the working class to the monarchy by appealing to the rank and file over the heads of their partisan and union leaders (Rimlinger 1971, 112–30; De Swaan 1988, 187–92). In essence, the Bismarckian social reforms represented an attempt to strengthen a conservative and authoritarian order against the growing threat of socialism.

If social reformers of the nineteenth century often were conservatives seeking support from the working class, as in Austria, Sweden, and Finland as well as in Germany, reformers of the early twentieth century more often came from the ranks of liberals. In Britain the Pension Act of 1908, which offered small, noncontributory, means-tested pensions to persons over the age of seventy, and the National Insurance Act of 1911, which established a national contributory pension plan, were the work of a liberal government (De Swaan 1988, 192–97). Although big business played a lesser role in the British reforms than in the German, British liberals who not long before had preferred private market solutions to social problems now came to believe that private insurance was inadequate to solve problems of poor health and economic insecurity in the working class, both of which were perceived to threaten economic efficiency (Rimlinger 1971, 60). The revelation of the pitiful state of health of working-class youth in recruitment for the Boer War; the strain on private retirement plans caused by an increasing lifespan and by the bankruptcy of employing firms; and the influential Booth study showing that 38 percent of persons surveyed over the age of sixty-five were paupers— all of these contributed to the conversion of liberal leadership. More importantly, and in sharp contrast to the Bismarckian reforms, a coalition of trade union leaders, friendly society officials and Labour politicians lobbied hard for a national pension system, convincing liberal leaders that reform was good politics (Heclo 1974, 158–78).

In chapter 2 below, Douglas Ashford shows clearly that there was at least as much debate about social insurance in France as in Britain in the 1880s and beyond. Those debates, and the succession of legislative proposals that they concerned, were of great importance in developing the notion of social solidarity. In larger private firms, company insurance developed rapidly in the first four decades of the twentieth century. No general government program was implemented, however, until the law of 30 April 1930, which established health, maternity, disability, death, and old-age insurance for all workers below a certain income level. There were significant precursors, including publicly mandated disability and old-age insurance for miners, sailors, and railroad workers in the 1890s, establishment in 1898 of employer responsibility for victims of industrial accidents (but without the creation of an insurance fund), and a more general pension plan that was enacted in 1910 but that died when the courts refused to enforce contributions. In 1930, only some 15 percent of the employed French population was covered by public pension insurance (compulsory or subsidized by the state), compared to 64 percent in Germany and 90 percent in the United Kingdom (Flora and Heidenheimer 1981, 76).

France adopted general and mandatory social insurance more than forty years after Germany and some twenty years after Britain. How can the French delay be explained? Why were ideas that were so much in the air left so long without fulfillment? The industrialization argument is suggestive, but finally inadequate, for although France was less industrial and much less urban than Britain in the early twentieth century, Germany in the 1880s was only beginning her industrial boom. A partial answer to this puzzle is offered by Abram de Swaan: the primary class enemy of the welfare state, small independent entrepreneurs and landholders, was stronger politically in early twentieth-century France than in either Germany or Britain (De Swaan 1988, 197–204, 216–17). Large-scale employers in all three countries tended ultimately, if reluctantly in the French and British cases, to accept mandatory social insurance as a way of improving labor-management relations and of relieving employers of responsibility for unfortunate employees. In France, small entrepreneurs, who enjoyed face-to-face relations with their employees and perceived of the good society in highly individualistic terms, saw no advantages and many inconveniences from social insurance, including increased costs and bureaucratic interference (Hatzfeld 1971 chaps. 3, 4). Unsurprisingly, attitudes tended to reflect economic interests. The petty bourgeoisie was particularly numerous in France. In the 1901 French census, 8 million people classified themselves as *patrons*, or owners of businesses, compared to 11 million workers and 7 million artisans (De Swaan 1988, 80). Small businessmen and property holders were strongly represented in centers of political power, particularly in the Senate, which overrepresented rural and small-town France and which regularly weakened or struck down social legislation passed by the Chamber (Hatzfeld 1971, 60–62). De Swaan explains the 1930 reform in terms of changes in class structure:

It was above all the gradual erosion of the political privileges that private property conferred, the irresistible increase of wage-earners and of the more privileged *salariés* among them, the growth of large enterprise and big government that finally shifted the balance and allowed a succession of center-right cabinets an opportunity to succeed where earlier governments had failed (De Swaan 1988, 203).

From 1906 to 1926, the proportion of the industrial work force employed in single-person firms dropped from 26.7 percent to 13.8 percent, while the proportion working in firms of more than one hundred employees increased from 24.8 percent to 36.8 percent (Hatzfeld 1971, 259). Policy changed as the ideas of policymakers changed. Ideas changed in part because of experience, but also because the social context out of which they emerged was also changing.

If France lagged behind most of Western Europe in instituting mandatory social insurance, she was a European leader in elementary education in the last three decades of the nineteenth century. The percentage of children of elementary school age enrolled in school in France rose from 57 percent in 1870 to 86 percent in 1900, while in the same period it rose in Germany from 67 percent to only 73 percent and in England and Wales from 49 percent to 74 percent (Benavot and Riddle 1988). One of the principal motives behind this massive effort was to form loyal republicans outside the now suspect Catholic schools, in order to bind a new generation to the young Third Republic (Prost 1968, 191–219). Another was to create the only kind of equality that was compatible with classical liberalism: equality of opportunity. Middle-class France could understand the logic of allowing each child the opportunity to rise to a place in society merited by his talent and effort. In France, as in the United States, classical liberals could support public education while denouncing most other government ventures into the social arena. Yet in France, unlike America, a full secondary education was reserved for a small elite until the dawn of mass secondary education in the 1950s. Although secondary enrollments of girls expanded under the Third Republic, as did enrollment of both sexes in "higher primary" courses, the number of boys in full secondary programs *(lycées* and *collèges)* was essentially the same in 1930 as it had been in 1880 (Prost 1968, 328–31). In its perspective on secondary and higher education, French liberalism in the early twentieth century was heavily laced with Malthusianism.

If the French bourgeoisie was divided over social insurance, so too was the French labor movement. Unlike the British labor movement, in which Marxism never played an important role, French labor already before the turn of the century was divided between radicals like Jules Guesde, who opposed all measures that might extend the life of capitalism, and reformers like Jean Jaurès, who believed that real improvements in the lives of workers could be achieved without revolution (Hatzfeld 1971, 184–216). This, of course, is the schism that has weakened the political influence of the Left throughout most of French republican history (Ambler 1985, 4–20). It was not until after World War II that the French Communist Party rallied to the idea of mandatory social insurance and participated in the coalition government that enacted the social security reforms of 1945 and 1946.

In the coalitions that have helped to build European welfare states, one often finds devout Catholics alongside moderate socialists and progressive liberals. Since World War II, Christian Democratic parties have contributed substantially to expansion of social programs in countries such as France, Germany, Austria, Belgium, and the Netherlands. Indeed, Christian Democratic support for the welfare state is one of the principal reasons why models that attempt to explain expansion of social expenditure in terms of the strength of parties of the Left have had such mixed results (Wilensky 1981; Castles 1982, 7–77, 83–88).

The French Catholic Church, we have seen, was the principal social welfare agency of the Old Regime. By attacking the Church as an institution, the French Revolution opened a schism between French Catholics and the republic that was not fully breeched until 1944, with the emergence of a new Christian Democratic party, the Popular Republican Movement. Particularly during the peak of anticlericalism, beginning with the Dreyfus Affair in the 1890s and culminating in formal separation of church and state in 1905, devout French Catholics were reluctant to support social reforms that might bind the public to the secular republic and extend the powers of its state apparatus. Nonetheless, there developed in the nineteenth century a school of social Catholicism that helped to shape the French climate of opinion on social policy (Ashford 1986, 82–85). Among the leading figures in this movement was an advisor to Napoleon III and founder of the influential journal, *Réforme Sociale*, Fréderic Le Play, whose social ideal was the extension to society as a whole of the virtues of the devout family: affection, harmony, morality. Other Catholic social reformers issued from the Ecole Polytechnique and the Ecole des Mines to play leading roles in the field of voluntary insurance and in the high civil service (Ashford 1986, 83). The Church hierarchy in the nineteenth century generally was unfriendly to any hint of socialism; yet by the 1890s there was a small group of Catholic socialists in the Chamber of Deputies. More important, an influential group of Catholic reformers, who believed that the social obligation of the state extended well beyond the defense of property, made its contribution to a growing national sense of social solidarity that provided the base for the later development of social security.

The great importance that French Catholics attached to protection of the family is reflected in their strong support for family allowances, which, as Rémi Lenoir argues in chapter 5, have been given an especially high priority in France. Catholic countries generally have devoted more resources to family allowances than have Protestant countries, but nowhere more than in France, where, on this issue, Catholics found common cause with republicans who sought to stimulate population growth through a system of payments for each child in a worker's family. Catholics made their own important contribution to the popular French doctrine of "familialism." Family allowances first were introduced by Catholic employers within private firms before they were generalized under state mandate in 1932. As one of the coalition partners in the first governments of the Fourth Republic, which sought to extend and integrate the social security system, the Popular Republican Movement insisted that family allowance funds should continue to enjoy privileged autonomy.

In chapter 5 below, Rémi Lenoir examines the ways in which French ideas and policies regarding the family have changed since 1932 in response to changes in social structure. In the early years of the family allowance program, family policy rested on a broad consensus in support of a conception of the "traditional family" in which the mother remained at home with her three or more children. By the 1970s, with the divorce rate rising, cohabitation by unmarried couples becoming more commonplace, the women's movement challenging traditional paternal privileges, and almost two-thirds of women under forty-five in the work force, the emphasis of policy shifted from keeping the mother at home to supporting costs of childrearing, whatever the occupational or marital status of the mother. Although family policy survived and retained some of its initial bias toward large families, it increasingly became a vehicle for aiding low-income families. Here is a fascinating example of social policy changing to reflect new social structures and new conceptions of social roles.

Many social and political groups, including the reformist Left, contributed to the growing consensus that resulted in the establishment of a national social security system in April of 1930. The final act, packaged to include government payment of a portion of the costs for farmers and placed along-side tax reductions to help overcome the reservations of the business community, was put in final form by a center-right government led by André Tardieu and passed by a National Assembly in which the Center and Right enjoyed more than a fifty-seat majority (Goguel 1946, 246; Hatzfeld 1971, 150–53). It was the French Right, not the Left of the Cartel des Gauches or of the Front Populaire, which gave France a social security system after decades of debate. The conversion of the French Right apparently was the result of a convergence of factors, including the hope for electoral gain, the growing size of firms, the inadequacies of private insurance in an increasingly urban society, the search of large employers for improved worker morale and increased efficiency, and the influence of reformist Catholics in some conservative circles. From a Marxist perspective, the French social security act, like the welfare state as a whole, was an attempt by the owning classes to pacify the working class (e.g., Offe 1984). From the perspective of social reformers who viewed harmony between the classes as a desirable and honorable goal, not as a cover for exploitation, social security served a high moral purpose as well as a practical one. In fact, the motives of French conservative social reformers no doubt were mixed, including a desire to win popular support (and in so doing to deny the Left credit for social security), a preference for social harmony as a contributor to economic efficiency, and a Catholic conception of the ideal society as a moral, caring community.

Interests

French conservatives not only presided over the inauguration of national social security; they sometimes contributed to its expansion, as did Christian Democrats in Germany after 1949, conservatives in Britain in the 1950s and 1960s, and the "bourgeois" government of Sweden from 1976 to 1982. As the welfare state expanded, conservatives found a new motive to protect it: their predominantly middle-class constituencies became beneficiaries along with the working class. In most of Europe, social insurance programs originally designed to protect limited groups of workers (miners, steelworkers, railroad workers, civil servants) from risk of accident, illness, disability, or poverty in old age had a tendency to expand over time to cover the whole of the working class and ultimately the entire population. As coverage and benefits expanded, so too did the social basis of political support for the welfare state. Once included in the social support system of national insurance, even more affluent occupational groups developed loyalty to it. As Goodin and LeGrand put it in the title of their book, in the developed welfare state "Not Only the Poor" benefit (Goodin and LeGrand 1987). Indeed, as these authors show for Britain, relatively affluent citizens get more than their share of such public services as health and education beyond the age of sixteen (Goodin and LeGrand 1987, 92). It is not surprising that conservative governments are almost as protective of the welfare state as those of the Left.

The reformist Left historically has viewed the welfare state as a device for redistributing income from the rich to the poor in order to create a more egalitarian society. Recent research has begun to shed some light on the very complex question of who actually benefits from the welfare state. Jean-Pierre Jallade and his associates, in a study of Germany, Great Britain, France, Sweden, and Hungary, conclude that social programs—particularly cash payments rather than services—do indeed redistribute income, although more from young people to older people (who are heavy users of health services, as well as the beneficiaries of pensions paid for by employed workers) than from rich to poor (Jallade 1988, introduction and conclusion). They find that the redistributive effect of the welfare state has decreased in the postwar period, largely as the result of three trends noted particularly in the 1970s: "earnings-related benefits expanded considerably at the expense of flat-rate benefits; reliance on social contributions, especially employers' contributions, increased at the expense of tax revenue; and non-state social programmes gained significant ground in the areas of retirement and health care" (Jallade 1988, 257). The general trend has been toward what Jallade calls the "Bismarckian tradition" of the welfare state, in which the emphasis is more on maintaining the individual's customary income than on equalizing incomes—that is to say, more on security than on equality.

Jallade places France very much in the Bismarckian tradition in that means testing is rare, most benefits are universal, many (pensions, unemployment compensation, and sickness pay) are linked to former income, and funding comes largely from contributions of employers and employees rather than from a progressive income tax. In 1982, social security contributions made up 43.2 percent of all French taxes and paid for over three-fourths of all social benefits (Jallade 1988, 11, 223). Although some two-thirds of the social security contribution is paid by the employer, the result is only mildly redistributive if one assumes that much of the employer's contribution otherwise would have gone to the employee in higher salary. Economists differ as to whether employers' contributions are shifted to consumers in higher prices or absorbed by employees in lower wages, yet figures on comparative wages in Europe, where wages typically are lower in countries, such as Italy and France, with high levels of employer contributions, suggest that at least within the European Community it is the employee who bears the primary burden (Jallade 1988, 232).

Social benefits as a percentage of household disposable income rose dramatically in France, from 19.3 percent in 1960 to 35.3 percent in 1983; yet out of this impressive total, in the latter year only 6 percent of all benefits were means-tested (Jallade 1988, 224, 226–27). The result is a fairly flat distribution of benefits. In one study using 1979 data, households headed by employed manual workers, with an average annual primary income of 58,200 francs (not counting social security contributions), received another 24,300 francs in social benefits, increasing their primary income by 42.7 percent, while households headed by professional and managerial personnel, with an average primary income of 162,700 francs, received 19,400 francs in benefits, representing 11.9 percent of their primary income (Gombert 1985, cited in Jallade 1988, 229). Apart from the retired and unemployed population, for whom social benefits were almost double all income from other sources, the net result was relatively "equal" in the sense that all occupational groups received roughly similar benefits. Since social benefits represent a much larger share of income for workers than for professionals, incomes after social transfers clearly are more equal than are primary incomes, as shown in table 1.2 (Jallade 1988, 231). If, however, one views the purpose of social benefits to be redistribution of income from the more affluent to the less affluent, the French welfare state contributes only modestly to this goal. The major beneficiaries are retired and unemployed persons, whose income index in 1979 rose from 35 percent of the average income before social benefits to 72 percent after benefits. The income gap between occupational groups narrows somewhat after social benefits, largely because of the dramatic redistribution to the nonemployed and some decline in the relative position of upper-income occupations. Manual workers, it will be noted, remain in virtually the same relative position—at about 80 percent of the average income—after social benefits have been distributed.

Some social programs are more redistributive than others, although most contain features that limit redistribution. Among the most redistributive are the "minimum insertion income," created in 1988 to support certain disadvantaged, unemployed persons during job training, and "social aid," this

TABLE 1.2

Effects of Social Benefits on Income Inequality, 1970–1979 (primary income excluding employees' social contributions)

	1970		1975		1979	
	Average Primary Income	Primary Income Plus All Social Benefits	Average Primary Income	Primary Income Plus All Social Benefits	Average Primary Income	Primary Income Plus All Social Benefits
Independent workers (Non-farm)	261	214	263	208	274	209
Professional and managerial workers	239	208	235	198	229	181
Independent farmers	143	125	137	118	138	118
Middle-level managerial workers	132	121	132	117	129	110
Clerical workers	93	90	93	88	94	85
Manual workers	79	80	80	81	82	82
Agricultural wage-earners	56	59	67	69	64	68
Nonactive persons	33	60	38	68	35	72
TOTAL	100	100	100	100	100	100

Source: Jean-Pierre Jallade, ed. 1988. *The Crisis of Distribution in European Welfare States.* Stoke-on-Kent: Trentham, 231.

Note: These index figures represent the income of each occupational group as a percentage of average income of all groups combined.

being the remnant of public assistance after most of its functions had been absorbed by social security (Thévenet 1989). Since 1988 social aid has been primarily a responsibility of the departments; it offers assistance to many of those who fall between the cracks of social security, particularly old people, children, and the handicapped. In 1987 all benefits paid out under social aid amounted to less than 4 percent of expenditures under social security (INSEE 1989, 158, 219).

The French system of compulsory health insurance distributes essentially the same level of benefits to all income groups, with the greater demand of low-income groups for hospital care and sickness benefits being offset by the greater demand of high-income groups for specialized medical and dental care; yet contributions rise with income (INSEE 1984, 366; Jallade 1988, 235). In January 1984, ceilings on wages subject to health contributions were eliminated, leaving employers to pay 12.6 percent of gross wages and employees an additional 5.5 percent on all wages paid. The result of level benefits, combined with contributions proportional to wages, represents a significant redistribution of income. Redistribution from rich to poor is limited, however, by the greater life expectancy of high-income groups. A study by the National Institute of Statistics and Economic Studies (INSEE) found that in the period 1975–1980, the probability of death among men in the thirty-five–sixty age group varied from 9.3 percent among teachers, liberal professionals, and high level managers to 20.9 percent among agricultural workers, unskilled and semiskilled workers, a difference attributable largely to higher death rates in the latter group from cancer, cirrhosis of the liver, alcoholism, and accidents (INSEE 1984, 355–56). In France as in most societies, older people are the heaviest users of health care. Those individuals from low-income groups who survive to old age receive on average far more in health benefits than they pay in through contributions; since in fact a disproportionate number of older people are from higher income groups, the overall redistributive impact of the health care system is more limited than it might appear.

Pensions under French social security are inherently less redistributive than health benefits. Since they vary according to past contributions and income, pensions serve to perpetuate into retirement differences in incomes established during years of employment. Redistribution is more between generations in this pay-as-you-go system than between income groups, again directing the greatest benefits to those who live longest. Nonetheless, certain features of social security narrow income differences among the retired. At the end of 1987, 1.4 million persons who had contributed too little to be eligible for a normal pension were receiving an "old-age minimum" benefit of 2,658 Fr per month for a single person and 4,746 Fr for a couple (CERC 1988, 106). Pushed upward by the Socialist Government after 1981, this *minimum vieillesse* reached the level of the minimum regular pension by the mid–1980s. Among a number of policies that particularly improved the situation of retirees from low-income groups in the 1970s and 1980s were the more rapid increase of basic pensions (12.5 percent annually from 1968 to 1979) compared to supplementary pensions (10.5 percent annually in the same period), the differential in compulsory health contributions owed by retired people from 1 percent on basic pensions to 2 percent on supplementary pensions, and lowering of the retirement age from sixty-five to sixty in the early 1980s, allowing workers who went to work at an early age the option of retiring at full pension at age sixty (Jallade 1988, 238–40, 246–47). Early retirement, which favors those who left school for the job market at age sixteen or eighteen, is partial compensation to the working class for the greater longevity of upper-income groups. By the late 1980s, social security pensions provided replacement ratios of 55 percent to 70 percent of preretirement income, with low- and middle-income pensioners near the top of that range. In sum, although pensions are designed more to allow retirees to maintain their accustomed standard of living than to equalize incomes, the redistributive impact of the French system is not inconsequential.

As shown by Rémi Lenoir in chapter 5, family benefits as a proportion of all social benefits have declined sharply since the 1950s and have been targeted more and more toward lower income groups. Basic family allowances are universal, but other types of family benefits such as the housing allowance, the "complementary" family allowance, and loans to young couples, are means-tested. The downward redistributive effect of means-tested programs is overridden, and even reversed, however, if one takes into account the effects of tax deductions for children, which award the greatest benefits to those in higher income groups. In 1982, a family with a gross monthly income of 6,597 Fr per month and with two children over the age of three was eligible for monthly family benefits of 621 Fr plus a tax advantage of 178 Fr, for a net gain of 799 Fr, compared to a family with the same number and age of children but with a gross monthly income of 19,792 Fr, which was entitled to benefits of 466 Fr plus a tax advantage of 898 Fr, for a net gain of 1,364 Fr (INSEE 1984, 211).

The Socialist Governments of 1981–1986 significantly increased family allowances and limited tax deductions to 7500 Fr per child, yet they also introduced two new benefits available to all families without restrictions on income. The tradition of universal benefits is far from dead. Although the various means-tested benefits administered within family policy are important income supplements for families at the lower end of the income hierarchy, French family policy viewed as a whole, taking tax benefits into account, is not an effective means of income redistribution from the affluent to the poor.

Unemployment compensation, like pensions, blends the principles of income maintenance and income redistribution. It serves as an important mode of income redistribution between the employed and the eligible unemployed. Yet its generosity depends largely on the former salary of the beneficiary. In 1982 replacement rates were set at 77 percent of former salary for workers earning only two-thirds of the average wage, 65 percent for those exactly on the average, and only 54 percent for those whose salary had been double the average. The highest compensation was set at 2.7 times the lowest compensation, still a substantial range of incomes, but narrower than within the employed population (Jallade 1988, 241). Faced with unemployment that eventually rose above 10 percent and an accompanying rise in the costs of compensation, the Socialist Government in the fall of 1982 tightened eligibility requirements, with the result that the proportion of all unemployed persons receiving compensation dropped from 70–72 percent in 1982 to 60 percent in 1984 (Jallade 1988, 247). Young people with little or no job experience were particularly affected by the tighter requirements. The growth in the number of unprotected "unemployables" presents a problem that Bruno Jobert addresses in the final chapter of this book.

Yet another policy area with mixed effects on social equality is education. The development of the French welfare state in the postwar period coincided with a dramatic expansion of secondary and higher education, as the government struggled to expand facilities to meet rapidly growing demand. Some scholars hold that education does not belong to the welfare state phenomenon in that it is inspired more by the principle of meritocracy than by that of equality (Wilensky 1975). A long series of sociological studies has demonstrated that, even in an era of mass secondary education, schools tend to reproduce existing elites, indeed to legitimate them by promoting a few exceptional offspring of the working class (e.g., Bourdieu and Passeron 1964 and 1970; Girard, Bastide, and Pourcher 1963; and Eicher and Mingat 1975). Higher education in particular is in good part a service paid for out of general taxation revenue for the primary use of the middle class; that is to say, it is a negative income transfer. Minimal tuition fees and guaranteed access to the university for all holders of the *baccalauréat* are rights every bit as important to middle-class as to working-class students, as shown by their repeated mass demonstrations against attempts to impose "selection."

Yet there are still good reasons to consider education along with other social services. As we have seen, education is not unique among social services in offering greater benefits to the affluent than to the poor. Moreover, free or low-cost education has come to be considered a right every bit as sacred to citizens of the welfare states as a pension or unemployment compensation. Without the social mobility that it allows, even the model welfare state could be led by a closed aristocracy of educated families.

Even though in France as elsewhere children from affluent and educated families succeed much better in school than those from poor and poorly educated families, one finds on close inspection that opportunities for upward mobility through education have improved since 1945. Important steps along the way were extension of the school-leaving age from fourteen to sixteen in the Debré Law of 1959, the creation after 1963 of a common middle school, the College of Secondary Education (CES), with a common trunk of liberal arts instruction for grades six and seven (6ème and 5ème), and the formal abolition of tracking in these middle schools in the Haby Reforms of 1975. Coupled with a growing popular appetite for education in a period of affluence, these reforms helped to transform French society from one, in the late 1940s, in which most children were out in the work force by age fifteen, to one in the late 1980s in which 87 percent of seventeen-year-olds were still in school (MEN, *Note d'Information* 90: 02, 2). The percentage of the age group passing one of the versions of the state secondary examination, the *baccalauréat*, rose from approximately 5 percent in 1950 to 36 percent in 1989 (*Le Monde de l'Education*, no. 168, 4). Enrollment in higher education grew from 210,000 in 1955–1956 to 1,300,000 in 1989–1990, en route to an official projection of two million by the year 2000 (*Le Monde de l'Education*, no. 172, 116–19).

Forty years ago the long jump in one generation from industrial worker to the liberal professions was almost unthinkable. Today it is still rare, but more possible. Children from families headed by an industrial worker (which comprise over a third of the French population) constituted 3.7 percent of all university students in 1959–1960 and approximately 13 percent in the 1980s (MEN, *Note d'Information* 1979: 42, and MEN 1985, 41). This gain is partially nullified by two factors, neither of which is unique to France: the tendency of working-class students to leave the university sooner than middle-class students, and the escalation of educational credentials required by employers as the pool of degree holders expands. Data for 1978–1979 show that students from families headed by an industrial worker made up 14.9 percent of all university students in the first two-year cycle, 10 percent of those in the second, full-degree cycle, and 7 percent of those in the third, doctoral cycle (MEN, *Note d'Information* 1979: 42, table III). They are poorly represented in the prestigious *grandes écoles* and in programs leading to the more lucrative professions. Raymond Boudon has offered a persuasive explanation of this phenomenon from a rational choice perspective: a student whose parents never took the *bac* is likely to feel himself a success at having completed a two-year diploma, while the child of professional parents must push ahead much further in order to avoid being the family failure (Boudon 1973). Incentives for children to succeed in school are also partly the function of the relative value that families place on education in different social milieux, whatever the educational achievements of the parents.

Despite recurring warnings of declining standards, the educational level of the French population as a whole is higher than at any time in history (Garin, Inciyan, and Lamoure 1989). The common middle school, even taking into account the informal tracking practices that frequently have developed, has contributed to equality of opportunity by delaying the age of academic segregation from eleven to approximately fourteen, allowing slightly more opportunity for late bloomers to prepare for the *bac* and higher education. Nonetheless French education, and hence French society, remains clearly hierarchical. The massive influx of *baccalauréat* holders into the universities has diminished the prestige of these institutions and enhanced that of the selective *grandes écoles*. It is the latter, and particularly the National School of Administration (E.N.A.), that serve as the royal gateway into high positions not only in public administration but also in politics and industry (Suleiman 1978). In few democratic societies are so many national leaders chosen from such a narrow educational elite. The *grandes écoles* emerged from the 1980s with their prestige and independence largely intact, despite earlier threats by the Socialist Party to merge them with the universities.

While still in opposition in 1978, the Socialist Party drafted a plan for education that acknowledged the educational handicaps of children of poorly educated parents and rejected meritocracy as an objective:

It is in no way a question of "equality of opportunity" understood as a kind of race where one tries to line up all candidates at the start and let the best one win. . . . The practice of class struggle teaches us that inequalities are primarily social in nature and that these are the ones that first must be remedied. To fight against inequalities is also to refuse an ideology that privileges the cadre of the nation, as opposed to other citizens (Parti Socialiste 1978, 19; translation mine).

More than a decade later, after experiments with "Priority Education Zones" and new secondary programs intended to bring "80 percent of the age group to the level of the bac," according to the slogan of Mitterrand's second education minister, Jean-Pierre Chevènement, French education remains meritocratic, with few second chances available to those who fail. Socialist governments in the 1980s essentially continued the expansion of education begun by their conservative predecessors (Ambler 1985, 116–44). As *baccalauréat* programs multiply, a new hierarchy emerges with the science-math *bacs* at the peak. As higher education enrollments explode, programs open to all *bacheliers* decline in value while those to which recruitment is by competitive examination rise. Here, as in other policy domains, the Socialists seem to have accepted a goodly measure of inequality of results (Charlot 1989).

With the exception of the chronically unemployed, the French safety net provides effective protection against the risks of illness, accident, and old age. If it maintains incomes more than redistributing them, if it is paid for by regressive payroll taxes rather than by a progressive income tax, the reason may be that the leading political parties as well as the population are accustomed to this style of welfare state. It emerged from the era of strong socialist majorities (1981–1986) with a slightly more egalitarian impact, but with its essential character intact: it is a system that lends security to the more affluent as well as the less.

Institutions

While it is true that all industrialized societies have moved toward the welfare state in the twentieth century, the rates at which they have adopted social protection and the forms that that protection has taken vary enormously. One of the causes of differences between nations is the impact of existing institutions, both governmental and private. Douglas Ashford, who is a leading exponent of an institutional approach to social policymaking, puts it this way: "Perhaps the welfare state was neither pushed nor pulled into existence by inexorable economic and social forces as much as it was the product of institutionalized searching, experimentation and accumulation within the democratic framework of each country" (Ashford 1986, 27–28). In chapter 2 below, he shows that in the French case the welfare state evolved out of a strong tradition of mutual societies (*mutualités*) and took the form of a complex system of multiple and partially self-administered plans in which the boundaries between public and private, state and society, were blurred. The argument is reminiscent of that of Peter Hall, who suggests that economic policymaking is best understood by examining the nature of private institutions (trade unions, employers associations, banks) as well as public institutions (Hall 1986).

According to another variant of the institutional perspective, the development of compulsory and universal social protection is the result of efforts by the state to strengthen its legitimacy while expanding its controls over society (e.g., Rimlinger 1971). While suggestive, the "state-building" interpretation of the growth of social protection overstates both the autonomy of political power and the unity of the state. In inaugurating compulsory social insurance in Germany, Bismarck did indeed seek to strengthen the state, but only because it was serving the goals of a socially and politically conservative monarchy. French Republicans in the Third Republic clearly favored the creation of mass elementary education as an instrument for strengthening the state, but only because the state was under their control.

Rather than risk reifying the concept of the state by assuming that it is a single, autonomous actor, we would do better to look closely at the variety of interests represented by governmental institutions (Suleiman 1987; Almond 1988; Ambler 1988). In the Third Republic, as we have noted, the Senate, "the Grand Council of the communes of France" in the famous phrase of Léon Gambetta, regularly rejected social legislation approved by the lower house. While the Senate acted as a brake on the development of social policy, representing small entrepreneurs and notables in France's many municipalities, the national civil service elite has played an important role in expanding social protection, particularly since World War II. As shown by Douglas Ashford in chapter 2, Pierre Laroque was one of the key architects of the emerging welfare state in France after 1945. The influence of men like Laroque and François Bloch-Lainé is understandable only in the context of the enormous prestige enjoyed by the high civil service in a country that long has taken pride in the quality of its central administration (Suleiman 1974, 1978).

Few democratic countries have a stronger tradition of centralized administration than does France, yet, as Ashford shows, the French welfare state is a complex mosaic of distinct plans with different levels of benefits for different occupational groups. The institutional untidiness of French social institutions can only be explained in terms of the pattern of private institutions in existence during the formative years.

Long before the central government saw fit to insure workers against accidents, illness, and death, apprentices within medieval guilds began pooling their resources to assist fellow workers. The guilds, like most other institutions surviving from medieval society, were outlawed in France in 1793 by a revolutionary government that viewed them as restraints on individual rights and threats to republican unity. In the course of the nineteenth century, workers in France, as elsewhere, sought to insure against risks by forming mutual societies. Emperor Louis Napoleon encouraged this development in the 1850s and 1860s and, by 1902, their number had grown to 13,677, with a total membership of over 2 million (Ashford 1986, 89). The *mutualités* were sufficiently powerful to impose compromises in the provisions of social insurance bills in 1910 and 1928.

The delay in enacting social insurance in France allowed private and single-industry plans to develop for much longer than in Germany and Britain, with the result that when a comprehensive social security plan was finally enacted in 1945, the constituents of existing plans were strong enough to force major concessions from government reformers who had hoped to create a unified social security system with uniform benefits. With the support of the General Confederation of Labor (CGT), miners, railroad workers, and various categories of civil servants maintained their own separate plans, within the framework of social security. As we have seen, the MRP and the Church insisted that family allowance funds retain their own autonomy. The result was great diversity of structure and of benefits, with elected union representatives directly involved in the administration of benefits alongside representatives of employers and of the state.

The evolution of social security institutions since 1945 is summarized by Ashford in chapter 2. Suffice it to say here that although there has been some tendency over time toward greater central controls and more standardized benefits, complexity and diversity on a scale that is rare in industrialized democracies have survived under the vigilant eyes of beneficiaries who prize the privileges and distinctiveness of separate plans. According to one count there were in 1984 no less than 117 distinct retirement plans within the social security system, including the "general plan," "complementary plan," and numerous "special plans" for various categories of civil servants, specific occupational groups, farmers, and self-employed persons (M. Laroque 1986, 78). There are no doubt instances where complexity allows flexibility in policy, as shown by Nathan Schwartz (chapter 6) with regard to housing, and by Douglas Ashford with respect to the financing of early retirement in the 1980s. There also, no doubt, are instances where institutionalized vested interests inhibit the reallocation of resources to groups that are not already included in the social security network, as Jobert (chapter 7) argues to be the case with the growing ranks of the unemployable. Whatever the merits and demerits of institutional complexity in the French welfare state, it has survived Gaullism and socialism to become a part of the French political tradition.

SURVIVING THE CRISIS

In France, as in most countries of Western Europe, the dramatic expansion of social expenditures largely coincided with the extraordinary period of almost three decades of economic growth that began not long after World War II. Under President Giscard d'Estaing in the years 1974–1981, French social expenditures continued to rise, at the rate of 6.2 percent annually in constant francs, even as the economy was slowing and other industrialized democracies were holding their social costs to a 4.8 percent annual increase (OECD 1985, 21). Before Giscard gave up the Elysée Palace to François Mitterrand, France had joined the international trend by shifting the priority of social policy to cost control.

The Socialist Party came to power in 1981 committed to changing the whole "economic and political system . . . on which an unjust and decadent society is built" (Mitterrand, in Parti Socialiste 1972, 8; translation mine). In a first year of frenzied activity, the government increased the minimum wage by 25 percent, family allowances by 25 percent (50 percent for those with two children), rent allowances by 50 percent, and minimum pensions by 38 percent, while reducing the allowable retirement age from sixty-five to sixty. By June of 1982, an inflation rate of 14 percent, an international run on the franc, and a stagnant economy forced the Socialists to adopt a policy of austerity. Nicole Questiaux, the Minister of National Solidarity, was quoted in the press as having told the Cabinet, when challenged on the large social security deficit, that "talking about numbers on this question is talking the language of the Right" (Ross and Jenson 1985, 45). She was replaced by

Pierre Bérégovoy, who understood that social expenditures could not be exempted from the rigors of budgetary restraint. Henceforth, until the conservative parties regained the majority in the National Assembly in the legislative elections of March 1986, socialist governments postponed costly social programs and searched eagerly for ways to control rising costs. As shown by David Wilsford in chapter 4, the French government under socialist control pursued policies of cost control in health that were basically similar to those designed by conservatives during the Giscard Presidency.

The financial problems of the welfare state were not simply the result of economic recession. Even in periods of economic growth, the welfare state in all Western democracies has been strained by an aging population, rising costs of health technology, and increasing public demand for social and educational services. For each French retiree in 1950 there were 4.62 workers on the job paying social security. By 1975, as the result of increasing longevity and moderate birth rates, the ratio had declined to 2.66 (Rosa 1982, 18). Total French expenditure on health rose from 4.3 percent of Gross Domestic Product (GDP) in 1960 to 8.6 percent of a much larger GDP in 1985 (Heidenheimer, Heclo, and Adams 1990, 85). In 1950 the majority of French children left school definitively at age fourteen and only approximately 5 percent entered institutions of higher education. By 1985, 96 percent of the twelve–seventeen age group were in school and close to 30 percent of the age group were continuing for higher education. At the lower end of the educational chain, 90.2 percent of all three-year-olds and 34.8 percent of all two-year-olds were enrolled in preelementary schools in 1981. By 1988, the respective figures were 97.4 percent and 36 percent, making France a world leader in child care and preschool education (MEN, *Note d'Information* 1989: 28).

As the proportion of national wealth being spent on social and educational programs approached or surpassed 30 percent in a number of countries in the 1980s, the "crisis" of the welfare state became a common subject of debate, even in such welfare leaders as Sweden. Everywhere governments sought to reduce costs in the 1980s, but in Britain under Prime Minister Thatcher and in the United States under President Reagan, conservative leadership mounted a fundamental assault on the whole concept of the welfare state. In these countries, as in some conservative circles on the continent, it was argued that private, market solutions to social problems are almost invariably more efficient than government programs.

Is it then the case that in the 1980s, unlike earlier periods, the welfare state became exclusively an idea of the Left? The evidence generally does not support this conclusion. Even Britain and the United States emerged from the 1980s with the basic structure of social security still intact. If there were reductions in public housing and in means-tested programs, the general entitlement programs in health, unemployment, and retirement survived largely intact. After a survey of the "welfare state crisis," Hugh Heclo concludes, "Nowhere in the developed OECD nations is it possible to find evidence of any major dismantling of the basic policy structures" (Heclo 1990, 265).

France followed this general pattern. The government of Jacques Chirac, which emerged from the legislative elections of March 1986, was more dedicated to a free-market economy than any other in the postwar period, perhaps more than any other in modern French history. The privatization drive of 1986–1987 was as dramatic as Mitterrand's nationalization drive of 1981–1982; yet social policy was largely spared the privatization cure, as shown in the chapters that follow.

The survival of the welfare state is hardly surprising, given the strength and breadth of the consensus that supports basic social security programs in most Western democracies (Smith 1987). In 1969, 1976, and 1983, the French polling institute, SOFRES, asked respondents to evaluate how serious it would be if various rights and institutions were abolished. In each of the three surveys, social security was perceived to be more important than all other rights and institutions mentioned. In 1983, 85 percent felt that the abolition of social security would be "very serious," compared to 81 percent for the right to vote, 80 percent for the right to choose one's place of employment, 70 percent for freedom of the press, 49 percent for the right to strike, and 33 percent for political parties (Schnapper 1986, 72; M. Laroque 1986, 13–14). Only 2 percent of the respondents felt that preservation of social security was "not important" or "not at all important." In view of this virtual unanimity of support, Jacques Chirac was far too skilled a politician to take on the welfare state, even if he had been inclined to do so.

Within the general consensus there is room for differences of emphasis. If moderate and conservative leadership was largely responsible for the dramatic increase of the real value of pensions in the 1970s (4.4 percent per year from 1970 to 1984), as well as for accommodating the explosion of school enrollments at the preschool, secondary, and higher education levels, it is nonetheless the Left that talks most often and most enthusiastically about social justice. In the wake of general disillusionment about government ownership of industry as the basis of the just society, European socialist parties find little to distinguish themselves from liberals and conservatives other than a commitment to greater equality among citizens. Upon coming to power in 1981, the French Socialist Party proposed a series of reforms designed to raise the floor of benefits and to target them more effectively on low-income families, including the designation of "Priority Education Zones," which received extra funds to reinforce schools with large numbers of low-income and immigrant families; increased housing allowances; and a higher floor on pensions. Although some progress was made, the results hardly matched the socialist campaign rhetoric of the pre–1981 years. The total value of social transfers increased by 5.4 percent in real terms from 1981 to 1983, but that must be compared with an average increase of more than 6 percent in the years 1974–1981 (Hall 1985, 103). The dramatic increases in social benefits of 1981–1982 were seriously eroded by high inflation, while the austerity program of 1982–1986 forced postponement of expensive new programs. Finally, the nation had become accustomed to a system of social insurance that maintains incomes more than it redistributes them.

At the end of the 1980s, France clearly was not an egalitarian society in a class with Sweden; yet the gap between rich and poor was not as great as suggested by several studies based on data from the early 1970s (Sawyer 1976; Van Arnheim and Schotsman 1982; Muller 1989; World Bank 1989, 229). Recent evidence gathered by the Centre d'études des revenus et des coûts (CERC), shows increasing equality of primary incomes after 1970 and a steady increase in social benefits. In 1962, the disposable (after tax and transfer) income of households in which the head was a senior manager was 2.9 times as great as that of households headed by industrial workers; by 1984, the gap had narrowed to 2.2 (CERC 1986). The narrowing of the gap was partly the result of a rapid increase in the number of women in the work force, particularly those in low- and moderate-income families. The biggest winners were the elderly and the unemployed. Families headed by nonemployed persons (most of them retired) had a per capita household income that was more than 25 percent below the average income in 1962; by 1984 it was 23 percent above as the result of more than a decade of real annual increases of 4.2 percent in pensions (CERC 1986). While the income gap was widening in the United States and in Britain, it seems to have narrowed in France in the 1970s and early 1980s (CERC 1986; Fourastié and Bazil 1980). This trend was most clear in the decade before the Socialist party came to power (Canceill 1990). Indeed, preliminary evidence suggests that the income gap has widened slightly since 1984, largely as a result of dramatic increases in income from investments coupled with stabilization of social expenditures (Chassard 1989).

In sum, the French welfare state emerged from the 1980s still under financial pressure, but strengthened by having survived (and tamed) the old socialism and the new liberalism. The present institutions may lack the uniformity and central controls that one might expect of a people who pride themselves in their Cartesian logic; yet, as Douglas Ashford argues in chapter 2, they seem to suit the preferences of the French, who may acclaim equality in the abstract, but rarely want it applied to their own particular privileges.

In addition to the imperative of controlling costs, a problem common to all industrialized democracies, the French welfare state in the 1990s will confront two relatively new problems. The first is structural unemployment. Unemployment rates hovered around 10 percent in the last half of the 1980s, and were much higher for young people. Bruno Jobert shows in the concluding chapter that existing institutions are designed to protect those who have been folded into the social security system through work experience. Young people who cannot find work, or long-term unemployables, who do not qualify for specific benefits like those for the handicapped, risk falling between the cracks. They fall back on the resources of their families or of local public assistance, each of which imposes a certain cost in social standing and self-esteem. Training and work-study programs designed to ease the transition into the work force will continue to have limited success so long as the economy fails to create new jobs. Policies that seek to create jobs by reducing payroll taxes undermine the already shaky financial basis of the welfare state.

A second problem is posed by rising anti-immigrant sentiment. The welfare state was built upon a growing sense of social interdependence and a resulting belief that the health and welfare of all members of society constitute public or collective goods (De Swaan 1988). Public support for means-tested programs—always less popular than entitlement programs—seems to depend upon empathy with the unfortunate, a sentiment that is strongest when all citizens can imagine themselves in the place of the poor, the disable, and the long-term unemployed. This capacity for empathy is reduced when the majority of recipients of social benefits are ethnically or culturally distinct from the majority of taxpayers. It is not surprising that there is greater resentment toward "welfare" recipients in the United States, where many belong to racial minorities, than in Sweden, where the population is ethnically quite homogeneous. In France, the immigrant population, and particularly the North African population, became a permanent presence and a volatile political issue at a time of high unemployment. Espousing such slogans as "two million unemployed = two million immigrants" and "the French first," Jean-Marie Le Pen and his Front National won 10 to 14 percent of the vote in a series of elections from 1984 to 1989. One of the tests of the welfare state in the years ahead will be the capacity of the French to extend the traditional idea of solidarity to those among them whose origins are in Algeria, Morocco, and Tunisia.

REFERENCES

Albers, Jens. 1982. "Some Causes and Consequences of Social Security Expenditure Development in Western Europe, 1949–1977." Paper presented to the International Political Science Association, Rio de Janeiro.
Almond, Gabriel. 1988. "The Return of the State." *American Political Science Review* 82: 853–74.
Ambler, John S., ed. 1985. *The French Socialist Experiment*. Philadelphia: ISHI.
———. 1988. "French Education and the Limits of State Autonomy." *The Western Political Quarterly* 41: 469–88.
Ashford, Douglas E. 1982. *Policy and Politics in France: Living with Uncertainty*. Philadelphia: Temple University Press.
———. 1986. *The Emergence of the Welfare States*. Oxford and New York: Blackwell.
Benavot, Aaron, and Phyllis Riddle. 1988. "The Expansion of Primary Education, 1870–1940: Trends and Issues." *Sociology of Education* 61: 191–210.
Boudon, Raymond. 1973. *Education, Opportunity and Social Inequality*. New York: John Wiley.
Bourdieu, Pierre, and Jean-Claude Passeron. 1964. *Les Héritiers*. Paris: Editions de Minuit.
———. 1970. *La Reproduction*. Paris: Editions de Minuit.
Canceill, Geneviève. 1990. "Le Revenu de ménages." In INSEE (1990), 138–144.
Castles, Francis G. 1982. *The Impact of Parties*. Beverly Hills: Sage.
Centre d'étude des revenus et des coûts (CERC). 1976. *Dispersion et disparités de salaires à l'etranger; Comparaisons avec la France*. Paris: Documents du CERC, no. 29–30.
———. 1986. *Le Revenu des ménages, 1960–1984*. Paris: Documents du CERC, no. 80.
———. 1988. *Constat de l'évolution récente des revenus en France (1984–1987)*. Documents du CERC, no. 89.
Charlot, Bernard. 1989. "1959–1989: Les mutations du discours éducatif." *Education Permanente* 98: 133–49.

Chassard, Yves. 1989. "La Croissance des inégalités." *Revue Politique et Parlementaire* 91: 943, 34–38.

De Swaan, Abram. 1988. *In Care of the State: Health Care, Education and Welfare in Europe and the USA in the Modern Era*. New York: Oxford University Press.

Eicher, Jean-Claude, and Alain Mingat. 1975. "Education et Egalité." In *Education, Inequality and Life Chances*. Vol I. Edited by O.E.C.D. Paris: O.E.C.D.

Flora, Peter, and Jens Albers. 1981. "Modernization, Democratization, and the Development of Welfare States in Western Europe." In Flora and Heidenheimer, eds., 37–80.

Flora, Peter, and Arnold J. Heidenheimer, eds. 1981. *The Development of Welfare States in Europe and America*. New Brunswick and London: Transaction Books.

Fourastié, Jean, and Béatrice Bazil. 1980. *Le Jardin du voisin: Les inégalités en France*. Paris: Librairie Générale Française.

Garin, Christine, Erich Inciyan, and Jean Lamoure. 1989. "Enquête: Le Niveau Monte." *Le Monde de l'Education* 156: 34–57.

Garnier, Maurice, Jerald Hage, and Bruce Fuller. 1989. "The Strong State, Social Class, and Controlled School Expansion in France, 1881–1975." *American Journal of Sociology* 95: 279–306.

Girard, André, Henri Bastide, and Guy Pourcher. 1963. "Enquête nationale sur l'entrée en sixième et la démocratisation de l'enseignement." *Population* 18: 9–48.

Goguel, François. 1946. *La Politique des partis sous la IIIᵉ République*. Paris: Seuil.

Goodin, Robert E., and Julian LeGrand. 1987. *Not Only the Poor: The Middle Classes and the Welfare State*. London: Allen and Unwin.

Hall, Peter A. 1985. "Socialism in One Country: Mitterrand and the Struggle to Define a New Economic Policy for France." In *Socialism, the State and Public Policy in France*, edited by Philip G. Cerny and Martin A. Schain. New York: Methuen.

———. 1986. *Governing the Economy: The Politics of State Intervention in Britain and France*. New York: Oxford University Press.

Hatzfeld, Henri. 1971. *Du Pauperisme à la sécurité sociale, essai sur les origines de la sécurité sociale en France, 1850–1940*. Paris: Colin.

Heclo, Hugh. 1974. *Modern Social Politics in Britain and Sweden*. New Haven: Yale University Press.

———. 1990. "Income Maintenance Policy." In Heidenheimer, Heclo, and Adams.

Heidenheimer, Arnold J., Hugh Heclo, and Carolyn Teich Adams. 1990. *Comparative Public Policy: The Politics of Social Choice in America, Europe, and Japan*. 3d ed. New York: St. Martin's.

Institut National de la Statistique et des Etudes Economiques (INSEE). 1984. *Données Sociales*. 5th ed. Paris: INSEE.

———. 1990. *Données Sociales*. 7th ed. Paris: INSEE.

———. 1989. *Annuaire Statistique de la France, 1989*. Paris: INSEE.

Jallade, Jean-Pierre, ed. 1988. *The Crisis of Distribution in European Welfare States*. Stoke-on-Kent: Trentham Books.

Jambu-Merlin, Roger. 1970. *La Sécurite Sociale*. Paris: Armand Colin.
Johanet, Gilles. 1986. *Contes et Mécomptes de la Protection Sociale*. Paris: Revue Politique et Parlementaire.
King, Anthony. 1973. "Ideas, Institutions, and the Policies of Government: A Comparative Analysis." *British Journal of Political Science* 3: 293–313, 409–23.
Laroque, Michel. 1986. *Politiques Sociales dans la France Contemporaine*. Paris: editions S.T.H.
Laroque, Pierre. 1983. *The Social Institutions of France*. New York: Gordon and Breach.
Maruo, Naomi. 1983. "The Development of the Welfare Mix in Japan." In *The Welfare State East and West*, edited by Richard Rose and Rei Shiratori. Oxford: Oxford University Press.
Ministère de l'Education (MEN). *Note d'information*. Paris: MEN (The first two digits indicate the year and the second two the number.)
————. 1985. *Tableau de Bord*. Paris: MEN.
Monde de l'Education, Le. 1990: 168.
Monde de l'Education, Le. 1990: 172.
Muller, Edward N. 1989. "Distribution of Income in Advanced Capitalist States: Political Parties, Labour Unions, and the International Economy." *European Journal of Political Research* 17: 367–99.
O'Connor, Julia S. 1988. "Convergence or Divergence?: Change in Welfare Effort in OECD Countries, 1960–1980." *European Journal of Political Research* 16: 277–99.
Offe, Claus. 1984. *Contradictions of the Welfare State*. Cambridge, Mass.: MIT Press.
Organization for Economic Cooperation and Development (OECD). 1985. *Social Expenditure, 1960–1990*. Paris: OECD.
Parti Socialiste. 1972. *Changer la Vie: Programme de gouvernement du Parti Socialiste*. Paris: Flammarion.
————. 1978. *Libérer l'Ecole: Plan socialiste pour l'éducation nationale*. Paris: Flammarion.
Pempel, T. J. 1982. *Policy and Politics in Japan*. Philadelphia: Temple University Press.
Prost, Antoine. 1968. *Histoire de l'Enseignement en France, 1800–1967*. Paris: Armand Colin.
Rimlinger, Gaston. 1971. *Welfare Policy and Industrialization in Europe, America and Russia*. New York: Wiley.
Rosa, Jean-Jacques. 1982. *The World Crisis in Social Security*. Paris: Bonnel.
Ross, George, and Jane Jensen. "Political Pluralism and Economic Policy." in Ambler (1985).
Sawyer, Malcolm. 1976. "Income Distribution in OECD Countries." In *OECD Economic Outlook: Occasional Studies*. July 1976.
Schnapper, Dominique, Jeanne Brody, and Riva Kastoryano. 1986. "Les français et la sécurité sociale, 1945–1982." *Vingtième Siècle* 10: 67–82.

Smith, Tom W. 1987. "The Polls—A Report: The Welfare State in Cross-National Perspective." *Public Opinion Quarterly* 51: 405–21.
Suleiman, Ezra N. 1974. *Politics, Power, and Bureaucracy in France.* Princeton: Princeton University Press.
———. 1978. *Elites in French Society.* Princeton: Princeton University Press.
———. 1987. *Private Power and Centralization in France.* Princeton: Princeton University Press.
Thévenet, Amédée. 1989. *L'Aide sociale aujourd'hui après la décentralisation.* Paris: E.S.F.
Van Arnheim, J. Corina M., and Guert J. Schotsman. 1982. "Do Parties Affect the Distribution of Income? The Case of Advanced Capitalist Democracies." In Castles (1982).
Wilensky, Harold L. 1975. *The Welfare State and Equality.* Berkeley: University of California Press.
———. 1981. "Leftism, Catholicism, and Democratic Corporatism: The Role of Political Parties in Recent Welfare State Development." In Flora and Heidenheimer (1981).
World Bank. 1989. *World Development Report 1989.* New York: Oxford University Press.

2

ADVANTAGES OF COMPLEXITY: SOCIAL INSURANCE IN FRANCE

DOUGLAS E. ASHFORD

The nature of the French welfare state is poorly understood in most English-speaking countries for two reasons. First, the notion of a powerful, centralized French state has often captured the imagination of both French and non-French social scientists so that the vast organizations such as the social security system that straddle the public and private sectors receive less attention. More recent scholarship has begun to uncover the complex institutional links between the state and society that make arbitrary definition of "state" and "welfare state" hard to defend (Ashford 1986). Second, for many years France, rather like the United States, was treated as a laggard among the contemporary welfare states and often excluded from early comparative studies of welfare states.[1] From a conservative perspective, it was comfortable to ignore the network of interdependency between French social policies and French politics. From a radical perspective, it was no less comfortable to think that French welfare and social services were meager concessions squeezed by weak unions from a dogmatically capitalist society.

Both of these interpretations are historically untrue and politically naive. According to Rosanvallon (1984), the concept of the *état providence* arose under the Second Empire, fostered by Le Play and Napoleon III in the form of expanded mutual insurance plans *(mutualité)*. Most of the major social debates in France take place at roughly the same time as similar debates in Britain, Germany, and the United States: social assistance for children in the 1880s; workmen's compensation in the late 1890s; social insurance experiments at the turn of the century; and, some years before their Nordic and Anglo-Saxon counterparts, family allowances in the 1930s (Levasseur 1903, 1907). To be sure, the product was not always substantial but important precedents were set that are firmly imprinted on modern French social institutions. Perhaps the best known is the solidarity movement of the radical republicans in the 1880s when the Ligue de prévoyance was second only to the Ligue de l'enseignement in advocating a fervent, secular republicanism (Stone, 1980). Preoccupied with the performance of welfare states rather than their aims and meanings, social science has seriously underestimated both the complexity and the promise of the French état providence and in doing so risks misinterpreting the meaning of the French state itself.

Instead of examining the French welfare state by means of a conventional social science design, this essay will seek to express the meaning of the French welfare state in terms of French historical experience and French political traditions (Ashford 1989). Seen in the context of French history and politics the French welfare state is an important affirmation of French political values and preferences, many of which are familiar to students of a wide variety of French policymaking situations.[2] Though the objectives and substance of policymaking on social protection and social equity may be radically different than the objectives and substance of policies dealing with economic management, industrial relations, or education, it should not be surprising that the French, like most nations, bring fundamental values and traditions to bear on social problem solving. Their concern with social issues is in many respects older than in most democracies. The revolutionary debates of 1793 outlawed vagrancy (mendacité) as a blot on society; the radical republicans and the early socialists fought bitter battles to replace the bureaux de bienfaisance (private local charity) with bureaux d'assistance publique (state-supervised local social assistance) (Ashford 1986, 135–37); and Millerand and his successors in the Ministry of Labor saw close connections between social insurance and labor policies (Derfler 1977). The French made social policies a basic instrument of state formation well before the more highly developed welfare states such as Britain and Germany.

Other major European welfare states made social insurance little more than an appendage to existing state structures. The British welfare state was left to function largely outside the sphere of government even though its progress was nonetheless frequently hampered by capricious, partisan intervention. The German welfare state never lost the authoritarian imprint of Bismarck and even in the early 1950s remained an object of intense discord between workers and employers. Perhaps because the French never proclaimed their social intentions as emphatically as other democracies, their efforts attracted less attention and on the whole are less well understood. But it is interesting to note that from its early stages the French concept of a welfare state was in many respects more comprehensive and more flexible than in most other democracies. There are no simple behavioral or quantitative measures of French "success" or "failure" but more accurately a variety of cross-cutting concerns that interlock to make the system appear more complex than it is. Outlining what these governing principles are helps us see why complexity makes sense to the French even if it makes little sense to some critics.

First, French social insurance is based on the idea of *mutualité*, or the idea that each person should voluntarily do as much as possible to provide for his or her own needs in cooperation with others. As noted, *mutualité* has an unfortunate association with the Second Empire, when the first legislation was passed, but mutual insurance was enthusiastically endorsed by the Third Republic and enormously popular in France well before there was state social insurance.[3] It is significant that in explaining the postwar social insurance legislation, the French Beveridge, Pierre Laroque (1961), assured the French people that the new system of national insurance was an extension of *mutualité*. Neither radical nor conservative critics of the contemporary welfare state are likely to agree, but the idea of mutual support enabled the French to organize a system that permits substantial redistribution among occupational groups. The French see nothing curious in the fact that the state retirement insurance (*régime général*) provides only a third of all retirement benefits while another third are provided by preexisting retirement plans (*régimes spéciaux*), most for workers considered essential to the state, while about a fifth of retirement benefits are provided by special occupational pension funds (*régimes complémentaires*) (Netter 1965, 1974). *Mutualité* is only one of many expressions in French policymaking that demonstrates how the French seldom polarize individual and public interests in devising policy solutions. Helping oneself and helping others are not mutually exclusive activities.

Second, the French have no difficulty accepting the principle that wage earners and the self-employed present fundamentally different social problems. Social insurance is basically divided between the *salariés* and the *nonsalariés*. This is in part an expression of the curious pragmatism that permeates French policymaking. Collecting funds from the self-employed is more difficult and of course the wage earners initially had more need of social protection. The result is that French social insurance is occupationally bifurcated with different conditions, benefits, and resources attached to persons in the two categories. There is one exception of great importance, the agricultural sector, where these categories have been differently applied and where, as in most countries, in one form or another farmers and farm workers get nearly all their social support from the state. This accounts for the anomaly that French agricultural *nonsalariés* (agricultural workers) got social insurance before the farm owners. Because social insurance for the entire agrarian economy is almost totally subsidized by the state through a mini–social system within the Ministry of Agriculture, the Mutualité sociale agricole (MSA), this is largely an academic distinction. The most important components of the *nonsalariés* are of course the *cadres*, who have two major funds to handle their retirement plans (AGIRC and ARRCO).[4] As will be explained below, the large reserves built up in these prosperous funds, intended to supplement white-collar pensions, enabled the Socialists to finance the costs of reducing the retirement age from sixty-five to sixty in 1983. In assessing the social insurance system, and other aspects of French policymaking, it would be misleading to convert French occupational differences into class differences.

Third, the French have always imagined social insurance systems in relation to all forms of social risk. This is not to say that all risks have been equally or even adequately treated, but since the late nineteenth century and earlier the government began to insure high-risk jobs, such as the merchant marine, mining, and railroads, while benevolent *patrons* established elaborate mutual insurance plans for their employees (Cheysson 1902; Guillot 1887; Hatzfeld 1971; Salais 1986). For example, there was never an impassioned debate over providing health insurance as part of social insurance although the liberal medical profession was fully protected and the hospital system only slowly brought under national supervision (Rodwin 1984; Jamous 1969). Many workers had some unemployment insurance well before de Gaulle created national unemployment insurance (UNEDIC) in 1958.[5] What is interesting in understanding the meaning of social insurance in France is that this decision was not considered terribly controversial. More important to an understanding of how the system acquires flexibility is the fact that unemployment insurance was not formally attached to the older system of social insurance but rests on voluntary agreements *(conventions collectives)* between the employers, negotiated by the CNPF and the unions.

Contrary to many neo-Marxist interpretations of the welfare state, the weakness and fragmentation of the French labor movement has little effect on unemployment benefits. Indeed, unemployment insurance is perhaps the most dramatic illustration of free riding in French policymaking. The three major unions, which represent no more than a fifth of French workers, monopolize the negotiations with the CNPF while the Communist unions accept the benefits while boycotting the procedures and condemning the results. All these paradoxes happily coexist because social insurance is defined to include all forms of social risk whether or not it lies within the formal state system.

Lastly, and in some ways most important in enabling the French system of social insurance to adapt to the stresses and strains of the 1980s, the French never singled out poverty as a peculiar problem nor have they ever placed fixed limits on state subsidies for social insurance.[6] This is partly due to historical accidents. In 1941, for example, Vichy had no funds to provide pensions for the thousands of unsupported elderly left without jobs and without families because of the war. The government simply seized the modest pension reserves that the first and fully capitalized pension plan had been accumulating since 1930. The entire pension system was shifted from capitalization to pay-as-you-go (*répartition*), thereby opening the way for more generous increases in better times and for inflation proofing once retirement incomes were threatened. The minimum pension (*allocation aux vieux travailleurs salariés*, or AVTS) was extended to the *nonsalariés* in 1946 and further supplemented with state funds for those outside the social insurance system with the Fonds national de solidarité (FNS) in 1956. There are to be sure poor persons in France but the exact meaning of the term is unclear (Rapport Oheix 1981; Rapport Wresinski 1987). Because these two benefits were superimposed on the entire insurance system before poverty was aggravated by recurrent inflationary spirals and because of the elaborate system of special benefits provided by the family fund (CNAF) for single mothers, handicapped children, disabled parents, etc., many of the most acute effects of poverty have been ameliorated if not eliminated. Unlike Britain, where poverty became a cause celebre as early as the 1950s, the French social insurance system does not pivot on a single, class-based issue but on the sharing of risk through multiple forms of benefits and diverse social funds.

For all these reasons, it is probably correct to say that the French find the distinction between the state and the *état providence* highly ambiguous.

Mutual support, social solidarity, risk sharing, and providing for the poor interlock in a complex set of social institutions that are an inextricable part of French political institutions. Key social and political groups are heavily involved in advisory roles, the main funds have *conseils d'administration* where employers and employees participate along with officials,[7] and the legal system provides a measure of semiautonomous decision making while still enabling government to provide fiscal and financial guidelines. The intricacies of French social insurance appear to make it obscure. In fact it is through its complexity that this system is able to provide numerous policy options, to offer alternative solutions to new needs and new risks, and to bridge, however tentatively, the interlocking aims of wage and social policies to make a step toward social democracy.[8] Thus, the French social insurance system is not only a demonstration of how a reluctant welfare state can become a leading welfare state but is also an important window through which to view the nature of the French state itself.

PUTTING THE SYSTEM IN MOTION

Unfortunately, the most detailed account of the postwar reconstruction of the French welfare state is not only in French but ends with 1952 (Galant 1955). This makes it difficult to trace the continuities of practice and preference that run through French social insurance. In France, as in Britain and Germany, there was until recently a tendency to see the postwar structure in isolation from earlier developments and to overlay evaluations of French social insurance with received knowledge on the deficiencies of the Fourth Republic. Indeed, from a comparative perspective the immediate postwar experience of France provides a better guide to the politics of policymaking than do events in Britain and Germany. The British welfare state was launched in the euphoria of victory and with almost no serious political debate while the resurrection of the German welfare state was an odd combination of Allied indecision and Adenauer's grim determination to see the prewar German welfare state reconstituted (Hockerts 1980). Though certain improvements were made by Vichy, constituting the French welfare state was a dramatic shift from the past policies and required an intense examination of French principles and preferences.

From the earliest days of the Liberation the comprehensive view of social protection prevailed. In February 1945, six months before the first order (*ordonnance*) on organizing social insurance, Blum's prewar factory committees were revived and *comités d'entreprise* were established in all firms with more than one hundred workers. Several months later another *ordonnance* created the *service national de logement*, the forerunner of the French public housing agency. Early the same year social insurance reform was introduced by appointing the Mottin committee to examine Laroque's proposals (Rapport Mottin 1945). The main dispute was over Laroque's plan to centralize all social insurance funds *(caisse unique)*, which the committee rejected by nine votes to eight, with fourteen abstentions. On the right the older occupational insurance funds considered the single national fund a financial threat and, on the left, the Catholic party (MRP) and well-developed local family associations regarded the proposal as a threat to the autonomy of the family benefit system. The CGT was so upset at seeing special retirement funds for miners and railroad workers merged with other funds that they told the Communist party they would leave the party were their privileges removed (P. Laroque 1983). The system of elections to the management committees was no less controversial. The CGT initially hoped to capture the system through factory-based elections while the family associations and the *mutualité* representatives were furious that their local powers might be jeopardized. Within a few months of Liberation social insurance was the focus of bitter political debate.

Despite the confused signals from the Mottin committee, the provisional government pressed on with its plans for a fully centralized system. Contrary to the notion of the French government as an omnipotent center of power, de Gaulle's Minister of Labor, Parodi, decided to compromise, diluting the *caisse unique* principle by agreeing on a single collection agency while restoring regional funds for medical and accident insurance and keeping locally administered social assistance *(aide sociale)*. There followed the parliamentary committee report by Buisson, a prewar social insurance official of the then non-Communist CGT. The *rapporteur* of the Consultative Assembly social affairs committee, Croizat, was a Communist deputy who later became Minister of Labor and oversaw the final passage of the law elevating the *ordonnance* to regular legislation. A moderate Communist at a time when the Parti Communiste Français (PCF) and Stalin still hoped that *tripartisme* might convert France to communism, Croizat was the author of the frequently misquoted tribute to French social insurance. "We conceived social legislation as a vast palace that could contain everyone. You know what happened to our palace: a number of small and separate pavilions were substituted, some by conversion, others without roofs, some furnished, and others not. We live in these modest lodgings. Afterwards we tried to install every comfort" (Rapport Buisson 1945, 727; my translation). The Rapport Buisson endorsed most of Parodi's proposals: the new pension plan was to be paid from annual revenues (répartition); collection was to be made by payroll taxes collected by firms; and the dispute over the autonomy of the family allocation fund was postponed. Only after the joint pleas of Parodi and Croizat, a strange combination of mortally opposed guardians of national virtue, did the leader of the Catholic Left, Tessier, withdraw his complaint that the centralized procedure still evoked "the principles of Vichy."

Early in 1946 the Socialist leader, Segelle, tried to patch up the scars that the social insurance debate had left on the tripartite government (Rapport Segelle 1946). His proposal was not to delay implementation entirely, as the Catholic Left wanted, but to stagger implementation so that sickness and health insurance would begin in 1946; accident insurance in late 1946; the reorganization of the various funds in 1947; and the integration of the family funds indefinitely postponed. Anticipating that the centralized social insurance system would be defeated, he promised that the government would protect the preexisting insurance funds (régimes spéciaux) for miners, railroad workers, the merchant marine, and the civil service (all of which had large Communist unions) while the alarmed cadre could keep their occupational pensions (régimes complémentaires). When de Gaulle resigned in January 1946 party competition over social insurance was vigorously revived. The electoral turning point was the second election of the Constituent Assembly of June 1946 when Socialist strength was deeply eroded and the Catholic Left, the MRP, was substantially enhanced against a still strong PCF. Essentially, the ideally nationalized system of social insurance died with tripartisme. Croizat remained at the Ministry of Labor but in the new government all the choice ministries were taken by the MRP.

From 1946 each step toward enlarging social insurance provided another opportunity to restructure Laroque's plan to meet French political necessities. The MRP social policy spokesman, Prigent, took his revenge on those who tried to merge family policy with national social insurance when a law was unanimously passed in mid–1946 enlarging birth benefits and redistributing family allocations to reward parents with larger families (Thebaud 1985; Ceccaldi 1962). The MRP announced plans to add all the nonsalariés to the social insurance rolls, to restore the full autonomy of the family fund (CNAF), and to enlarge family fund representation on all the management committees. As so often happens in French policy reforms, Croizat had little alternative but to promise the Constituent Assembly that all the *droits acquis* would be honored under the new system of social insurance. The fatal blow came in early 1947 when a parliamentary committee under Surleau investigated better pensions to the *nonsalariés*. The Rapport Surleau (Galant 1955, 113–15) recommended that each self-employed occupational group, the artisans, the professions, and agriculture, have its own collection agency. Driving home their political advantage, family benefits were extended to the entire population, making it an irreversible concession. By the end of 1946 accident compensation insurance had been more effectively decentralized and the liberal professions acquired health and sickness insurance. French pensions were irreversibly diversified in late 1946 when the numbers of retired in the two branches, state pensions *(régime générale)* and occupational pensions *(régime complémentaire)*, became roughly the same.[9] A balance of political forces had been achieved within the social insurance system. Depending on one's partisan preferences, a familiar model of policymaking in France had been repeated by reproducing within social insurance the same political tensions, compromises, and diversity that characterized French politics.

The sequel to the political fragmentation of social insurance was to restore the internal autonomy of the *régimes complémentaires*, a task left to the "social partners" of government. In 1947 the employers, led by the CNPF and the main union of the cadre, the CGC, signed a *convention collective* converting occupational pensions to pay-as-you-go. Contributions were only on the amount of wages above the ceiling for state pension contributions but *cadre* could voluntarily agree to have larger portions of their salary taxed for occupational pensions. Starting in 1946 from two hundred thousand persons, mostly highly skilled white collar employees, by 1964 occupational pensions had grown to include 7 million persons who paid supplementary pensions for about 5 million retired employees. In much the same way that the state social insurance funds developed ways to transfer surpluses to accommodate demographic and economic shortages in particular state insurance benefits, a new organization, AGIRC, was established to move surpluses among the then fifty-eight different occupational funds designed to fit the French occupational structure. Because under French law these funds were *établissements publiques*, they could retain their surpluses and accumulate large reserves that, as we shall see, became crucial to the Socialist pension reform of 1983.

Although incrementalist explanations of the growth of social spending have tended to lose favor in recent years, it should be clear that the interfund and interoccupational complexities of French social insurance are ideally suited to generate uncontrollable growth. Having established the minimum pension (AVTS) for workers who did not qualify for pensions, it was only a short step in 1952 to extend it to the self-employed under the same handicap. Because workers were entitled to sickness and health benefits under the AVTS, it was only logical to add these benefits to the self-employed who were unqualified for state pensions and received the AVTS. These charges against the *régime générale* were passed on to the entire working population, both *salariés* and *nonsalariés,* who contributed to all these funds up to the ceiling on social insurance contributions.

But unlike the British and American social insurance, which perpetuated the stigma of poverty, the French made an additional provision for those who could not participate in national social insurance, in part because the growing charges on the *régime générale* troubled those who wanted to accumulate supplementary or occupational pensions. This is why the loi Pleven of 1956 created a national solidarity fund (FNS) to be paid from the state revenues in order to provide additional means-tested *allocations supplémentaires* to low-income noncontributors.[10] Because a wide variety of disadvantaged mothers, children, handicapped, and disabled were already receiving additional income support from the family fund (CNAF), the addition of means-tested supplements for low-income workers did not create a feeling of poverty or, much to the disappointment of some neo-Marxists, inflame class politics. In effect, help for those outside the system was propelled by the system itself rather than isolated from the social insurance as in Britain and the United States.[11] In a political sense France has a less severe poverty problem than other democracies because social insurance interlocks with minimum retirement benefits. Because the social assistance funds come from three different sources they can more easily respond to changing dimensions of poverty.

PERFECTING THE SYSTEM

In the areas of foreign policy, and to a lesser extent economic and industrial policy, the transition from the Fourth to the Fifth Republic marked substantially policy changes. In retrospect, it now seems clear that much of the controversy these decisions generated eventually focused on important reorganizations of French social insurance over the 1960s even though several French social security experts (Rapport Boutbien 1974), including Laroque himself (Interview, May 1987), feel that the reforms of 1961 and 1967 were not as fundamental as de Gaulle's political adversaries on both the Right and the Left chose to label them. On returning to power de Gaulle commissioned two major economic studies, one of French finances by his trusted economic advisor, Rueff (1972), who soundly castigated social insurance for its waste and inefficiency, and one of the future of social insurance by Laroque, who basically recommended the full *fiscalisation* or transfer of social insurance to the state budget. An indication of how successfully social insurance had been institutionalized under the Fourth Republic was that the extreme advice of both experts was largely ignored.

In assessing the progress of French social insurance over the 1960s it is important to recall that when the Fifth Republic was launched very few democracies had highly developed welfare states. Germany was the largest social spender but was still spending less than a fifth of GNP for social programs while Britain lagged well behind. Sweden, often appealed to as the model welfare state, had not begun the spurt of social spending growth that later drew attention and in 1960 spent less than Britain or Germany. The Benelux countries, whose welfare states exploded over the 1960s and 1970s to over half their GNP, still lagged behind the larger democracies. In aggregate terms, the growth of social spending in the early Fifth Republic was comparable to changes taking place throughout Europe. In fact, from 1960 to 1965, years often regarded as the height of social neglect in France, social spending increased at the rate of 15 percent per year and continued to grow at almost 10 percent per year for the rest of the decade (Barjot 1971). In 1958 pensions were increased roughly 15 percent at a cost of 14 billion francs, the largest increase since the war. But the internal changes in the system are more indicative of how social policy was changing the basic structure of French politics.

Throughout the steady growth of social insurance over the 1960s, French social institutions underwent dramatic reorganization. In part because of the bitter attacks on the Gaullists from the Left and in part because of scholarly disinterest in social policy at the time,[12] the institutionalization of French social welfare has been neglected. The first wave of reorganization consisted of the decrees of 1960, which most French social security experts regard as more important than the controversial reforms of 1967 (Laroque Interview, January 1987). The plight of the Gaullists, and other governments who have wished to restructure social insurance since 1960, is suggested by the furious rejection of their 1960 proposals by both the UIMM, the major private sector agency reporting on social insurance for businesses, and the unions. Both thought the menace of *étatisation* completely intolerable. Despite these fears, the overall effect of the 1960 reforms was to increase the political and administrative status of social institutions within the government. The position of the Ministry of Labor as a spokesman for social policy was enhanced by giving it supervisory powers over the social budget. The prestige of the neglected administration of social services and social programs was enhanced by creating an inspection corps, the Inspection générale des affaires sociales (IGAS) to attract high-quality young civil servants to the social sector. The organization of social security civil servants was clarified by creating a new management agency with the same participatory control given to the major social funds.[13] For the first time in the history of sickness and health insurance the government persuaded doctors to sign a *convention collective* regarding their fees and duties. Though outside the organization of social insurance, but nonetheless overlapping in important ways, the first national unemployment agency (UNEDIC) was created by voluntary agreement between the CNPF and the unions. In 1966, 4.5 million persons were added to the sickness and health beneficiaries, making health insurance nearly universal for the *salariés*.

Although many measures to modernize France were resented by the Right and despised by the Left, economic growth made the expansion of benefits possible. Rather like the British Labour government of the same time, the Gaullist government only became aware of the financial implications of their rapidly expanding welfare state in the mid–1960s.[14] In 1966 de Gaulle and Pompidou appointed J.-M. Jeanneney minister of the strengthened and unified Ministry of Social Affairs to try to bring the system under control (Ferry 1972; Guillaume 1971). The popular outrage that greeted his proposals suggests that social insurance in France, as elsewhere by the 1960s, had acquired a political constituency of its own. Few took time to note that the Friedel inquiry (1966) clearly revealed that the enormous administrative structure managing social insurance was virtually autonomous, nearly immune to political guidelines, and barely accountable to democratic government. In his highly technocratic manner, Jeanneney understood the underlying issue but totally failed to realize its political significance. Primarily, his aim was to follow the dictates of sound microeconomics by separating out the various "risks" within different social insurance funds: CNAV for retirement insurance, CNAMTS for sickness and health insurance, and CNAF for family benefits.

The vain hope of the CNPF [15] to restore the giant social security system to "insurance principles" became a travesty and only served to deprive the Gaullists of the credit they might have had for expanding social insurance over the 1960s while making them vulnerable to the charges of catering to business. But the most offensive change was to alter representation on the management committees of the three main funds. Since 1946 labor (meaning in fact only the four major labor unions) had been given two-thirds of the seats and the employers (meaning the CNPF) had one-third. Jeanneney introduced parity, which meant to French social insurance contributors and unions that they were being deprived of supervision over their own savings, however questionable it may be whether social insurance in 1966, much less 1986, was covered by contributions. Indeed, the rough estimate today is that the French state budget provides roughly 40 percent of retirement benefits. [16] With a view toward making the unwieldy and almost completely subsidized social benefits for the agrarian sector visible, if not politically manageable, the Ministry of Agriculture was directed to construct a single social budget (BAPSA). For a government that actually made substantial progress in improving and expanding social benefits, [17] Jeanneney was an enormous political handicap, as he again proved to be in 1969 when he was in the main presidential advisor advocating the referendum that destroyed de Gaulle.

Much less attention is paid to other substantial and expensive modifications made by the 1967 reforms. Unemployment insurance was extended to nearly the entire population. A special benefit (indemnité de licencement) was created for workers losing their jobs for economic reasons (industrial conversion and adaptation). A new national training agency (ANPE), largely supported by unemployment insurance contributions from employers and employees, was established. Sensing the importance of technical education in sustaining German competitiveness and labor harmony, vocational training funds were tripled. Lastly, the first of many contractual arrangements provided tax breaks for employers encouraging on-the-job training programs for obsolete workers, the allocation de conversion. While clearly not of the proportions of the more elaborate labor market policies that interlock wages and social benefits in Scandinavia and Germany, the Gaullists made important steps toward reshaping industrial relations and social policy along social democratic lines. [18]

A second wave of major Gaullist reforms came in the early 1970s, with finishing touches added by Giscard d'Estaing in the late 1970s. In France and elsewhere, alarm over inflationary damage to social insurance and social services has almost obscured important political changes of this period. By 1970 the administration and regulation of social insurance had achieved political recognition equal to any other major government task. Able and ambitious ministers established their reputations in social ministries, among them Robert Boulin in the early 1970s and Simone Veil in the late 1970s. Though viewed with some skepticism by President Pompidou, the *nouvelle société* of Chaban-Delmas elevated social issues to the top of the political agenda and such bright young civil servants as Jacques Delors made their names designing programs intended to integrate social, wage, and industrial policies in ways distinctive of a social democratic state. Indicative of the changing attitudes, by the late 1960s the *troisième age* had become a French political slogan.

In the area of social insurance, the most important change was the Boulin law of 1971.[19] It followed a detailed inquiry into aging by the Secretary of State for Social Action, a special report on aging by the social security inspectors (IGAS), and the massive four-party study of social problems in the Sixth Plan. Boulin's subgroup, the Intergroupe pour l'étude des prestations rélatifs aux personnes agées, reported in 1971 and his law is among the most sweeping reorganizations of retirement insurance among the many taking place in Europe at about the same time. For the first time the question of retirement at sixty years of age was broached, although at reduced rates. The base for calculating pensions was enhanced by averaging the last ten years. Essentially, Boulin laid the groundwork for the integration of state and supplementary pension plans. The minimum pension was to reach one-half of lifetime average earnings. The effect was to make the idea of a minimum income rather than a minimum pension the basis for retirement. An important side effect was to avoid institutionalizing poverty within the insurance system, as did the British. By putting benefits for low-income retired on a more flexible foundation, social support for elderly *nonsalariés* was stimulated. In 1975 the notion of a *minimum de retraite garanti* became law and the government compensated the social insurance funds for retirement credits lost for reasons of maternity, military service, and unemployment. Without resorting to elaborate means-testing, the government gradually introduced variable incomes for vulnerable and unfortunate aged and unemployed, thereby adding an entirely new dimension of equity to social insurance and avoiding the menace of unavoidable poverty.

THE SOCIALISTS DISCOVER THE WELFARE STATE

When the Socialists came to power in 1981 the basic structural reforms making the French welfare state indistinguishable from the French state itself had been accomplished. All three major funds operated on common principles of contribution, the compensation among the three funds as well as between *salariés* and *nonsalariés* had been worked out, a variety of social assistance benefits for single-parent families, children, and child care had been merged into a single family support benefit *(complément familial)* to support poor families (not including the additional local social assistance, or *aide sociale*), and virtually the entire French population was covered by social insurance. It is perhaps for this reason that the Socialist trial bill of 1980 (*Journal Officiel* 1980), clearly part of the run-up to the 1981 elections, contains few major reforms. Indeed, the readiness of the Left to accept the institutionalized welfare state as complete is all the more remarkable because outside France, in Britain and the United States, uncritical acceptance became the springboard for the arch-conservative attack on the welfare state over the 1980s.[20]

Although Nicole Questiaux, Mitterrand's choice for Secretary of State for Social Affairs and National Solidarity (the latter a Socialist appendage), was an ambitious and active minister, she had few ideas about basic structural reform of French social security. The main briefing document (Blum-Girardeau 1981) prepared for her arrival at the place de Fontenoy is sadly reminiscent of a doctoral thesis. There were of course, as in most democratic governments, important internal political tensions limiting her possibilities. As a rather disappointed Minister of Agriculture, Rocard, with his eye on 1988, could not be expected to make major concessions in the 60 billion franc social budget for the agricultural sector. With growing unemployment, social insurance funds could not expect concessions from the Ministry of Labor or unemployment insurance funds. Indeed, to find additional funds the party reversed its preelection stand and added a new Fonds de solidarité pour l'emploi to be financed with additional contributions from secure public sector employees. Many proposed reforms were blocked by the Minister of Finance, Delors, who refused to allow social expenditure to become the driving force of inflation.[21]

But before Bérégovoy's elevation to finance in 1982, Questiaux's ministry had increased social benefits by roughly 40 billion francs. More innovative reforms and more diverse social experiments were foreclosed by the natural

TABLE 2.1

Distribution of Social Security Taxes by Type of
Protection in 1984 (in percentages)

	Total Taxes	Régime Général
Pensions	41	27
Health	34	50
Family	14	22
Unemployment	11	—

Source: L'Année métallurgique 1985, 125.

tendency to do the most simple and most visible increases first. Questiaux's future was no doubt sealed when she commented that she was not responsible for keeping the accounts. Her 1 percent reduction in social insurance contributions of February 1981 had to be rescinded in November 1981. Perhaps the most important promise made by the Socialists was retirement at sixty years of age, a promise deeply rooted in Socialist concern for humanizing labor and redistributing income to the aged through pension reform.

Further reform was complicated as well as enhanced by the intricacies of French social insurance organization. By 1980 the main fund *(régime général)* accounted for only 27 percent of pension contributions and was heavily committed to providing huge transfers for the ever-rising costs of sickness and health insurance (see table 2.1). Nearly half of all pension contributions were for supplementary pensions *(régimes complémentaires)* and a fifth were for the privileged pension plans for public employees *(régimes spéciaux)*. Lowering the pension age was obviously a problem of persuading the more viable funds to contribute to the cost of pensions for those wholly dependent on state pensions, much like similar pension reforms in Britain, Sweden, and West Germany. But the politics were completely different. A second possibility was to raise the ceiling, or *plafond*, so that the cost of earlier pensions was directly shifted to higher income persons. The main problem with this solution was that it would impose an enormous disincentive on employers, still paying roughly two-thirds of all social insurance contributions in 1984 (see table 2.2) and, in 1982, bitterly complaining about the cost of unemployment insurance. Employer cooperation was essential to propel France's economic recovery from the oil crisis. With soaring medical costs and high unemployment the conventional route of interfund transfers was closed.

The only remaining choice, therefore, was to persuade the supplementary

TABLE 2.2

Division of Social Security Taxes among Contributors (in billions of francs and percentages)

	1970	%	1975	%	1980	%	1984	%
Employers	73.3	73	160.7	73	399.7	68	546.8	66
Salariés	18.7	19	45.2	21	128.9	26	223.1	27
Nonsalariés	7.5	8	13.2	6	32.9	7	61.6	7
Total	99.5		219.1		501.7		831.5	

Source: Ministère de la Finance 1984.

pension funds (*régimes complémentaires*), under the semiautonomous management described above, to share their reserves in order to finance the transition to early retirement (Mecereau 1987; Chadelat 1983, 121–27). By the early 1980s they had become an integral component of French social insurance, paying out nearly 8 billion francs in pension benefits in 1984, collecting contributions from 20 million employees in more than 4 million firms (see tables 2.3 and 2.4). Moreover, early retirement held attractions to the *cadre* and skilled employees enrolled in supplementary plans. Nor was the issue entirely unknown. Civil servants and military had long been able to retire at sixty years while railroad workers, miners, and members of other hazardous professions could retire at fifty-five years and even earlier in some cases. The estimate was that of the roughly two hundred thousand persons retiring each year about eighty-five thousand would take the sixty-year option. The anticipated cost of extending the pension system, essentially finding the money to pay contributions into the existing pensions of each early retiree

TABLE 2.3

Membership by Adherents and Firms of the *Régimes Complémentaires*

	1966	1976	1981	1985
Adherents (in millions)				
AGIRC	.9	1.9	2.4	2.8
ARRCO	7.4	15.1	14.0	15.7
UNIRS	4.8	5.7	5.8	6.5
Firms (in thousands)				
AGIRC	195	336	556	391
ARRCO	1,600	1,946	3,000	3,200
UNIRS	370	456	577	680

Source: L'Année métallurgique as indicated from the respective annual publications.

TABLE 2.4

Division of Contributions among Social Security Programs (in percentages)

	1975	1980	1981	1982	1983	1984
Régime général[1]	66.4	66.6	65.9	66.5	65.3	65.1
Régimes statutaires[2]	7.5	6.6	6.9	6.7	6.5	6.3
Régimes spéciaux[3]	8.5	9.0	9.0	8.9	8.9	8.8
Régimes complémentaires[4]	—	12.5	12.9	12.4	12.3	11.9
Assurance chômage[5]	17.7	5.3	5.3	5.5	7.0	7.9

Source: Ministère de la Solidarité Nationale 1984.

1. The *régime général* received 545 of 831 billion francs in contributions in 1984, which is distributed among the four *caisses* for pensions (CNAV), health (CNAMTS), family protection (CNAF), and accident compensation.
2. The *régimes statutaires* are funds organized before the nationalization of social insurance in 1946: SNCF, RATP, Banque de France, local government workers, EDF, and GDF.
3. The *régimes spéciaux* are private sector workers who organized pension funds before 1946 and refused to join the *régime générale*: miners, merchant marines, artisans, merchants, professions, etc.
4. *Régimes complémentaires* are additional earnings-related pension funds organized after 1946 for high-level *cadre* (AGIRC), mid-level *cadre* (ARRCO), and white collar workers (UNIRS), plus a few small funds of technical experts.
5. Unemployment contributions are held by UNEDIC, organized in 1958 to distribute funds for unemployment and related labor market programs, largely through ASSEDIC.

for five years, both public and private, was anticipated to be 5.3 billion francs. Early retirement was not such a gigantic task as political and industrial rhetoric made it sound. By skillful manipulation of the interdependent social insurance funds it was not too difficult to find an acceptable solution. Once policymakers agreed to overlook ideological positions and partisan self-interest, the complexity of the system helped provide a solution.

Among employers the most detested benefit was the *garantie de ressources*, a cornerstone of the unemployment insurance system erected in the prosperous days of the early 1970s. At sixty years of age the unemployed were guaranteed 70 percent of their salaries. With additional social benefits this meant that some *salariés* could retire at more than their salaries. This generous agreement had no formal legal foundation but was a voluntary agreement between employers and employees that was rather unwisely renewed in 1974 to attract labor support for the Right. A more rash extension was added in 1977 to when Giscard agreed to provide *any* worker retiring at sixty with the *garantie de ressources* to tide him or her over until the regular pension became available at sixty-five years (Chadelat 1983, 335). By 1981 the burden of the *garantie de ressources*, two-thirds of which fell on the employers, was 14.5 billion francs. Essentially early retirement was made possible by a compromise between two funds: unemployment insurance, which remained outside the legal orbit of social insurance, and the state pension system. The achievement is the product of interfund solidarity that had attracted a Labour party social insurance expert to the French system twenty years before. Lateral transfers within the system helped rescue social groups in jeopardy. The *régimes complémentaires* agreed to borrow funds against their substantial reserves over ten years in order to permit the state system to absorb the costs of early retirement and to reach a decade when the burden of retirement is expected to decrease. Paradoxically perhaps, under a Socialist government the *patrons* agreed to a small increase in unemployment taxes in order to finance the change. Both government and *patrons* benefitted by being relieved of the less predictable and countercyclical burden of the *garantie de ressources*.

In some respects the early retirement agreement marks the frontier of social democracy in France, not because there is any highly developed welfare state model as in Sweden, but because French social politics permit the movement of funds between the public and private sectors.[22] The accord of February 1983 is not even within the realm of public law but is private law. Starting in 1984 the supplementary pension plans borrowed 4 billion francs though normal banking procedures. Lest anyone think that this outcome is less than mutually beneficial, interviews with the Director of the UIMM social insurance research office, the Director of the Social Security in the Ministry of Social Affairs, and Mitterrand's social security advisor were unanimous in their approval of the plan (Moreau, 1987). The successful outcome contributed to Bérégovoy's reputation as Minister of Social Affairs and opened the way for his promotion to Minister of Finance. His two equilibrium plans for social insurance of 1982 and 1983 curbed social spending by about 40 billion francs, hardly an awesome amount when France was spending over 600 billion francs on social insurance of all kinds. In fact, the coming of age of French social insurance, as in other democracies, was the realization that social insurance is integral to the state and to the economy. To be sure, it was becoming a matter for experts. In 1984 a .5 percent error in forecasting social spending produced a deficit of 6 billion francs; the loss of contributions from .5 percent of the active population represents a 1.5 billion franc loss of revenues.

Perhaps more clearly than any other social insurance system, the French experience over the 1980s reveals how fully institutionalized welfare programs and policies have become in the democracies, so much so that social and partisan politics have in some ways become indistinguishable. But each country makes the metamorphosis toward the merger of social and labor interests in its own distinct pattern. Much of this accomplishment is unanticipated, and at times, as with the costly *garantie de ressources*, inadvertent. But certain features of a social democratic model were always visible within the French social insurance system. From the turn of the century, employers and employees were important partners in developing social benefits and social protection and agreed that they should have a significant representation in the management of the system. While *solidarité* was always vulnerable to partisan rhetoric, the layered funds meant that even the so-called private or occupational pensions are linked to government and yet able to enjoy many advantages of being organized under private law. The French never permitted the social insurance system to off-load its problems onto social assistance and local charity to the extent found in many other countries. Though the question of poverty has become a political issue, most recently addressed in the plan for minimum incomes (*revenue minimum d'insertion*, or RMI) (*Le Monde* 1988), contrary to the fears of some conservatives and to the hopes of some radicals, income policies have not polarized around the social insurance system. Whatever the early excesses of the Socialist government, the system now functions as well as or better than most major social insurance systems of Europe and North America while remaining imbedded in the republican principles that first inspired it.

NOTES

1. Nearly all the inadequacies found in American social security by Margaret Weir, Ann Shola Orloff, and Theda Skocpol (1988) could be found in France. Though the nature of the centrifugal political forces is different in the two countries, in both, in the early years of national social insurance, the main issue was to keep the system from fragmenting. The similarity casts some doubt on the Weir-Orloff-Skocpol assertion about America's retarded welfare state.
2. The intricacy of policymaking networks in France appears in many policy areas. See, for example, Peter Hall (1986). For an evaluation of additional cases of French policymaking complexity, see Douglas E. Ashford (1982).
3. Much as the boundaries between the public and private economic sectors are blurred in French policymaking, the distinction between *mutualité* and social insurance is also unclear. Historically, the idea of earners voluntarily sharing risks under state supervision blurs with national social insurance partly because the myth of participant management and individual prudence, as in the United

States, was preserved for many years. At the beginning of the Third Republic there were twenty-six hundred mutual insurance societies with 289,000 members. By 1902 there were 13,677 societies with about 2 million members.

4. AGIRC was created by mutual agreement in 1947 as part of the reaction against the nationalization of French social insurance. ARCCO was established in 1961 to extend supplementary pensions to lower-level *cadre*. The final step was the organization of UNIRS to manage supplementary pensions to virtually all of the *salariés* in small firms. Part of the complexity of French pensions arises from the fact that French retirees receive payments from three pension funds or more.

5. Contrary to the frequent assertion that unemployment protection was late in France, there is a long and suggestive history of labor protection. See, among others, François Sellier (1984); on the complex history of labor law and labor protection, Yves Delamotte (1984); and on recent progress, UNEDIC (1983). Contrary to the common question about weak French unions delaying social insurance, a more interesting question is why they are so influential and politically privileged in social insurance policymaking despite their weakness.

6. Central to the Socialist reforms of social insurance after 1982 was Mitterrand's promise to reduce the *prélèvement obligatoire*, or total tax burden of social expenditure, by 1 percent per year for the next few years. The calculation of the *prélèvement* is itself an interesting indication of how the French generalize about social insurance. It is the percentage of GDP paid by individual contributions or social taxation to social insurance funds plus the contribution from national budget. It rose from 39 percent of GDP in 1976 to nearly 43 percent in 1981 and to 45.6 percent from 1981 to 1984. See *Les Prélèvements obligatoires* (1986). A readable history of the early struggle to contain social security costs is Henri Roson (1974).

7. The political quarrels over control of the *conseils d'administration* are poorly understood. The issue was not, nor could it conceivably have been, that participants should manage such intricate funds but that each *caisse* has a discretionary fund, sometimes running to millions of francs, which can be used for summer camps, vacation supplements, etc., for persons employed in the system. Since 1953 union representation on the councils has, in a characteristically French solution, been portioned out, with the FO having CNAMTS, the CGC given the CNAV; and the CFTC with its old liberal Catholic roots, the CNAF. The best account of these and other internal political problems is Antoinette Catrice-Lorey (1981). A recent study assessing how powers are distributed within the various *caisses* is the annual IGAS.

8. Though hardly the intensive form of social democracy familiar to Scandinavians, the French have many links between social and wage policy, the most important being the SMIC, or *salaire minimum interprofessionel de croissance*. Rather than make the wage gap, i.e., the difference between the minimum wage and minimum social assistance, into an adversarial political issue, as it has become in Britain, the French use changes in the AVTS to rachet the SMIC upward and vice versa. Poverty is not a zero-sum game in France.

9. Similar to Britain, the United States, and Germany, social insurance was rapidly

expanded after the war to include nearly all workers. In early 1946 the National Assembly did so at a cost of 38 billion old francs. See *Journal Officiel* (1946).

10. Despite the Fourth Republic's political instability, social policy enjoyed remarkable ministerial stability and the 1956 law was instrumental in avoiding grinding poverty in France. Few countries have sufficiently flexible social institutions to readily make such combinations of resources. See the high praise for this decision by Tony Lynes (1967). In contrast, the only way British politicians could acquire more funds for the aged poor was to increase means-tested social assistance, which is paid entirely from Treasury revenues.

11. The simple solution to this problem is of course to nationalize all social insurance, the course favored by Weir, Orloff, and Skocpol (1988, 287, 423), to eliminate the so-called bifurcation of American social security. Equating territorial and social class divisions is a risky business and to some extent spatial tensions may actually help the worst off. In some measure, all systems of social insurance have awkward spatial problems that, as the French case shows, are not likely to become simpler simply by nationalizing social insurance.

12. It is interesting to note that what was widely regarded as an authoritative introduction to developments in France at the beginning of the Fifth Republic, Hoffman (1963), has no article on social policy or social insurance although it does include an article on family structure.

13. Though a rather technical point, it was regarded as a fundamental change in the internal politics of social security. The postwar organization of social security workers, FNOSS, or the Fédération nationales des organismes de la sécurité sociale, was split into two organizations: ACOSS, or the Agence centrale des organismes de la sécurité sociale, to handle personnel policies; and UCANSS, or the Union des caisses nationales de sécurité sociale, to be a collection agency for contributions to the *régime général* (family and unemployment funds have their own). On the unionization of the roughly two hundred thousand French social security employees, see Catrice-Lorey (1981, 220–30).

14. The Gaullists actually kept the earlier MRP Minister of Labor, Bacon, in place until 1962, when he was succeeded by Grandval, generally thought to be a weak minister and not a Gaullist. The social insurance functions were merged in a single ministry, the Ministry of Social Affairs, in 1966, when Jeanneny took the post.

15. During the expansion throughout the early Gaullist years the CNPF unsuccessfully lobbied the government to restrict social spending. The formal proposal was the Rapport Picketty submitted in 1965. When the CNPF Social Committee was chaired by a more liberal businessman, Chôtard, in the late 1960s and early 1970, the CNPF dropped its adamant opposition.

16. This includes a charge of 10 billion francs per year accepted by the state in 1983 to reduce the retirement age to sixty; about 20 billion in various state subsidies to agricultural social insurance and to the nearly bankrupt *régimes spéciaux*; and allocations through the FNS to top off low pensions and to pay pension contributions during pregnancy, military service and unemployment, etc.

17. Between 1962 and 1964 pensions doubled. In 1963 an *allocation d'éducation*

spéciale was added to family benefits for handicapped children; the *allocation de logement* grew to include over 2 million families; and medical insurance was expanded to include nearly all the population. In addition, supplementary pension funds grew hugely during the economic take-off of the 1960s.

18. There was an entire battery of social insurance studies in the mid–1960s. The Rapport Ortoli under the umbrella of the Fifth Plan recommended a national manpower training program undertaken by the ANPE in 1966. The Rapport Rivero studied the problems of reaching agreements with the doctors. The Rapport Dobler, also part of the Fifth Plan, studied inequalities among benefits. In addition, talks were underway between the CNPF and the unions to reduce the work week to forty-two hours.

19. Boulin chaired the Sixth Plan Intergroup, *Personnes agées* (1971). See the discussion of his contribution in Anne-Marie Guillemard (1980, 74–76).

20. There were to be sure important reflections on the Left about the future of social security, such as Jacques Fournier and Nicole Questiaux (1979); and, more moderate, Michel Laroque (1984). Characteristically, these studies paid little or no attention to the political and financial implications of social insurance nor did they attempt to realistically assess political obstacles and popular preferences that might qualify their suggestions. Though certainly not a repeat of lost opportunities after the war, when the political potential of the welfare state was regularly underestimated, the French scene was not unlike the situation in Britain and the United States insofar as the Left failed to take new initiatives to protect gains against conservative attacks. The difference in France was that the Right chose not to make such an attack. A sober post-mortem is Gilles Johanet (1986); a fascinating account of changing social definitions is Jacques Donzelot (1984).

21. There were of course some aspects of Bérégovoy's economies that drew stiff fire from the Left, such as minor charges of medical visits for the elderly, but they were a very small decrease and were mainly designed, like similar restraints in Britain and the United States, to keep medical costs under control. The clearest exposition of the impact of his reforms is found in Jean-François Chadelat (1983, 59–63). It is surprising what simple mistakes allowed the Socialists to lose the initiative in 1981. For example, the abrupt cancellation of the 1 percent increase in social security taxes cost 21 billion francs, roughly half the social security deficit at the end of 1981. Only 8 billion of the 40 billion franc deficit was caused by new initiatives.

22. The French have never subscribed to the Swedish idea that pension funds might be used to socialize the private sector nor, aside from their pragmatic efforts to link pensions to the cost of living, have they seen pensions as a form of income redistribution. This is why the notion of "sectoral blurring" described by Martin Rein and Lee Rainwater (1986, 202–14) is inappropriate for much of Europe and North America even though dependence on social insurance in old age and many other critical moments of life has substantially increased client or consumer concern with social insurance in all the democracies. It should be noted that the deficits of 10 or 15 billion francs in social security funds that are

immediately emblazoned in French headlines are about .5 percent of total social expenditure.

REFERENCES

Année métallurgique, L'. 1985. Paris: Union Interprofessionnelle Métallurgique et Minière (UIMM).

Ashford, Douglas E. 1982. *Policy and Politics in France: The Politics of Uncertainty*. Philadelphia: Temple University Press.

———. 1986. *The Emergence of the Welfare States*. Oxford and New York: Blackwell.

———. 1989. "L'Etat-providence à travers l'étude comparative des institutions." *Revue Française de Science Politique* 39: 276–95.

Barjot, Alain. 1971. "L'Evolution de la sécurité sociale (juin 1960–juin 1966)." *Revue Française des Affaires Sociales* 25: 61–79.

Blum-Girardeau, Catherine. 1981. *Les Tableaux de la solidarité*. Paris: Economica.

Catrice-Lorey, Antoinette. 1981. *Dynamique interne de la sécurité sociale*. Paris: Economica.

Ceccaldi, D. 1962. *Histoire des prestations familiales en France*. 2 vols. Paris: CNAF.

Chadelat, Jean François. 1983. *La Protection sociale*. Paris: Institut des Actuaires françaises. Mimeo.

Cheysson, Emile. 1902. *L'Evolution des idées et des systèmes de retraite*. Paris: Society of Political Economy.

Delamotte, Yves. 1984. *Le Droit de travail en pratique*. Paris: Les Editions d'Organisations.

Derfler, Martin. 1977. *Alexandre Millerand: The Socialist Years*. The Hague: Mouton.

Donzelot, Jacques. 1984. *L'invention du social*. Paris: Fayard.

Ferry, Antoine. 1972. "La sécurité sociale depuis les ordonnances de 1967." *Revue d'Economie Politique* 82: 983–87.

Fournier, Jacques, and Nicole Questiaux. 1979. *Le Pouvoir du social*. Paris: Presses Universitaires de France.

Galant, Henri C. 1955. *Histoire politique de la sécurité sociale en France, 1945–1952*. Paris: Colin.

Guillaume, Michel. 1971. "L'Evolution de la sécurité sociale, 1966–1977." *Revue Française des Affairs Sociales* 25: 81–97.

Guillemard, Anne-Marie. 1980. *La Vieillesse et l'état*. Paris: Presses Universitaires de France.

Guillot, Paul. 1887. *Les assurances ouvrières: accidents, maladies, vieillesse, chômage*. Paris: Impriméries Centrales.

Hall, Peter. 1986. *Governing the Economy: The Politics of State Intervention in Britain and France*. Oxford and New York: Polity Press.

Hatzfeld, Henri. 1971. *Du paupérisme à la sécurité sociale, 1850–1950*. Paris: Colin.

Hockerts, H. G. 1980. *Sozialpolitische Entscheidungen in Nach Kriegs-Deutschland.* Stuttgart: Klett.

Hoffman, Stanley, ed. 1963. *In Search of France.* Cambridge: Harvard University Press.

Jamous, Haroun. 1969. *Sociologie de la décentralisation: la réforme des études médicales et des structures hospitalières.* Paris: Editions du CNRS.

Johanet, Gilles. 1986. *Contes et mécomptes de la protection sociale.* Paris: Presses Universitaires de France

Journal Officiel. 1946. Annexe no. 1215. Assemblée Nationale Constituante, séance du 25 avril, pp. 1945–46.

————. 1980. Annexe no. 1856. Assemblée Nationale, 25 juin.

Laroque, Michel. 1984. *Politiques sociales dans la France contemporaine: le social face à la crise.* Paris: Editions STH.

Laroque, Pierre, 1961. *Succés et faiblesses.* Paris: Colin.

————. 1983. Interview, November.

————. 1987. Interview, January, May.

Les Prélèvements obligatoires, Cahiers Français. 1986. No. 225 (mars–avril).

Levasseur, E. 1903. *Histoire des classes ouvrières et de l'industrie en France, 1798–1870.* Paris: Rousseau.

————. 1907. *Questions ouvrières et industrielles en France sous la Troisième République.* Paris: Rousseau.

Lynes, Tony. 1967. *French Pensions.* Occasional Papers in Social Administration, no. 21. London: Bell and Sons.

Mercereau, François. 1987. Interview, April.

Ministère de la Solidarité Nationale. 1984. *Comptes de la protection sociale.* Paris.

Ministère de la Finance. 1984. *Comptes de la nation.* Paris.

Monde, Le. 1988. October 12.

Moreau, Yannick. 1987. Interview, June.

Netter, François. 1965. "Les retraites en France au cours de la période 1895–1945." *Droit Social* 28: 514–26.

————. 1974. "Histoire des retraites complémentaires des salariés." *Droit Social* 40: 58–63.

Rapport Boutbien. 1974. "Les problèmes poses par la sécurité sociale." *Journal Officiel,* Conseil Economique et Social, Avis, et Rapports, 26 septembre, pp. 1317–26.

Rapport Buisson. 1945. *Journal Officiel,* annexe no. 554. Documents de l'Assemblée Consultatif, 24 juillet, pp. 725–34.

Rapport Friedel. 1966. *Commission d'études des structures de la sécurité sociale.* Paris, Prime Minister. Mimeo.

Rapport Mottin. 1945. *Rapport relatif aux travaux de la commission charger d'étudier le project d'ordonnance relatif à l'organisation de la sécurité sociale.* Paris, 9 juillet. Mimeo.

Rapport Oheix. 1981. *Contre la précarité et la pauvreté.* Paris, Ministry of Social Affairs. Mimeo.

Rapport Segelle. 1946. "Rapport fait au nom de la commission de travail et de la sécurité sociale sur l'organisation de la sécurité sociale," *Journal Officiel*, annexe no. 698. Assemblée Nationale Constituante, séance du 19 mars, pp. 667–70.

Rapport Wresinski. 1987. "Grande pauvreté de précarité économique et sociale." *Journal Officiel*, Conseil Economique et Social, Avis et Rapports, session de 28 fevrier.

Rein, Martin, and Lee Rainwater. 1986. "The Future of the Public/Private Mix." In *Public/Private Interplay*, edited by M. Rein and L. Rainwater. Armonk and London: M. E. Sharpe.

Rodwin, Victor. 1984. *The Health Planning Predicament*. Berkeley and Los Angeles: University of California Press.

Rosanvallon, Pierre. 1984. *Crise de l'état providence*. Paris: Seuil.

Roson, Henri. 1974. "Les grandes tendances de l'évolution de la sécurité sociale en France." *Bulletin de l'Institut International de l'Administration Publique* 37:7–29.

Rueff, Jacques. 1972. *Combat pour l'ordre financier*. Paris: Plon.

Salais, Robert. 1986. *L'invention du chômage*. Paris: Presses Universitaires de France.

Sellier, François. 1984. *La Confrontation sociale en France, 1936–1981*. Paris: Presses Universitaires de France.

Sixth Plan Intergroup. 1971. *Personnes agées*. Paris: Documentation Française.

Stone, Judith. 1980. *The Search for Social Peace: Reform Legislation in France, 1890–1914*. Albany: State University of New York Press.

Thebaud, F. 1985. "Le mouvement nataliste dans la France de l'entre-deux guerres: l'Alliance national pour l'accroissement de la population francaise." *Revue d'Histoire moderne et contemporaine* 32: 272–301.

Tutelle et contrôle dans le domaine social. 1986. Paris: Ministère des Affaires Sociales.

UNEDIC. 1983. *Historique du régime d'assurance chômage, 1959–1982*. Paris.

Weir, Margaret, Ann Shola Orloff, and Theda Skocpol, eds. 1988. *The Politics of Social Policy in the United States*. Princeton: Princeton University Press.

3

CONTINUITY AND CHANGE IN FRENCH SOCIAL POLICY: THE WELFARE STATE UNDER GAULLISM, LIBERALISM, AND SOCIALISM

DAVID R. CAMERON

The French social security system has been described as an "unfinished cathedral" (Dumont 1978b). Like one of the great cathedrals in France, the system is a vast monument to an epoch. It is, as Ashford notes (1982, 228), replete with numerous chapels, altars, offices, and a few old relics—as well as the ever-present scaffolding for repair work and, of course, the numerous unobtrusive collection boxes for contributions. Like a cathedral, it is somewhat musty and poorly illuminated. But, like a cathedral, it offers refuge, sanctuary, and relief from the noise, din, and trauma of the world outside, and within its walls, under its vaults and arches, gather those seeking shelter from the tribulations of life. As does the cathedral, it brings together men and women of several generations. There are large numbers of the elderly, especially elderly women. But there are also many younger persons, including young parents with their children. And there are the sick and infirm and disabled of all ages. Each has a reason for being there, although the reasons differ.

If the task of describing the long process of construction of the cathedral belongs to the art historian, the task of describing the long, gradual, and

An earlier version of this chapter was presented at the 1988 Annual Meeting of the American Political Science Association in Washington, D.C. The author is grateful to John Ambler and Douglas Ashford for extensive comments and suggestions.

piecemeal construction of the system of social security and assistance in France belongs to the student of politics and public policy. A full description of that system, even over the finite life of one republic, would far exceed the confines of a single chapter and for such descriptions we must refer the reader elsewhere (see, among many, Ashford 1982; Barjot 1971; Doublet 1971; Dumont 1981b; Galant 1955; Guillaume 1971; Hatzfeld 1971; Laroque 1948, 1961, 1971, 1980; and Rustant 1980). In this chapter, I shall pursue the more limited objective of outlining some of the salient features of the French system of social security when viewed from a comparative perspective. The comparisons will involve both space and time. I shall consider how the French system compares with those of other nations. And I shall compare how the French system itself has changed over the past four decades. For these comparisons, I shall use measures of total spending effort for social security and social assistance. While the simplicity and crudeness of such measures cannot be overstated, they nevertheless *do* enable one to make systematic and parsimonious comparisons across space and time.

The chapter is organize in three parts. In the first section, the total spending effort for social programs in France is compared with that in other nations. This comparison indicates the extent to which the social security "cathedral" in France, although still incomplete, looms above many of the smaller "chapels" elsewhere in Europe—including nations that are usually presumed to have highly developed "welfare states." In the second section, the total spending effort for social programs in France is compared diachronically over the period 1950–1987. Against an incremental model that views policy, and aggregate spending, as highly dependent on past policy and largely the result of small changes—usually additions—to the prior base, this section considers whether regime and partisanship have discernible effects. In particular, we consider whether, how, and to what extent the change from the Fourth to the Fifth Republic affected the aggregate spending for social programs. And we consider whether, and to what extent, the tenure of the four presidents of the Fifth Republic affected spending for social programs in a distinctive manner. The analysis suggests that both the change from the Fourth to the Fifth Republic and, within the Fifth Republic, those involving the occupant of the *Elysée* palace had distinctive effects on spending. The chapter concludes with a consideration of the complex relationship between social spending and distributive outcomes in French society. In particular, we note one of the major paradoxes that appears when France is compared

TABLE 3.1

Total Outlays of Government as a Percent of Gross Domestic Product

	1960	1970	1980	1986	Increase, 1960–86
France	34.6	38.5	46.1	51.8	17.2
Australia	22.1	26.8	33.8	37.9	15.8
Austria	32.1	39.2	48.9	52.4	20.3
Belgium	30.3	36.5	50.7	53.5	23.2
Britain	32.6	38.8	44.9	45.5	12.9
Canada	28.9	34.8	40.5	46.4	17.5
Denmark	24.8	40.2	56.2	56.0	31.2
Finland	26.7	30.5	36.6	41.9	15.2
Germany	32.0	38.6	48.3	46.9	14.9
Ireland	28.0	39.6	50.8	54.7	26.7
Italy	30.1	34.2	41.9	50.9	20.8
Japan	17.5	19.4	32.6	33.1	15.6
Netherlands	33.7	43.9	57.5	59.4	25.7
Norway	29.9	41.0	48.3	49.9	20.0
Spain	17.0	22.2	32.9	41.7	24.7
Sweden	31.1	43.3	61.6	63.6	32.5
United States	27.8	31.6	33.7	36.9	9.1

Sources: OECD Economic Outlook 46 (December 1989): table R-14, p. 179; OECD Economic Outlook 32 (December 1982): table R-8, p. 161.

to other nations—the juxtaposition of an unusually high level of aggregate spending for social security and social assistance, on one hand, and an unusually inegalitarian size distribution of income, on the other.

I. FRENCH SOCIAL SPENDING IN COMPARATIVE PERSPECTIVE

Government plays a significant role in the economic life of all of the advanced capitalist nations. A simple, yet illustrative, measure that suggests the importance of that role is provided by the ratio of public revenues or expenditures to the economic product of a nation. Table 3.1 presents such a measure for seventeen of the relatively developed capitalist democracies of Western Europe, North America, and the Pacific. As the data in table 3.1 indicate, the "public economy" is large and expansive throughout the advanced capitalist world (see Cameron 1978). Three decades ago, all levels of government, taken together, spent an amount equivalent to approximately one-quarter to one-third of the Gross Domestic Product in most of the seventeen nations. But by the late 1980s, that proportion had risen dramatically and total public expenditures exceeded 40 percent of G.D.P. in most of the nations. Indeed, in some, such as Belgium, Denmark, Ireland, the Netherlands, and Sweden, aggregate public spending had risen to well over one-half of G.D.P.

Despite decades of conservative rule until the 1980s, the fiscal role of the French government was, by the measure used in table 3.1, among the largest in the advanced capitalist world. And it had held that rank throughout the post–World War II era. Thus, in the early 1960s, when it epitomized the activist, interventionist state (see, among many, Shonfield 1965), the French government spent a larger share of the nation's economic product on public programs and services than did government in any other capitalist democracy. And while a number of nations—Sweden, Denmark, Norway, Ireland, the Netherlands, Belgium, Spain, Austria, and Italy—experienced unusually large increases in public spending relative to their economic product in recent decades, France remained among the highest-spending nations, in terms of G.D.P. Thus, in 1986, for example, public expenditures in France represented approximately 52 percent of its G.D.P.

If the fiscal role of government has been large and expansive in France and throughout the advanced capitalist world in the post–World War II era, so too the amount of funds spent on social programs has expanded more rapidly than the economy in most nations. Table 3.2 presents the proportion of G.D.P. spent on social programs in 1960, 1970, and 1980 in the same seventeen nations. The data in table 3.2, reported by the International Labour Organization in its most recent international inquiry (I.L.O. 1985), include benefits for medical care, sickness, unemployment, old age, work injury, families, maternity, invalidity, survivors, and public assistance, as well as the administrative expenses associated with the provision of these benefits and services. As such, the data in table 3.2 represent the broadest, and most cross-nationally comparable, measures of the relative magnitude of the welfare state in the advanced capitalist world.

The data in table 3.2 suggest that France has one of the most highly developed welfare states, in a fiscal sense, in the advanced capitalist world. In 1960, most governments spent between 5 and 15 percent of the nation's economic product on social security and social assistance. France, which spent 13 percent of its G.D.P. on social programs in that year, ranked, with Austria, Belgium, and Germany, among the leaders in national spending effort.

TABLE 3.2

Total Government Expenditures on All Social
Security Schemes as a Percent of G.D.P.: 1960,
1970, and 1980

	1960	1970	1980
France	13.2	15.3	26.8
Australia	7.7	8.0	12.1
Austria	15.4	18.6	22.4
Belgium	15.3	18.1	25.9
Britain	10.8	13.8	17.7
Canada	9.2	11.8	15.1
Denmark	11.1	16.4	26.9
Finland	8.8	12.8	18.6
Germany	15.4	17.0	23.8
Ireland	9.3	11.6	21.7
Italy	11.7	16.3	18.2
Japan	4.9	5.4	10.9
Netherlands	11.1	20.0	28.6
Norway	9.4	15.5	20.3
Spain	na	na	16.1
Sweden	10.9	18.8	32.0
United States	6.8	9.6	12.7

Source: I.L.O. (1985, 56–59).

Over the two decades after 1960, the share of the economic product
devoted to social programs rose substantially in every nation, and by 1980
most nations were spending between 15 and 30 percent of their G.D.P. on
such programs. In spite of the unusually large increases in spending in such
nations as Denmark, the Netherlands, and Sweden, and in spite of the
decades of rule by the Gaullists, neo-Gaullists, and other conservative parties, France remained among the leaders in its fiscal commitment to social
policy. Thus, in 1980, it spent approximately 27 percent of its G.D.P. on
social security and social assistance.

The data in tables 3.1 and 3.2 indicate that total public expenditures, and
spending on social security and social assistance, expanded more rapidly than
the economy in all of the advanced capitalist nations in the post–World War
II era. What those data do not show is that in most nations spending for
social programs not only grew more rapidly than the economy but also grew

TABLE 3.3

The Proportion of All Public Expenditures
Allocated to Social Security Schemes in Seventeen
Nations, 1960–1980

	1960	*1970*	*1980*
France	38.2	39.7	58.1
Australia	34.8	29.9	35.8
Austria	48.0	47.4	45.8
Belgium	50.5	49.6	51.1
Britain	33.1	35.6	39.4
Canada	31.8	33.9	37.3
Denmark	44.8	40.8	47.9
Finland	33.0	42.0	50.8
Germany	48.1	44.0	49.3
Ireland	33.2	29.3	42.7
Italy	38.9	47.7	43.4
Japan	28.0	27.8	33.4
Netherlands	32.9	45.6	49.7
Norway	31.4	37.8	42.0
Spain	na	na	48.9
Sweden	35.0	43.4	51.9
United States	24.5	30.4	37.7

Source: Calculated from tables 1 and 2.

more rapidly than spending for other public programs and, as a result, came to absorb a larger share of total public expenditures.

Table 3.3 presents the share of total government spending allocated to social security and social assistance in the seventeen nations in 1960, 1970, and 1980. The data in table 3.3 suggest that in almost every nation spending on social programs constituted a significantly larger share of total public expenditures in the 1980s than in the 1960s. Thus, whereas spending for social programs ranged from one-quarter to one-half of all public spending in the early 1960s, by the 1980s such spending generally accounted for at least 40 percent of all public expenditure (except in the United States, Canada, Australia, and Japan). And in several nations, social spending accounted for *more* than one-half of all public spending.

The data in table 3.3 clearly demonstrate that, as was the case with total public expenditures and social spending relative to the economic product of the nation, France is among the leading nations in the share of total public spending devoted to social policy. Indeed, table 3.3 suggests that although France lagged behind several of its neighbors—most notably, Germany, Belgium, Austria, and Denmark—in the share of its considerable "public economy" that was devoted to social programs in the 1960s, by the 1980s France was leading all nations in that regard—even those such as Belgium, the Netherlands, Sweden, and Denmark, which are renowned for their highly developed welfare states. Some might argue that it is somewhat misleading to speak of the "welfare state" in France, for reasons having to do with the forms of funding, organization, and administration of the French social security system (see Ashford 1982, 229–35; and Freeman 1985). Nevertheless, to the extent that a state is defined by its activities, and by the programs to which it devotes its resources, the data contained in table 3.3— especially the most recent entry for France—suggest that, more than is the case in almost any other nation, the French state is a "welfare state."

Correlates of Cross-National Variation in Social Spending Effort

The preceding comparisons among the advanced capitalist nations demonstrate the universality of increasing public spending in general, and social spending in particular, in recent decades. That universal experience implies that the sources of the expansion in the fiscal role of the state were supranational, or at least present among most of the nations. That, in turn, implies that at least a portion of any explanation of the increase in social spending in a particular nation, such as France, lies beyond the realm of national politics. Nevertheless, it is also true that the nations reveal a remarkable diversity in the extent to which they support social programs, and diversity may reflect the impact of politics or other attributes and characteristics of the nations. In this section, I shall explore that diversity in an effort to understand why, in spite of the common pattern of an expanding fiscal commitment to social policy, some nations, of which France is one, commit a much larger share of their economic resources to social programs than do other nations.

The most elementary way in which to comprehend why nations differ in this fiscal commitment to social policy is to compare the variation across the nations in such measures as social spending as a fraction of G.D.P. (reported in table 3.2) and of total public spending (reported in table 3.3) with the variation in particular aspects and characteristics of polity and economy. Table 3.4 reports the simple, bivariate correlation coefficients between the

TABLE 3.4

The Political, Social, and Economic Correlates of Spending on Social
Security in Seventeen Nations, 1980

	Expenditures on Social Security	
	As % of G.D.P.	As % of All Expend.
Percent of Cabinet Portfolios, 1965–85, held by:		
Social Democrats & Labor parties	.53	.39
Christian Democratic parties	.32	.31
Centrist parties	−.23	−.17
Conservative parties	−.45	−.37
Social Democratic, Labor, *or* Christian Democratic parties	.64	.52
Percent of Workforce Unionized, 1970–85	.49	.24
Organizational Unity of Labor Movement	.51	.30
Power of Labor Confederations over Unions	.54	.28
Scope of Collective Bargaining	.65	.50
Exports as a Percent of G.D.P., 1965–85	.62	.35
Percent Change in Constant-Currency ("Real") G.D.P., 1965–85	−.56	−.48
Percent of Population, 15–64, in Labor Force, 1975–85	.03	−.14
Percent Change in Total Labor Force, 1974–85	−.42	−.57
Percent Change in Total Employment, 1974–85	−.32	−.53
Percent of Total Labor Force, Unemployed, 1965–85	−.17	−.04
Federal System of Government	−.36	−.38
France ("dummy variable")	.26	.50

two measures of social spending effort and measures of various aspects of
political and economic life in the seventeen nations.

Table 3.4 includes measures of the frequency with which distinctive
families of political parties, such as Social Democratic, Labor, and other
leftist parties, or Christian Democratic parties, or conservative parties, have
governed in recent years. (For the technique of constructing these measures,
and their sources, see Cameron 1984 and 1988a.) Included also are several
measures that describe the density, inclusiveness, and organizational power

of some of the most important political-economic actors in advanced capitalist society; thus, I have included measures of the degree of unionization, the
organizational unity of the labor movement, the power of labor confederations over their affiliates, and the scope of collective bargaining. (For an
elaboration of these measures, see Cameron 1984.) Table 3.4 also includes a
variety of economic attributes, such as the degree of openness (as measured
by exports relative to G.D.P.; see Cameron 1978), the rate of economic
growth, the size of the active labor force, growth in the labor force and in
total employment, and the level and increase in the rate of unemployment.
(The measures of the labor force and unemployment were obtained from
O.E.C.D. 1988.) Finally, table 3.4 includes two "dummy variables"—one
of which distinguishes between nations according to whether their governments are federal or unitary in structure, the other of which distinguishes
between France and all other nations.

The data in table 3.4 reveal that certain political and economic attributes
of the nations are clearly associated with the variation among nations in
spending effort on social programs—regardless of whether that effort is
measured relative to G.D.P. or to total public spending. Thus, one observes
that the partisanship of government over a long period may have a systematic
effect on social spending effort. For example, nations in which leftist parties
have dominated government tend to spend a larger share of their G.D.P. on
social programs (r = .53) and tend, also, to spend a larger share of total public
expenditure on such programs (r = .39). But leftist parties are not alone in
promoting the welfare state; table 3.4 suggests that Christian Democratic
parties may have almost the same effect as leftist parties in promoting social
spending, and that the most important distinction among the partisan families with regard to social spending is between the leftist parties and the
Christian Democratic parties, on one hand, and the centrist and conservative
parties, on the other.[1]

The partisan correlates of social spending reported in table 3.4 suggest a
plausible distinction among the political parties. But they also suggest that
the French experience is somewhat anomalous and deviant from the general
pattern observed across the seventeen nations. For more than two decades
prior to 1980 (the date for which the social spending measures were obtained), France was governed neither by Social Democratic or Labor parties
nor by Christian Democratic parties, and, indeed, both of those partisan
families have been quite weak, relative to their strength in several neighboring countries. France is the only nation among the seventeen in which social

spending was highly developed in spite of domination of the government for several decades by various coalitions of conservative parties.

If France appears as an anomaly in the light of the partisan correlates of social spending, that is even more true when one considers the social organizational correlates of spending. Table 3.4 indicates that the nations in which social spending effort is most highly developed are ones in which a relatively large share of the work force is unionized, in which there is a relatively high degree of organizational unity (as opposed to fragmentation) in the labor movement, in which labor confederations have considerable power over their affiliates, and in which collective bargaining is centralized. France is one of the nations in which the work force is *least* organized, in which the labor movement is *most* fragmented, in which labor confederations have relatively *few* powers over their affiliates, and in which collective bargaining is *de*centralized rather than concentrated at the economy-wide level. And yet France is one of the leading spenders on social programs, in spite of the organizational weakness of the labor movement during much of the post–World War II era.

Beyond these political and social correlates, table 3.4 also suggests that the level of spending on social programs, relative to G.D.P. and to total public spending, is associated with various economic attributes. The nations in which social spending is most developed are those in which the economy is relatively open and export-dependent, in which the long-term rate of economic growth has been low, in which the labor force increased by a relatively small amount in recent decades, and in which total employment likewise increased by a small amount (or even decreased). These correlates— especially those involving growth and employment—suggest that the development of the contemporary welfare state has been greatly influenced by adverse developments in the economy and that it expanded in recent years— most notably, the 1970s—as the economies of the advanced capitalist nations deteriorated.

In order to account for the variation among the nations in social spending in a manner that is both more parsimonious and more complex than is made possible by the compilation of a large number of bivariate correlations, tables 3.5 and 3.6 report multiple regression analyses of the two measures of social spending. The analyses in the two tables are the result of an identical procedure: first, the five most highly correlated variables not contaminated by excessive amounts of multicollinearity were included in a regression.[2] The five variables are the proportion of cabinet portfolios held by Social Demo-

TABLE 3.5

Multiple Regression Analyses of Spending on Social Security, as a Percent of G.D.P., in Seventeen Nations, 1980

	(1)	(2)	(3)	(4)
Constant	19.5	18.8	19.6	17.8
	(3.03)	(3.18)	(3.38)	(3.21)
Percent of Cabinet Portfolios,	0.030	0.041		
Social Democratic, Labor, or	(0.54)	(0.89)		
Christian Democratic parties				
Scope of Collective Bargaining	10.378	9.723	12.992	14.26
	(1.48)	(1.48)	(2.41)	(2.78)
Percent Change in G.D.P.	−0.056	−0.056	−0.067	−0.064
	(1.66)	(1.73)	(2.28)	(2.31)
Percent Change in Total Labor	−0.066			
Force	(0.39)			
Federal System of Government	−3.50	−3.83	−3.89	−3.19
	(1.38)	(1.66)	(1.70)	(1.46)
France				6.85
				(1.65)
Coefficient of Determination (R^2)	.66(.50)	.65(.53)	.63(.54)	.70(.60)

Notes: Parentheses contain t-statistics.
Parentheses beside R^2 of equations contain the $\bar{R}^2$, adjusted for degrees of freedom.

cratic and Labor *or* Christian Democratic parties; the scope of collective bargaining; the rate of economic growth; the change in the total labor force; and the "dummy variable" for a federal form of government. After conducting the analyses with this initial set of variables, subsequent analyses deleted sequentially the single most statistically insignificant variable as long as the coefficient of determination adjusted for degrees of freedom ($\bar{R}^2$) increased.[3] Once the final, pared-down analysis had been obtained, the "dummy variable" for France was included in order to ascertain the extent to which the analysis accounted for the relative magnitude of the French spending effort.

Table 3.5 presents the results of the multiple regression analysis of all public spending on social security and social assistance as a fraction of G.D.P. The analysis indicates that the three most significant explanatory variables are the scope of collective bargaining, the rate of economic growth, and the distinction between federal and unitary systems of government. The presence of highly centralized collective bargaining—bargaining that occurs at the economy-wide level as opposed to bargaining that is highly decentralized and occurs at the firm or plant level—is strongly associated with high

68 DAVID R. CAMERON

TABLE 3.6

Multiple Regression Analyses of Spending on Social Security, as a Percent of Total Public Expenditure in Seventeen Nations, 1980

	(1)	(2)	(3)
Constant	50.2	49.7	45.9
	(6.39)	(6.88)	(8.01)
Percent of Cabinet Portfolios,	−0.016		
Social Democratic, Labor, or	(0.24)		
Christian Democratic parties			
Scope of Collective Bargaining	9.509	8.321	10.871
	(1.11)	(1.26)	(2.10)
Percent Change in G.D.P.	−0.058	−0.055	−0.052
	(1.42)	(1.48)	(1.82)
Percent Change in Total Labor	−0.330	−0.305	−0.245
Force	(1.59)	(1.78)	(1.83)
Federal System of Government	−3.20	−3.31	−2.33
	(1.04)	(1.13)	(1.02)
France			12.70
			(3.01)
Coefficient of Determination (R^2)	.58(.38)	.57(.43)	.77(.66)

levels of social spending. Thus, most of the countries with such centralized bargaining—Austria, Sweden, Denmark, and, to a lesser extent, Belgium and the Netherlands—spend at least one-quarter of their G.D.P. on social programs. One reason, of course, may be that centralized bargaining is, at least in part, the product of a strong and inclusively organized labor movement that actively advocates the development and funding of social programs. Another, to which I have alluded elsewhere (see Cameron 1978, 1984), may be the tendency for governments to use social policy as a means of obtaining labor's acquiescence to policies of wage restraint—policies that are most likely to develop in the smallest (and thus most open) economies and that depend for their negotiation and enforcement on the presence of highly centralized collective bargaining.

Table 3.5 indicates that the rate of economic growth has a significant and consistent effect on social spending across the advanced capitalist world. Social spending tends to be high, relative to that elsewhere, in nations that have experienced unusually low levels of growth over the long term. There are, of course, some nations—most notably, Britain and the United States —that appear at or near the bottom of *both* the measures of economic growth over the long term[4] and the measures of social spending as a portion of G.D.P. In general, however, social spending tends to be highest in those nations, such as Belgium, the Netherlands, Sweden, Denmark, and Germany, that experienced the lowest rates of economic growth over the better part of two decades.

Table 3.5 also suggests that the institutional structure of government has a consistent effect on the level of spending for social programs. In particular, social spending tends to be highest in nations in which government is organized on unitary rather than federal principles. Thus, table 3.5 indicates that the presence of federalism, independent of all other factors, reduces social spending levels by three or four percentage points of G.D.P. relative to those observed in unitary systems.

The last, and most condensed, regression in table 3.5 includes the "dummy variable" for France. The rationale for including this variable is simply to test the proposition that the high level of social spending in France is largely or solely the result of political and economic forces that affect social policy throughout the advanced capitalist world. To the extent that this were the case, one would have little reason to resort to extensive analysis of social policy in France in order to account for its relatively high level of spending. The results reported in table 3.5 suggest, however, that that is not the case. The *t* statistic for the "dummy variable" is quite significant (1.65) and the regression coefficient is quite large (6.85). That suggests that the general, cross-national explanation does not fully account for France's high level of spending—something that is immediately apparent if one considers that, contrary to most of the high-spending nations, France has had in recent decades a relatively *decentralized* system of collective bargaining and (at least until the 1980s) a relatively *high* rate of economic growth. In short, then, France emerges from this cross-national analysis of social spending as something of an anomaly or a "deviant case" that warrants further examination.

Table 3.6 presents the results of multiple regression analyses of spending on social security and social assistance as a fraction of total public expenditure. Given the strong association across the seventeen nations between the two measures of social spending (r = .81), it is not surprising that the results are similar to those reported in table 3.5. Thus, one observes that a relatively high share of total public expenditure devoted to social spending is associated with centralized collective bargaining, a relatively low rate of economic growth over the long term, and a unitary form of government. In addition, however, the analysis in table 3.6 suggests that high levels of social spending, relative to total public spending, are most likely to occur in nations in which the labor force has experienced the slowest rate of growth—an indicator of the extent to which the development of social spending in the advanced capitalist world in recent decades is affected by the performance of the economy, defined not only in terms of growth but also the rate of job creation.

Table 3.6 also demonstrates, as did the preceding analysis, that the cross-nationally general explanation of social spending as a share of total spending does not fully account for the French experience. Indeed, the very high t statistic (3.01) and regression coefficient (12.70) for the "dummy variable" for France indicate that the cross-national explanation may be of limited use in accounting for why that nation allocates such a large share of its public spending to social programs. The image that has already been invoked, of France as an anomaly or a "deviant case," is only reinforced by the results in table 3.6. And as with any anomaly or "deviant case," these results not only arouse one's curiosity about the dynamics of social policy in France but imply that, in order to comprehend why France spends as much as it does on social policy, one must examine in detail the evolution of social policy in France over the past decades. It is to that subject that I now turn.

II. FRENCH SOCIAL SPENDING SINCE 1950

In most of the years since 1950, social spending in France increased by a larger percentage than the economic product of the nation, and as a result the ratio of spending to G.D.P. drifted upward over time. Figure 3.1 presents the ratio of total spending on social security and social assistance to G.D.P. for each year between 1950 and 1987.[5] One observes a gradual upward movement over time in that ratio. Thus, while such spending was equivalent to about 11 percent of G.D.P. in 1950, the share of G.D.P. rose to slightly more than 13 percent in 1960, 17 percent in 1970, 24 percent in 1980, and by 1987 represented roughly 27 percent of G.D.P.

As one would expect of a domain of policy that is very large—in 1985, for example, social security benefits totaled 998 billion francs, and social assistance totaled another 115 billion francs—and that is organized, as Ashford notes, in a complex array of regimes, funding sources, and administrative councils (see Ashford 1982; 232–35), change in the share of G.D.P. consumed by these programs has been piecemeal and incremental. A telling indicator of the degree of incrementalism and, therefore, continuity over

FIGURE 3.1
Public Spending on Social Security and Social Assistance in France, 1950–1987

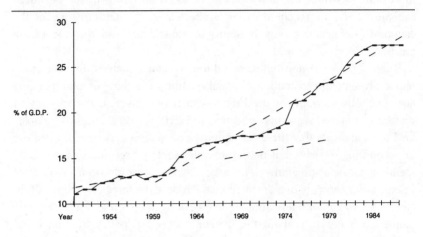

time, is the exceptionally high correlation between the share of G.D.P. spent on social security and social assistance in each year and the share in the prior year; for the period 1951–1987, the correlation between the share of G.D.P. in year i and the share in year i-1 is .995! Thus, if one were to regress the former upon the latter, one could explain fully 99 percent of the variation in the level of spending as a function of the prior year's level of spending. In statistical terms, the time series contains a very high degree of autocorrelation, which can be taken as a measure of the high degree of continuity over time. That being the case, there would not appear to be much room in the explanation of spending, statistically speaking, for all the factors, such as partisanship of the government, the identify of the president, the proximity of elections, or even the distinction between the Fourth and Fifth Republics, that might plausibly cause social spending to fluctuate from year to year.

The image of continuity is reinforced if one fits a regression line to the data in figure 3.1 in order to estimate the annual change in the share of G.D.P. spent on social programs. The regression, in the form $y = a + b(x)$, where the dependent variable, y, is the share of G.D.P spent on social security and social assistance and the independent variable, x, is simply a time counter (1950 = 1, 1951 = 2, . . .), explains fully 95 percent of the variation over the period. In that regression, a (the estimated value in the year prior to the first in the series, i.e., 1949) equals 9.29. The estimated annual increment in spending as a share of G.D.P., *b*, equals 0.461. That is, the share of G.D.P. absorbed by social spending increased almost one-half of one percentage point *every* year over the nearly four decades. Put in nonstatistical language, these results suggest a pattern of *dynamic incrementalism*—that is, a process that is highly incremental, in which each year's spending is largely a function of the previous year's, but one that is also consistently expansionary to such a degree that the annual increments, when taken together, cumulate into a significantly and nonincrementally larger share of G.D.P. spent on social programs.

However much the time series of the share of G.D.P. spent on social policy is characterized by continuity and a uniform gradual rate of change, there *are* significant differences in the rate of change over the period. As pervasive as the autocorrelation and serial correlation are, a cursory examination of the data in figure 3.1 suggests a wave-like oscillation in the upward-drifting series, with periods of relatively small annual increase followed, in turn, by later periods of relatively large increase. Although at first glance there appeared to be little statistical space for such political factors as partisanship, the presidency, or even regime and republic, the presence of that wave-like oscillation may provide an opening for a more political, and less uniformly incrementalist, explanation.

A first step in establishing whether there are differences in the rate of change over time in social spending that are significant and that are associated with such political factors as parties, presidents, and republics is to compare the average rates of change for politically demarcated periods of time. Table 3.7 presents such a comparison. The table presents the results of regressions of the share of G.D.P. spent on social policy upon a time counter for several different periods. The initial values listed in the table are the constant terms in the regressions; the annual increases are the slope estimates obtained from the regressions. By comparing the latter, one can ascertain whether politically distinctive periods were marked by different average rates of growth in social spending relative to G.D.P.

The results presented in table 3.7 suggest that there were, in fact, marked differences in the growth of social spending in politically distinctive periods. Of course, spending increased relative to G.D.P. in *all* periods—something that suggests that politics (at least in this domain of policy in this country over this period) did not involve choices over increasing or decreasing spending as much as choices among policies that, taken together, would alter the rate of increase in spending. Nevertheless, in some politically demarcated

TABLE 3.7

Estimated Annual Increases in Expenditures for Social Security and Social Assistance in Politically Demarcated Periods in France, 1950–1987

Period	Initial Value	Annual Increase	$\bar{R}^2$
1950–87:	9.29	0.461	.95
Fourth Republic (1950–59)	11.09	0.282	.91
Fifth Republic (1959–87)	11.94	0.543	.96
Fifth Republic President:			
De Gaulle (1959–69)	12.76	0.476	.89
Pompidou (1969–74)	16.84	0.274	.82
Giscard d'Estaing (1974–81)	18.72	0.779	.93
Mitterrand (1981–87)	25.40	0.325	.66

Note: Estimates are generated by regression of social expenditures as a percent of G.D.P. upon annual counter. The initial value is the constant, a, in the regression. The annual increase is the regression coefficient, b, in the regression. For simplicity, the t-statistics have been omitted; all are obviously very high.

periods, spending increased at a markedly more rapid rate than in other periods. Thus, for example, the annual rate of change, expressed in terms of the increase in the share of G.D.P. spent on social policy, was twice as large in the Fifth Republic as it had been in the Fourth Republic (0.543 vs. 0.282).

To give some visual meaning to these estimates, and to demonstrate the significant difference between the republics, one can return to figure 3.1. The figure includes a broken line that represents the slope estimates from the regressions reported in table 3.7. A sense of the magnitude of the impact on social policy of the change from the Fourth to the Fifth Republic can be obtained by extrapolating the rate of increase in social spending as a share of G.D.P. observed in the Fourth Republic through the years of the Fifth Republic. By this obviously simplistic device, France might now be spending roughly 18 percent of its G.D.P. on social programs, rather than the 28 percent it currently does. In other words, the difference between spending at a level that now puts the country among the leaders, with Sweden, Denmark, Belgium, and the Netherlands, and spending at a level that would put it, with Britain, Canada, Spain, and Italy, well below the international average in terms of the portion of G.D.P. devoted to social policy, can apparently be attributed to the change from the Fourth to the Fifth Republic.

If the change from the Fourth Republic to the Fifth set in motion a variety of forces that caused a marked acceleration in the rate of increase in social spending, relative to that of the economy as a whole, the estimates reported in table 3.7 indicate that spending did not increase at a uniform rate throughout the Fifth Republic. Thus, the annual rate of increase in social spending increased dramatically during de Gaulle's tenure as president, relative to the rate of increase in the last decade of the Fourth Republic (0.476 per year vs. 0.282), largely because of a dramatic wave of reforms in health and unemployment insurance in the early years of the Fifth Republic (on these reforms, see Ashford 1982; Barjot 1971; Doublet 1971; and Laroque 1980).[6] But as de Gaulle was followed by Pompidou, the annual rate of increase in social spending as a fraction of G.D.P. receded, from 0.476 to 0.274—in spite of the commitment of Chaban-Delmas, Pompidou's first prime minister, to the creation of a "new society."

Figure 3.1 and the estimates reported in table 3.7, taken together, indicate that after the upward surge in the rate of acceleration in social spending in de Gaulle's first term as president, and then the slowdown in the general's last years in office and throughout the Pompidou presidency, a second upward surge occurred during the Giscard presidency. During each of Giscard's seven years in office, social spending increased by almost eight-tenths of 1 percent of G.D.P. (0.779). But that second period of accelerated expansion was in turn followed by a period of considerably slower expansion (0.325) percent annually during the Mitterrand presidency—in spite of the partisan base of support and programmatic commitments Mitterrand and his government brought to office in 1981.

This disaggregation of the rate of increase in social spending relative to the economy during the Fifth Republic reveals, then, two periods of especially dramatic increase in spending. One occurred in the early years of the Republic, during the de Gaulle presidency; the other occurred in the late 1970s, during the Giscard presidency. As a result, the two most expansionary presidents of the Fifth Republic, from the perspective of social policy were, perhaps surprisingly, de Gaulle himself and the fiscally conservative minister of finance who, after the Pompidou interlude, followed him to the Elysée. And the two least expansionary presidents were Pompidou and Mitterrand.

The differences in the rate of increase in social spending relative to G.D.P. among the republics and the presidents of the Fifth Republic are certainly marked. But are they significant? They may appear so at first glance. But it is possible that the differences reflect other unspecified factors that

TABLE 3.8

The Annual Change in Gross Domestic Product and in the Proportion of G.D.P. Spent on Social Security and Social Assistance in France, 1951–1987

Period	Average % Change in Constant-Price G.D.P.	Average Change in % of G.D.P. Spent on Social Security & Assistance
1951–87	4.0	0.43
Fourth Republic (1951–59)	4.4	0.25
Fifth Republic (1959–87)	3.9	0.48
Fifth Republic President:		
De Gaulle (1959–69)	5.7	0.37
Pompidou (1969–74)	5.1	0.25
Giscard d'Estaing (1974–81)	2.5	0.86
Mitterrand (1981–87)	1.7	0.51

influence the share of G.D.P. spent on social programs, in which case the politically demarcated differences might disappear once those other factors were taken into account. Perhaps the most obvious exogenous factor is the performance of the economy. As the cross-national analysis discussed earlier suggests, the share of G.D.P. spent on social policy may fluctuate inversely with the rate of growth in the economy, increasing at a more rapid rate in economic downturns (both because of the relatively fixed nature, at any time, of old-age payments and the larger amounts that must be spent on unemployment compensation) and increasing at a slower rate in periods of high economic growth (when the denominator of the ratio increases by a relatively large amount). When one is considering, as we are here, a long period that encompasses periods of high growth as well as world recession, it would be foolish to attribute the different rates of growth in social spending to presidents, parties, ideologies, or regimes without first taking into account the fluctuations—both those that are short term and cyclical as well as those that are longer term—in the economy.

Table 3.8 presents a summary of the average rates of change in the constant-price G.D.P. over the entire period since 1951 as well as during the various politically demarcated periods. The table also includes, for the sake of comparison, the average first-order change in the proportion of G.D.P. spent on social security and social assistance. These data suggest, in a preliminary way, that some of the unusual growth experienced during the

Giscard presidency in social spending relative to G.D.P. may be attributable to the drop in the rate of economic growth that occurred during those seven years—largely the product of the recession of 1974–1975, the slowdown in growth in the late 1970s, and the second major recession in 1980–1981.

While the data in table 3.8 suggest that the rate of increase in social spending relative to G.D.P. may have varied inversely with the rate of economic growth, those data also suggest some anomalies. For example, during the de Gaulle presidency, *both* the rate of economic growth and the rate of increase in social spending increased relative to what they had been during the Fourth Republic. (Likewise, both decreased during the subsequent Pompidou presidency.) And in contrast to the experience during Giscard's presidency, social spending increased by no more than the average for the three decades of the Fifth Republic during the Mitterrand presidency —in spite of the fact that France experienced, during his tenure, the lowest rate of economic growth over the long term in the post-World War II era.

In order to ascertain the significance, if any, of the distinctions I have noted in the rate of increase in social spending between the republics and the presidents of the Fifth Republic once the fluctuations in economic performance have been taken into account, table 3.9 presents the results of several multiple regression analyses. Because of the exceptionally high autocorrelation and serial correlation in the time series of the measure of social spending effort, any estimates obtained by regressing the percent of G.D.P. spent on social programs upon the independent variables—even if one of those was the lagged dependent variable—would be severely biased. The best way of dealing with that problem is to create a measure of change in the dependent variable and regress that measure upon the independent variables. The coefficient of determination will be much lower, of course, but the estimates will be more reliable.

The regression analyses reported in table 3.9 treat as the dependent variable the first-order change in social spending as a portion of G.D.P. over the period from 1951 to 1987. All of the regression equations reported in that table include the percent change in constant-price G.D.P. as an independent variable. In addition, they include as independent variables an election-year "dummy variable"—to test for the plausible hypothesis that social spending tends to increase in election years and has been driven up over time by the cumulative effects of elections in the Fourth and Fifth Republics. Also, table 3.9 includes "dummy variables" that distinguish the Fourth from the Fifth Republics and, within the latter, among the four occupants of the Elysée.

TABLE 3.9

Multiple Regression Analyses of Expenditures for Social Security and Social Assistance as a Percent of G.D.P. in France, 1951–1987

	(1)	(2)	(3)	(4)
Constant	0.816	0.615	0.769	0.729
	(4.42)	(2.39)	(2.29)	(2.08)
Change in G.D.P.	−0.096	−0.092	−0.117	−0.113
	(2.29)	(2.18)	(1.75)	(1.68)
Election Year		0.119		0.068
		(0.82)		(0.47)
Fifth Republic		0.182		
		(0.94)		
Fifth Republic President				
De Gaulle			0.266	0.257
			(1.18)	(1.12)
Pompidou			0.038	0.036
			(0.15)	(0.14)
Giscard d'Estaing			0.421	0.424
			(1.55)	(1.54)
Mitterrand			−0.195	−0.173
			(0.65)	(0.56)
Coefficient of Determination (Adjusted)	.11	.09	.19	.17

The results reported in table 3.9 suggest that the share of G.D.P. consumed by social spending does indeed vary inversely, and to a statistically significant degree, with the rate of economic growth. They indicate that a change of one percentage point in the rate of growth over the period was associated with an inverse change of about one-tenth of 1 percent in the share of G.D.P. consumed by social programs. That is, a drop in the rate of growth to 1 percent below the long-term average rate of growth produced an increase in the share of about one-tenth of 1 percent of G.D.P.; conversely, an increase in the rate of growth to 1 percent above the long-term average rate of growth produced a decrease in the share of about one-tenth of 1 percent. Thus, for example, if (from table 3.7) the share of G.D.P. devoted to social programs increased by 0.779 of 1 percent each year of the Giscard presidency, about 20 percent of that annual increase (from table 3.8, $[(4.0 - 2.5) \times 0.1]/0.779$) can be attributed to the lower rate of growth during the Giscard presidency. And of course, much of the unusually large increases in social spending, relative to G.D.P., in such years as 1975 and 1981 can be attributed to the even lower rates of growth in those recession years. ·

Table 3.9 also contains regression estimates of the impact on social spending, after controlling for the fluctuating rate of economic growth, of the change in republics (the second equation in the table), the impact of elections (the second and fourth equations in the table), and the change in presidents during the Fifth Republic (the third and fourth equations). The results suggest that elections had a consistent, albeit modest, effect on social spending, raising the ratio of social spending a fraction of G.D.P., by about one-tenth of 1 percent in each election year ($b = 0.119$ in equation 2 and $b = 0.068$ in equation 4). They also suggest that both the change from the Fourth to the Fifth Republic and the change in Fifth Republic presidents had marked consequences for spending, above and beyond the changes associated with the performance of the economy. After taking into account the fluctuations and longer-term trends in the rate of economic growth, as well as the presence or absence of elections, the analysis indicates that the spending ratio increased by about one-fifth of 1 percent during each year of the Fifth Republic ($b = 0.182$ in equation 2), relative to the average rate of increase in the Fourth Republic.[7]

The analyses reported in table 3.9 also suggest, as did the earlier perusal of figure 3.1, that the largest average increases in spending occurred during the de Gaulle and Giscard presidencies. After controlling for the fluctuations in the economy and the timing of elections, the spending ratio increased in each year of the de Gaulle presidency by approximately one-quarter of 1 percent of G.D.P. more than it had in the Fourth Republic ($b = 0.257$). And it increased in each year of the Giscard presidency by almost one-half of 1 percent more than it had in the Fourth Republic ($b = 0.424$). For both of these presidencies, the rate of growth in social spending associated with the presidency independent of the rate of economic growth is statistically significant.[8]

In contrast to the estimates reported in table 3.9 for the de Gaulle and Giscard presidencies, the estimates associated with the Pompidou and Mitterrand presidencies are quite insignificant, which is to say that virtually all of the modest increase in social spending observed during those presidencies can be attributed to the rate of economic growth, to the presence or absence of elections, or to the various inertial forces present in social policy. Insignificant as they are, however, those estimates are useful as first approximations of the magnitude of increase in social spending during those presidencies, independent of the rate of economic growth. Thus, they suggest that, after controlling for the rate of growth, the proportion of the economic product devoted to social spending increased during the Pompidou years at about the same rate as it did during the Fourth Republic ($b = 0.036$). And they suggest, surprisingly, that the ratio of social spending to G.D.P. during the Mitterrand years actually increased at a markedly *lower* rate than in the Fourth Republic ($b = -0.173$)—which, itself, experienced a rate of increase considerably below that of the Fifth Republic!

In the analyses reported thus far, the dependent variable was the ratio of all social spending by the French government to the nation's G.D.P. Those analyses accurately depict the extent and sources of fluctuation over time in the country's aggregate spending effort in social policy. However, it is possible that the observed increase in social spending effort over the long term may reflect, at least in part, the simultaneous growth of *all* public spending over the long term. That is, social programs may simply have received a constant share of a government budget that was expanding relative to the economic product of the nation. If that were the case, any explanation of growth in social spending would have to be cast at the level of public expenditure in general, rather than at the level of social policy in particular.

One means of assessing whether the sources of fluctuation in aggregate social spending effort lie in the realm of public expenditure in general, or in social policy in particular, is to replicate the analyses presented earlier with a dependent variable that measures social spending as a fraction of all public expenditure rather than as a fraction of G.D.P. If the growth in aggregate spending effort on social programs was in fact simply the product of a constant share of an expanding "public economy," one would expect to find no significant increase over the long term in the share of all public expenditures devoted to social programs. And one would expect, also, that the effects, noted earlier, of the change in republics and in occupants of the office of president during the Fifth Republic on social spending would be greatly diminished or altogether absent.

Table 3.10 presents an analysis of aggregate social spending as a fraction of all public expenditure in France over the period 1953–1987. Replicating the analysis presented in table 3.7, table 3.10 presents the initial values for that measure for each of the politically distinctive periods considered earlier. And it presents the regression-derived estimate of the average annual change in the ratio of social spending to all public expenditure for each of those periods.

TABLE 3.10

Estimated Annual Increases in Expenditures for Social Security and Social Assistance as a Portion of Total Public Expenditures in France in Politically Demarcated Periods, 1953–1987

Period	Initial Value	Annual Increase	$\bar{R}^2$
1953–87	34.7	.558	.96
Fourth Republic (1953–59)	35.6	.189	.08
Fifth Republic (1959–87)	38.3	.545	.93
Fifth Republic President:			
De Gaulle (1959–69)	37.2	.705	.75
Pompidou (1969–74)	42.4	.786	.96
Giscard d'Estaing (1974–81)	47.1	.631	.85
Mitterrand (1981–87)	51.6	.021	−.16

Note: Calculated as in table 7.

The analysis in table 3.10 suggests that the increase in social spending effort over the past four decades in France was *not* simply the product of a constant share of the budget for social programs applied to an ever expanding "public economy." Rather, the share of aggregate public expenditure allocated to social programs increased in every politically distinctive period—so much so that social policy increased from approximately one-third of all public expenditure in the early years of the Fourth Republic to more than one-half by the advent of the Mitterrand reign in 1981.

Table 3.10 also suggests that the rate of expansion in social spending, relative to all public expenditure, fluctuated over the four decades. And as with the measure of social spending relative to G.D.P., those fluctuations depended, in part, on politics. For example, social spending's place in the budget of French government increased *three times* faster in the Fifth Republic than in the Fourth (0.545 vs. 0.189). And confirming the earlier results that appeared to contradict a conventional view about partisanship and social policy, table 3.10 suggests that social spending's share of all public expenditures increased significantly during the administration of each conservative president—0.705 per year during de Gaulle's reign, 0.786 per year during Pompidou's, and 0.631 per year during Giscard's—and significantly more under conservative rule than under rule by the leftist parties (0.021 for Mitterrand).

Table 3.11 presents several multiple regression analyses of the annual

TABLE 3.11

Multiple Regression Analyses of Expenditures for Social Security
and Social Assistance as a Percent of Total Public Expenditure
in France, 1953–1987

	(1)	(2)	(3)	(4)
Constant	0.159	−0.254	−0.326	−0.234
	(0.48)	(0.52)	(0.47)	(0.32)
Change in G.D.P.	0.065	0.077	0.087	0.076
	(0.87)	(1.01)	(0.66)	(0.55)
Election Year		−0.073		−0.119
		(0.28)		(0.42)
Fifth Republic		0.477		
		(1.26)		
Fifth Republic President:				
De Gaulle			0.368	0.396
			(0.81)	(0.85)
Pompidou			0.638	0.648
			(1.25)	(1.25)
Giscard d'Estaing			0.777	0.764
			(1.42)	(1.37)
Mitterrand			0.205	0.154
			(0.34)	(0.25)
Coefficient of Determination (Adjusted)	.01	.02	.03	.05

change in social spending as a fraction of total public expenditure. Replicating the analysis presented in table 3.9, the results in table 3.11 suggest that the place of social policy in the larger budget varied *directly*, rather than inversely, with the rate of economic growth. That is, the share of spending allocated to social policy increased a bit more rapidly in periods of high growth than in periods of low growth—in spite of the greater needs that typically became evident in the latter.

More important than what they convey about the relationship between economic growth and social policy, the results in table 3.11 clearly indicate that the political effects identified earlier applied to social policy in particular rather than just to public expenditure in general. Table 3.11 does suggest that the impact of elections on social policy disappears once one treats it in terms of the share of total public expenditure rather than in terms of the share of G.D.P. But the impact of the change from the Fourth to the Fifth Republic remains significant and considerable. Thus, social policy's share of the budget increased almost one-half of one percentage point faster in each year of the Fifth Republic than it had in each year of the Fourth ($b = 0.477$ in equation 2).

The results in table 3.11 indicate, also, that the differential impact of the presidents of the Fifth Republic on social spending remains discernible and significant when one considers spending relative to the entire budget of government rather than relative to the economic product of the nation. Thus, one observes that the conservative presidents—especially Pompidou and Giscard—presided over large annual increases in social spending's share of the budget—increases that far exceeded the modest ones that occurred during Mitterrand's presidency. The estimates for the de Gaulle presidency are somewhat smaller than those reported in table 3.9, indicating that a considerable portion of the apparent increase in social spending effort in the first decade of the Fifth Republic should be attributed to the growth in public expenditure in general, rather than to social policy in particular. Conversely, the estimates for the Pompidou presidency are considerably greater than those reported in table 3.9, indicating that the modest increase in social spending relative to G.D.P. masked a substantial increase in the portion of public expenditure allocated to social programs as other nonsocial spending programs, and the overall share of the economy absorbed by public expenditure, were cut back by the Pompidou governments. Nevertheless, the overall message remains clear: over the past four decades in France, it has been during the administrations of the Gaullist and "liberal" presidents of the Fifth Republic that spending for social programs has increased most rapidly.

CONCLUSION

We began this paper with a comparison of the spending effort, relative to the economic product, of governments in the domain of social security and social assistance. By the measures used here, France appears as one of the leaders among the advanced capitalist nations, spending a considerably larger share of its economic product on social programs than such nations as Britain, Italy, the United States, Japan, and Canada. Indeed, France spends as much on social programs, relative to its economic resources, as such highly developed "welfare states" as Sweden, Denmark, the Netherlands, and Belgium.

The cross-national analyses presented in the first section of this chapter revealed a quite parsimonious, multivariate explanation of the variation across the nations in social spending relative to the economic product of the nation and to the total public expenditures of the nation. But France spends considerably more on social programs than those cross-national analyses predict—indeed, so much more that France appears as something of an anomaly or a "deviant case" in those analyses. That being the case, the chapter turned to a detailed examination of the change in social spending within France over the past forty years in order to understand why social spending had grown to consume such a large share of the economic product of the country.

The analysis of the growth in social spending within France since 1950 suggested several reasons for that large increase. For one thing, the analysis revealed that the advent of the Fifth Republic, with de Gaulle's accession to power in 1958, apparently put into motion a variety of forces that caused the rate of increase in social spending to accelerate. Foremost among these were the accumulating perceptions of the need to reform, modernize, and extend the benefits of the social security system inherited from the Fourth Republic —perceptions that culminated in a series of important reforms and extensions of coverage in the late 1950s and early 1960s.

The analysis of social spending within France over the past four decades also revealed a complex relationship between the partisanship of government and the rate of change in social spending. Contrary to much conventional wisdom—and to the earlier results of our cross-national analysis—the largest increases in social spending did not occur in periods when leftist parties (or Christian Democratic parties) controlled government. Indeed, the largest increases occurred not during the Mitterrand government, or even during the "new society" era when Chaban-Delmas served as Pompidou's prime minister. Instead, they occurred in the first years of the Fifth Republic, when de Gaulle was President, and later, during the 1970s, when Giscard held the Elysée.

In short, then, the diachronic analysis of social spending in France suggests that, despite the considerable degree of continuity and incremental change exhibited over the past several decades, politics *has* had a marked and significant impact on the development and expansion of the contemporary French welfare state. In particular, the advent of the Fifth Republic, as well as the fiscal policies of the de Gaulle and Giscard governments, exerted a significant upward thrust in social spending.

Having emphasized throughout the chapter the high levels and large increases in spending for social programs in France, it is appropriate, in concluding, to inquire about the *consequences* of a highly developed welfare state. For example, what are the distributional consequences of the French welfare state? To what extent has social policy, absorbing as it does more than one-quarter of the nation's G.D.P., alleviated or at least provided a partial remedy for the burdens imposed on individuals by sickness, unemployment, work injury, child-rearing, and old age? And to what extent, if at all, has the extensive system of social security and social assistance lessened the poverty and the distributional inequalities present in French society?

One cannot, of course, comprehensively address these, and similar, questions in the concluding paragraphs of a chapter, and for such a treatment the reader must turn to such works as Fourastié and Bazil (1980) and the periodic reports of the Centre d'Etude des Revenues et des Coûts (1990). Nevertheless, it is possible to marshal some evidence that allows one to hazard an educated guess about the social and economic consequences of the French welfare state. Tables 3.12-3.15 present that evidence.

One of the enduring distributional paradoxes about France is the coincidence of a highly developed welfare state, through which more than one-quarter of the nation's G.D.P. is allocated to various social programs, and a relatively high degree of distributional *inequality among incomes. Table 3.12 presents two measures of the degree of distributional inequality among incomes in France and the other advanced capitalist nations. These data, from Cameron (1988a, 223), suggest that, despite its unusually high level of spending on social programs, France ranks among the most inegalitarian of the advanced capitalist democracies. What is that? And does the paradoxical coincidence of high levels of social spending and a high degree of distributional inequality indicate that social policy in France has no redistributive effect?

One means of ascertaining whether social policy has a redistributive effect is to examine the allocation of social benefits among individuals or households ranked by income. Table 3.13 presents such an analysis of the recipients of transfer payments in France and five other nations. At first glance, it would appear that social policy in France indeed has little or no redistributive effect. The data in table 3.13, based on those reported by Sawyer (1976, 34–35), indicate that in most of the six nations the lowest-ranking quintiles of

TABLE 3.12

Two Measures of the Degree of Inequality in the Size
Distribution of Income among Households in Sixteen Nations

	Gini Coefficient	Difference Between Top 20% and Bottom 20% of Households in Shares of Income Received
France	.342	36.7
Australia	.384	41.7
Belgium	.265	28.1
Britain	.315	32.7
Canada	.330	34.7
Denmark	.320	33.2
Finland	.304	31.3
Germany	.295	31.6
Ireland	.300	32.2
Italy	.347	37.7
Japan	.270	28.8
Netherlands	.260	27.9
Norway	.304	32.2
Spain	.308	33.1
Sweden	.290	30.0
United States	.329	34.6

Source: Cameron (1988a, 223).
Note: The lower the Gini coefficient, the less the inequality among household incomes.

TABLE 3.13

Distribution of Transfer Payments to Quintiles of Households Ranked by
Income in Six Nations

	France (1970)	Britain (1973)	Canada (1972)	Germany (1969)	Norway (1970)	Sweden (1972)
Top 20 Percent of Households	24.3	9.3	14.6	19.1	10.5	10.7
Next 20%	17.7	10.9	13.5	17.0	11.2	12.2
Middle 20%	19.5	12.6	16.0	16.7	14.5	13.8
Next 20%	20.9	24.9	28.2	23.5	30.6	26.1
Bottom %	17.8	42.4	27.8	23.7	33.2	37.3

Source: Sawyer (1976, 34–35).

households receive a disproportionately large share of benefits. Thus, in Norway, Sweden, and Britain, more than 60 percent of all transfer payments are distributed to the poorest 40 percent of households. Conversely, the households ranking in the top quintiles receive considerably less than they would if benefits were allocated equally among all households regardless of income. In France, however, there appears to be no concentration of benefits among the poorest households; instead, benefits appear to be distributed quite evenly across all of the quintiles without regard to their position in the size distribution of income.[9]

The pattern observed in table 3.13, of a proportional distribution of social benefits without regard to income, suggests that social policy may have little consequence for the size distribution of income in France. To establish whether that in fact is the case, it is necessary to examine the size distribution of income in France. In particular, it is necessary to consider the distribution of income before and after transfer payments. Table 3.14 presents that analysis. Composed from data reported in Sawyer (1976, 14, 35), table 3.14 compares the distribution of income among households ranked by income before taxes and transfer payments, after transfer payments and before taxes, and after both transfer payments and taxes. While somewhat dated, the figures in the table allow one to assess the extent to which—if at all—transfer payments effect a reduction in distributional inequality among incomes in France.

The data in table 3.14 on the size distribution of income in France before and after transfer payments and taxes indicate quite clearly that social policy does indeed have a discernible redistributive effect. This is true, we should note, despite the essentially proportional allocation of social funds among all households regardless of income. Considering only old-age pensions—which, although the largest component of social security, are not necessarily the most redistributive of social benefits—table 3.14 suggests that transfer payments reduced the share of income received by the top quintile of households by about three and one-half percentage points and increased the share of income received by the two lowest quintiles by about four percentage points. Given that those two lowest quintiles, representing the poorest 40 percent of French households, received only slightly more than 11 percent of total income before taxes and transfers, and given that they received 15 percent after transfers, there can be little doubt that social policy did in fact provide some remedy for those with the lowest incomes in French society. Obviously, the poorest 40 percent still received a very disproportionately small

TABLE 3.14

The Impact of Transfer Payments and Direct Taxes on the Distribution of Income among Households in France, 1970

Households Ranked by Income:	Effect of Transfer Payments			Effect of Direct Taxes		
	Share of Income			Share of Income		
	Pre-Transfer, Pre-Tax	Post-Transfer, Pre-Tax	Change in Share	Pre-Tax, Post-Transfer	Post-Tax, Post-Transfer	Change in Share
Top 20%	50.2	46.7	−3.5	47.0	46.9	−0.1
Next 20%	23.4	22.6	−0.8	23.0	22.7	−0.3
Middle 20%	15.2	15.8	+0.6	15.8	16.3	+0.5
Next 20%	8.5	10.2	+1.7	9.9	9.8	−0.1
Bottom 20%	2.8	4.8	+2.0	4.3	4.3	0.0

Source: Sawyer (1976, 14, 35).

TABLE 3.15

The Change in Shares of Income Received by Quintiles of Households, Ranked by Income, Attributable to Transfer Payments in Six Nations

	France (1970)	Britain (1973)	Canada (1972)	Germany (1969)	Norway (1970)	Sweden (1972)
Top 20% of Households	−3.5	−3.1	−2.3	−4.3	−3.0	−6.7
Next 20%	−0.8	−1.4	−0.9	−1.3	−1.4	−2.7
Middle 20%	+0.6	−0.6	−0.2	−0.3	−0.3	−0.9
Next 20%	+1.7	+1.4	+1.5	+2.3	+1.8	+4.2
Bottom 20%	+2.0	+3.6	+1.0	+3.5	+2.8	+5.9

Source: Sawyer (1976, 34–35).

share of income, even after the receipt of transfer payments, and France remained a relatively inegalitarian society. Nevertheless, the share of total household income received by those poorest households was considerably larger—by some 36 percent—than it had been prior to the transfer payments.

The data in Table 3.14 enable one, also, to compare the magnitude of the redistributive impact of social policy with that produced by direct taxes on income. They suggest that social policy has a considerably greater redistributive effect on incomes in France than does taxation. Indeed, social policy accounts for virtually *all* of the redistributive effect of fiscal policy. Direct taxes appear to have no discernible redistributive effect at all—largely, no doubt, because of the exceptionally modest levels of taxation of incomes in France.[10]

If it is true that French social policy—despite the nearly proportional distribution of pension benefits—has a significant redistributive effect, how does the magnitude of that effect compare with those observed in the social policies of other nations? Table 3.15 presents a summary of the changes in shares of income received by each of the quintiles of households, ranked by income, in France and five other nations. The data in table 3.15 suggest that the other European nations for which comparable data are available—Norway, Sweden, Britain, and Germany—effect a somewhat greater reduction of the market-generated inequality among incomes via social policy than does France. It would be wrong to assume or assert that French social policy has no ameliorative effect on inequality in the size distribution of income. But it would be equally wrong to assume that, because it involves a relatively large share of the country's economic resources, French social policy is more redistributive—or even *as* redistributive—as that in other European nations. In fact, French social policy, although mildly egalitarian and redistributive, appears to be *less* egalitarian and redistributive than is social policy in any other European nation for which we have comparable data. And therein may lie both the resolution of the apparent paradox of a high level of social spending and a relatively high degree of distributional inequality, and the enduring dilemma facing contemporary French policy makers: high levels of social spending, if distributed in a proportional manner throughout the society rather than concentrated among the poorest households, and if unaccompanied by significantly higher levels of income taxation, will do little to mitigate the inequalities endemic in any capitalist economy.

NOTES

1. For a discussion of Christian Democracy that is congruent with this argument, see Cameron 1988a, 236–39.
2. As I have demonstrated elsewhere (Cameron 1984, 166), the measures pertaining to the organization and structure of the labor movement are highly correlated with each other and with the measure of openness. For that reason, tables 3.5 and 3.6 include only one measure from that group of variables, although most are highly correlated with the spending measures.
3. To compare the degree of statistical significance of the independent variables in a multiple regression analysis, one can compare the *t*-statistics (reported in parentheses under the regression coefficients in tables 3.5 and 3.6). Those statistics are calculated by dividing the coefficient by its standard error.
4. The percent change in constant-currency G.D.P. between 1965 and 1985 was 49 percent in Britain and 76 percent in the U.S. No other country among the seventeen considered here had a lower long-term rate of growth than Britain. And only Sweden, Denmark, and Germany (and Britain) had lower long-term rates of growth than the U.S.
5. The measure of social spending effort used in figure 3.1 was calculated from data reported by the Organization for Economic Cooperation and Development in its annual publication, *National Accounts of OECD Countries*. These data include all public expenditures for social security and social assistance except that portion of public final consumption expenditure associated with social programs.
6. This analysis thus supports Laroque's contention that the reforms of the late 1950s and early 1960s, which attempted to bring some order to the various social security *régimes* and extended sickness, unemployment, and other benefits to workers and employees outside industry, were more consequential than the more

widely publicized administrative reforms of 1967. On the 1967 reforms, see Guillaume (1971).

7. Since the rate of increase in social spending, independent of economic growth and elections, was 0.182 for each year of the Fifth Republic relative to each year of the Fourth Republic, the rate of increase for each year of the Fourth Republic, relative to each year of the Fifth, was −0.182.

8. For our purposes, an appropriate definition of statistical significance—somewhat relaxed but still quite restrictive—requires a probability of 90 percent for a one-tailed test.

9. It must be noted here that the category "transfer payments" includes, for France, only pensions. This undoubtedly accounts, to some degree, for the near-proportional distribution of benefits throughout the population regardless of income.

10. Among all the O.E.C.D. nations, only two—France and Greece—received less than 20 percent of all government revenues from taxes on personal and corporate incomes. And over the period 1965–1983, only in Greece did taxes on personal income represent a smaller share of G.D.P. than in France. See O.E.C.D. (1985b, 20, 87).

REFERENCES

Andrews, William G., and Stanley Hoffmann, eds. 1981. *The Fifth Republic at Twenty*. Albany: State University of New York Press.
Ashford, Douglas E. 1982. *Policy and Politics in France: Living with Uncertainty*. Philadelphia: Temple University Press.
———. 1986. *The Emergence of the Welfare States*. Oxford: Blackwell.
Barjot, Alain. 1971. "L'Evolution de la Sécurité Sociale (Juin 1960–Juin 1966)." *Revue Française des Affaires Sociales* 25: 61–79.
Cameron, David R. 1978. "The Expansion of the Public Economy: A Comparative Analysis." *American Political Science Review* 72: 1243–61.
———. 1984. "Social Democracy, Corporatism, Labour Quiescence, and the Representation of Economic Interest in Advanced Capitalist Society." In *Order and Conflict in Contemporary Capitalism*, edited by John H. Goldthorpe. Oxford: Oxford University Press.
———. 1985. "Public Expenditure and Economic Performance in International Perspective." In *The Future of Welfare*, edited by Rudolf Klein and Michael O'Higgins. Oxford: Blackwell.
———. 1986. "The Growth of Government Spending: The Canadian Experience in Comparative Perspective." In *State and Society: Canada in Comparative Perspective*, edited by Keith Banting. Toronto: University of Toronto Press.
———. 1988a. "Politics, Public Policy, and Distributional Inequality: A Comparative Analysis." In *Power, Inequality, and Democratic Politics: Essays in Honor of Robert A. Dahl*, edited by Ian Shapiro and Grant Reeher. Boulder: Westview.

———. 1988b. "The Colors of a Rose: On the Ambiguous Record of French Socialism." *Working Paper Series*. Cambridge: Center for European Studies, Harvard University.

Centre d'Etude des Revenus et des Coûts. 1990. *Constat de l'Evolution Récente des Revenus en France (1986–1989)*. Paris: C.E.R.C.

Commissariat Général du Plan. 1983. *L'Avenir de la Protection Sociale*. Paris: Documentation Française.

Doublet, Jacques. 1971. "La Sécurité Sociale et son Evolution (Octobre 1951–Juin 1960)." *Revue Française des Affaires Sociales* 25: 27–60.

Dumont, Jean-Pierre. 1978a. "La Sécurité Sociale et les Projets des Partis." *Le Monde*, February 21.

———. 1978b. "Une Cathédrale Inachevée." *Le Monde*, May 23.

———. 1981a. "L'Heure des Comptes." *Le Monde*, August 30–31.

———. 1981b. *La Sécurité Sociale: Toujours en Chantier*. Paris: Editions Ouvrières.

Fourastié, Jean, and Béatrice Bazil. 1980. *Le Jardin du Voisin: Les Inégalités en France*. Paris: Librairie Générale Française.

Freeman, Gary. 1985. "Socialism and Social Security." In *The French Socialist Experiment*, edited by John S. Ambler. Philadelphia: Institute for the Study of Human Issues.

Galant, Henry C. 1955. *Histoire Politique de la Sécurité Sociale Française, 1945–1952*. Paris: Armand Colin.

Gordon, Margaret S. 1988. *Social Security Policies in Industrial Countries*. Cambridge: Cambridge University Press.

Guillaume, Michel. 1971. "L'Evolution de la Sécurité Sociale, 1966–1970." *Revue Française des Affaires Sociales* 25: 81–97.

Hatzfeld, Henri. 1971. *Du Paupérisme à la Sécurité Sociale: Essai sur les Origines de la Sécurité Sociale en France, 1850–1940*. Paris: Colin.

International Labour Organisation. 1985. *The Cost of Social Security: Eleventh International Inquiry, 1978–1980*. Geneva: I.L.O.

Kuisel, Richard F. 1981. *Capitalism and the State in Modern France*. Cambridge: Cambridge University Press.

Laroque, Pierre. 1948. "From Social Insurance to Social Security: Evolution in France." *International Labor Review* 57: 565–90.

———, ed. 1961. *Succès et Faiblesse de l'Effort Social Français*. Paris: Colin.

———. 1971. "La Sécurité Sociale de 1944 à 1951." *Revue Française des Affaires Sociales* 25: 11–26.

———. 1980. *Les Institutions Sociales en France*. Paris: Documentation Française.

Organisation for Economic Cooperation and Development. 1982. *OECD Economic Outlook*. 32.

———. 1985a. *OECD Economic Studies: The Role of the Public Sector*. Paris: O.E.C.D.

———. 1985b. *Revenue Statistics of OECD Member Countries*. Paris: O.E.C.D.

———. 1988. *OECD Labour Force Statistics, 1966–1986*. Paris: O.E.C.D.

———. 1989. *OECD Economic Outlook*. 46.

Roson, Henri. 1976. "Les Grandes Tendances de l'Evolution de la Sécurité Sociale en France." *Bulletin International de l'Institut d'Administration Publique* 37: 7–20.

Rustant, Maurice. 1980. *La Sécurité Sociale en Crise*. Lyon: Chronique Sociale.

Sawyer, Malcolm. 1976. "Income Distribution in OECD Countries." *OECD Economic Outlook: Occasional Studies*. Paris: Organization for Economic Cooperation and Development.

Shonfield, Andrew. 1965. *Modern Capitalism*. New York: Oxford University Press.

United States Department of Health and Human Services. 1980. *Social Security Programs Throughout the World, 1979*. Washington, D.C.: U.S. Government Printing Office.

4

THE CONTINUITY OF CRISIS: PATTERNS OF HEALTH CARE POLICYMAKING IN FRANCE, 1978–1988

DAVID WILSFORD

We're insured against the big health risks—everything major medical, for example—but it's abnormal, aberrant that we're also insured against the little risks—like colds and the flu. You can even get reimbursed for aspirin, as long as you have a prescription for it.
—French physician speaking in 1984

We lived in the middle of Paris, so we took a taxi to the hospital when my wife went into labor. At the emergency room, I paid the driver and turned to follow my wife in. The driver stopped me to ask if I wanted a receipt. In reply to my "Why?" he riposted, "Because Social Security will reimburse you!"
—American social scientist reflecting on a stay in France, 1984–1986

The French health care system is characterized by a strong, centralized state authority. However, health professionals, especially physicians, are splintered into competing groups, constituting a weak, fragmented interest sector.

This chapter is a revised version of a paper originally presented at the annual meeting of the American Political Science Association/French Conference Group, 1–5 September 1988, Washington D.C. Translations from French are my own. My thanks go to John Ambler, Philip Cerny, Henry W. Ehrmann, Arend Lijphart, and Pascale Canlorbe Wilsford for suggestions and assistance. All unattributed quotations are taken from confidential interviews with the author.

(Wilsford 1988a lays out the details of these characteristics of state and society in France.) This chapter will explore how these independent variables affect patterns of policymaking in French health care.

I will first describe the French health care system and then turn to three examples of state reform of health policy during socialist rule from 1981 to 1986. These cases are the institution of the *budget global* for public hospitals, the reform of graduate medical education, and the proposed departmentalization of hospitals. Finally, I will look at more general issues of health care policymaking during socialist rule and contrast them to policymaking in health care in the 1986 Chirac government. One principal conclusion to be derived from this contrast will be that in health care in France, the political party in power makes little difference to policy outcomes, chiefly because of the overriding salience of the high and incessantly increasing cost of health care. The issues explored in this chapter also point up the prevalence of polemic in French health care politics and the overarching importance that all the French attach to providing comprehensive health care coverage to virtually all the population through national health insurance. This last goal serves to persistently undercut the traditional prerogatives of the medical profession and thus reduce the political influence of organized medicine.

1. "LA MÉDECINE LIBÉRALE"

The French think of their medical system as a treasured mix of socialized access to health care, which fulfills the important goals of national solidarity, combined with the private practice of medicine, which preserves the freedom and independence of the physician and of the patient. This latter aspect is known as *"la médecine libérale,"* or liberal medicine. *La médecine libérale* is composed of the four sacred principles of French medicine first set forth in the 1927 manifesto known as the Medical Charter, or *Charte médicale:* (1) freedom of physician choice by the patient, (2) freedom of prescription by the physician, (3) fee for service payment, and (4) direct payment by the patient to the physician for services rendered. These principles apply to the organization of health care delivered by private practitioners, both generalists and specialists. Private practitioners constitute roughly 57 percent of French physicians. They are private not because their incomes are financed privately —except in rare cases they are not—but because they work on the fee-for-service basis in their own offices and are paid directly for their services by their patients, who are then reimbursed by the sickness funds.

In France a large proportion of medicine is practiced in hospitals, as well. Hospital physicians constitute roughly 35 percent of the practicing medical corps. Most of these physicians are paid on a salaried basis. The remainder of French physicians—about 8 percent—work in various salaried capacities: in public health centers, as sickness fund inspectors, as plant physicians for private businesses, for schools, and so on. Eighty percent of French hospitals are public; their administration falls under the purview of the national health ministry. Public hospitals range from small provincial establishments in rural areas to the most prestigious and very large research hospitals in the large university cities, such as Paris. The remainder, 20 percent, are private hospitals, or *cliniques*. These are owned and operated for profit. Patients in them are covered by the national health insurance, but at a lesser rate. *Cliniques* may also charge whatever they want. In general, they are reserved to the upper classes, for obvious economic reasons, and tend to be concentrated in the large cities or spa towns, like Vichy, Aix-en-Provence, or Aix-les-Bains.

This short description shows clearly that the character of the French health care system is heavily public. In fact, state intervention in health care has a very long history in France. Henri IV issued an edict dated 16 May 1604 that established salary deductions from miners' wages so that a surgeon could be employed and medicines bought to care for those injured in mining accidents. According to the edict, "the injured poor could [thereby] be freely cared for, and by this example of charity, others shall be the more encouraged to work." In 1673, Colbert issued similar ordinances concerning sailors of the merchant marine.

With the rise of industrialization in France—in the mines, in steel, in ship building, in heavy construction, in textiles—coupled with advances in medicine and science—a collective protection of the health risk gradually supplanted individual and familial protection. Zola gives compelling accounts of the dangerous conditions surrounding the industrial workplace in France during the latter nineteenth century and of how workers often suffered. But there was a more utilitarian concern as well. Injured workers are not productive. The law of 9 April 1898 instituted workers' compensation and required industrial employers to subscribe to private insurance for industrial accidents.

In 1930, general social protection was finally established after a decade of opposition by the medical corps to various specific provisions. This national health insurance was essentially a "legislative support" for the numerous previously private sick funds. Employees covered were required to enroll in a fund, and the state paid the premiums out of taxes levied on wages and on employers (Glaser 1970, 17–18). After World War II, the ordinances of 4 and 10 October 1945 further extended the principle of social protection— health care, retirement, and family allowances—to the entire population.

The 1945 ordinances were originally designed by the Conseil national de la résistance to extend health care, retirement coverage, and family allowances in a unitary administrative system. The interwar system established in 1928–1930 covered only a small percentage of salaried workers, those below a relatively low wage ceiling. In the postwar politics of generalizing social security, however, miners, the merchant marine, functionaries, and employees of the national railroads fought to keep their own individual health care and retirement regimes. Initially, then, in addition to these specialized regimes, one general regime covered all other wage laborers and another specialized regime covered agricultural workers. In subsequent years, social security protection was extended to students, writers, artisans, and independent shopkeepers. In the 1970s, the remaining margins of the population were covered: handicapped adults, widows, and divorced women in 1975: single parents in 1976; and all others theretofore uncovered in 1978. This last category constituted little over 2 percent of the general population, including—ironically—physicians. As of 1985 only 0.4 percent of the French population (defined to include all citizens and residents) remained uncovered; these 0.4 percent are normally treated through public welfare funds.

Throughout its historical evolution, the character of the French national health insurance system has always been critically influenced by two forces. The first, the concept of "solidarity," underpins the development of social security since the nineteenth century. By "national solidarity," I refer to the agreement by all elements of an otherwise highly divided French society that social assistance was necessary to the strength and well-being of France— both to its internal cohesiveness and to its power in the international order. This unity of purpose was focused around the concepts of both mutual dependence and national obligation, and it was directed toward social welfare goals concerning unemployment, family allowances, retirement pensions, and health care. The theme of national solidarity dates to at least the French Revolution and has historically attracted all shades of French intellectual thought, ranging from that of the Radical Socialists of Blanc's time to that of the Gaullists and neo-Gaullists of the Fifth Republic. This sentiment was particularly strong in France at the close of World War II. It was a crucial support in the coming together of all ideological factions in favor of a reformed social security system.

The second force, particularly important to all that has to do with the financing and administration of the French health care system, is the corps of civil servants imbued with a strong sense of bureaucratic mission. By "bureaucratic mission" I mean that French high functionaries felt—and still feel—that they act with the authority to perform a special duty. This duty involves the constant definition and defense of the general interest in the face of all who would assert particular or partisan interests contrary to the interests of the whole, or of France. This sense of mission is not unlike the preaching, teaching, and proselytizing of a religious order. The order in French bureaucratic politics is the *grand corps*. Its training grounds are the *grandes écoles*. The mission gives high functionaries in France the perception that the state has an interest that is both definable and defendable. It also shapes their understanding of where interests lie, which of these are compatible with the state's interest, and what types of conduct by decision makers and outside groups are appropriate to this administrative-political universe. High functionaries in French health care policymaking defined their duty as improving and extending social security protection, especially in the postwar period. In executing this mission, they also made use of extensive appeals to the ideology of national solidarity.

Currently, the main sickness fund, the Caisse nationale de l'assurance maladie des travailleurs salariés (CNAMTS) covers the health care expenditures of 80 percent of the French population. The remainder are divided between specialized regimes and the agricultural regime. At the national level, the CNAMTS governs a system of sixteen *caisses régionales* and 129 *caisses locales*. The regional sickness funds coordinate prevention and development, in particular of hospital facilities. The local sickness funds, usually corresponding to departments, oversee the enrollment of those covered by the system and the collection of the employee/employer contributions. They also are charged with the reimbursement of all claims. The national sickness fund fixes all general policy—often at the direction of the government— regarding levels of contribution, levels of reimbursement, and levels of charges and fees. It also generally oversees the administration of the system. This system is vast. In 1985, there were over one hundred thousand administrators, agents, clerks, and physician-inspectors employed by the CNAMTS. Of these, seventy-six thousand worked in the local funds. In 1984, 393 million

TABLE 4.1

Average Levels of Reimbursement Fixed by the CNAMTS, 1985
(in percentages)

	Reimbursement Level	Patient Copayment
Physician fees	75	25
Other personnel expenditures	65	35
(e.g., nurses, physical therapists, etc.)		
Hospitalization	80	20
Prescription drugs	70	30
Special medications	100	none
Eyeglasses, prostheses	70	30
Laboratory analyses	65	35

Source: CNAMTS.

payment operations were executed. The average levels of reimbursement are displayed in table 4.1. In 1984, the CNAMTS administered 267 billion francs in payments.[1]

Physicians in private practice in France must adhere to the *convention* for their patients to be reimbursed for their services. The *convention* is the standard fee schedule for all procedures and consultations that is periodically negotiated between the sickness funds and organized medicine. Physicians are paid directly by their patients, excepting most surgical procedures and consultations associated with hospitalization. If the physician is *conventionné*, the patient is then reimbursed the specified percentage of the scheduled fee.[2] All the sickness funds together count only 734 physicians in private practice in France who are not *conventionnés*. Their patients are therefore not eligible for full reimbursement.

The history of the *convention* has been complex. The 1945 ordinances established a *convention* at the departmental level between funds and medical unions. But beginning in 1946, the Confédération des syndicats médicaux français (CSMF)—at that time, the sole principal union representing private practitioners—opposed the fee negotiating system altogether. The national sickness funds were also dissatisfied, for many of the departmental agreements sanctioned fee levels that they considered too high. This system led to substantial disparities in payment percentages. In theory, the social security system was supposed to cover an individual's health care expenditures, especially physician fees, at 75 percent. But in fact, reimbursement levels varied widely from department to department and from individual physician to individual physician (Wilsford, 1988b).

Against the backdrop of widely varying levels of reimbursement, in 1960 the French state imposed a new system of binding fee negotiations. With the decree of 12 May 1960, the state instituted a crucial change: henceforth, negotiations would still take place at the departmental level between sickness funds and the medical union, but physicians would have the right to adhere to the negotiated fees—or, in the absence of agreement, to the fee schedule published by the sickness fund—*individually*. This reform—imposed by the state—was akin to an open-shop rule and greatly damaged the medical union's strategic position, for it meant that the union no longer spoke for the entire medical corps. Further, the patients of physicians who did not sign— in the absence of a union agreement—would be reimbursed at ridiculously low levels, from 5 to 10 percent of the customary fees charged by physicians in most areas. The imposition of the decree of 12 May 1960 and the subsequent fee system led to a schism in French medical syndicalism (Wilsford 1987b).

As of 12 December 1984, 69,094 physicians had signed the 1984 fee agreement, or 79.7 percent of private practitioners. Another 7,186 physicians (8.3 percent) benefited from a sanctioned right to exceed the fee schedule without the loss of their patients' right to reimbursement (the *droit de dépasse- ment*). These are usually physicians who are either very celebrated in their specialty or practice a specialty that is in exceedingly great demand. The *droit de dépassement* is no longer granted. Another 9,740 physicians (11.2 percent) had opted for Sector 2, a parallel fee system created in 1980 that permits physicians who choose it to exceed the negotiated fee schedule "with tact and reasonableness."[3] In return, they must pay their own social insur- ance premiums. In practice, Sector 2 physicians generally exceed Sector 1 fees by about 35 percent. Naturally, they tend to be those physicians with specialties in demand, or those who enjoy a stable surplus of patients, much like the physicians who were formerly granted the *droit de dépassement*. Sector 2 replaces the *droit de dépassement* as a safety valve, or exit option, for physicians in high demand to get around the restrictions of the national health insurance system. The state and the sickness funds assumed that with a large and growing supply of physicians, fees in Sector 2 would be kept more or less in check. Further, the financing of the higher fees of Sector 2 would fall on the consumer. He or she would be reimbursed by the sickness fund at

TABLE 4.2

Number of Private Practitioners Adhering to the *Convention*,
31 December 1984

	Without DP	With DP	Conventioned Sector 2	Total Conventioned	Non- conventioned	Total
Generalists	43,454	1,149	5,505	50,108	549	50,657
Specialists	25,640	6,037	4,235	35,912	186	36,098
Total physicians	69,094	7,186	9,740	86,020	735	86,755
Percent	79.7	8.3	11.2	99.2	0.8	100.0

Source: CNAMTS (1985a, 16).
Notes:
1. These figures do not include full-time hospital personnel.
2. "DP" signifies "*dépassement permanent*" and permits those practitioners so designated to exceed the official fee schedule at their discretion. The *dépassement permanent* is no longer granted.
3. The Sector 2 was established by the 1981 Convention to permit physicians to opt out of the negotiated fee schedules without losing the right of their patients to be reimbursed at normal levels.

the Sector 1 rate (Godt 1987). Finally, the 735 private practitioners who are not *conventionnés* comprise only 0.8 percent of total private practitioners in France (CNAMTS 1985a). These figures do not count hospital or other salaried physicians (see table 4.2).

2. EXPLOSIVE DEMOGRAPHIC GROWTH OF THE FRENCH MEDICAL CORPS

There was a terrible shortage of doctors [in the 1950s and 60s] and then . . . UP! We trained *plenty* of them. And now, there are way too many. — French physician speaking in 1984

The French state has used its tactical advantages to greatest effect in influencing the demographic growth of the medical profession in France. That growth has helped it and the sickness funds to keep fee increases down, for supply of physicians has come to exceed demand.[4] The explosive growth of the French medical corps and its changing demographic character have increasingly weakened the strategic position of organized medicine.

Growth of physician supply began in 1967 when the French state dramatically increased medical school enrollments. One reason it did so was because as late as 1965, for example, medical demographic studies predicted

FIGURE 4.1

Medical Graduates in France, 1919–1986

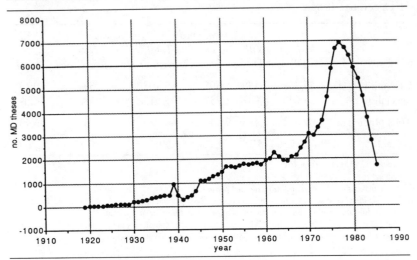

Source: French Ministry of Education, mimeo (September 1986).
Note: Figures for 1983 through 1986 are provisional.

that France would experience a growing *shortage* of qualified physicians. According to the most optimistic hypothesis, there were to be more than seven thousand fewer physicians than needed in 1970 and nine thousand fewer than needed in 1975. Under more pessimistic assumptions, shortages were to amount to 11,500 physicians in 1975 (Bui-Dan-Ha-Doan 1965). The French state thus increased the number of medical students by increasing the quota of students permitted by competitive examination to pass from the first to the second year of medical studies. This competitive quota system is known as the *séléction* in French and the quota is fixed annually by the Ministry of Education. Consequently, the numbers of medical graduates dramatically increased as well, especially beginning in 1975. The number of French physicians has tripled in a quarter-century and more than doubled in the last decade (see figure 4.1). In 1983, there were 147,402 physicians— both private practitioners and hospital physicians—licensed to practice medicine by the Ordre des Médecins. In January 1987, there were 157,527 practicing physicians (excluding retirees). Medical density in France has grown from two hundred practicing physicians per one hundred thousand inhabitants in 1979 to 256 per one hundred thousand in 1984 (see figure

FIGURE 4.2

Growth in Number of Practicing Physicians in France, 1970–1984

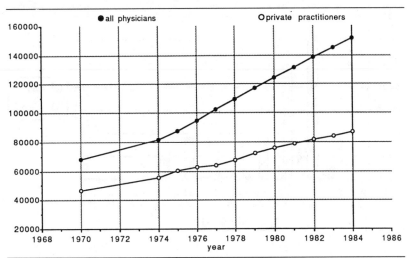

Source: Calculated from CNAMTS (1985a, 8).

Notes:

1. The difference between the number of practicing physicians (the top graph line) and the number of private practitioners (the bottom graph line) represents the number of full-time hospital physicians.
2. The figure for each year is that taken on 31 December of that year.

4.2). Medical demographers predicted in 1984 that the number of physicians would continue to increase at an average annual rate of 22 percent in the next five years. All categories of medical personnel have grown—excepting midwives.

Nevertheless, recent statistics show a slowing of the growth of the medical corps. The average physician age will also begin to gradually rise. The same state that increased enrollments in medical schools so rapidly in the 1960s was also able to restrict them when it became apparent that having too many physicians causes its own problems as well, namely a great many unemployed and underemployed young physicians. The quotas for admissions into second-year medical school have been cut by more than half in eleven years, from 8,661 in 1976–1977 to only forty-one hundred in 1987–1988. Of all physicians who opened a private practice between 1975 and 1979, 3.4 percent had ceased practicing medicine altogether by 31 December 1982. In March 1985, 980 physicians were collecting unemployment benefits (*Le Monde*, 8 May 1985). In April 1988, the state also authorized the sickness

FIGURE 4.3

Number of Private Practitioners in France by Age Group and by Sex, 1984

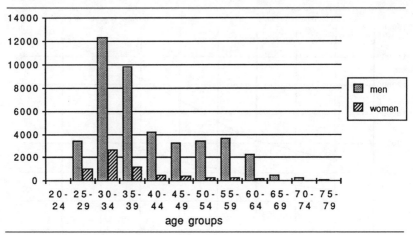

Source: CNAMTS (1985a).

fund to reach an agreement with the medical unions (CSMF and FMF) on an early retirement program. Physicians between sixty and sixty-five years of age would be eligible to retire on advantageous pensions for two years. Altogether, seventy-five hundred physicians were eligible for the program (*Quotidien du Médecin,* 7 April 1988).

The current plethora of physicians in France has three notable characteristics. First, there is the "feminization" of the medical corps. In 1968 women constituted 13.6 percent of all physicians; they constituted 17.6 percent in 1979 and 26.2 percent in 1984. A feminization of the medical corps has also occurred in all countries of the European Community. Second, the average French physician is far younger now—only 42.5 years old (see figure 4.3). Over half of all physicians have graduated after 1974. Third, there are more salaried physicians, a phenomenon tied in part to the feminization of the medical corps and in part to the surplus of all physicians. It is very difficult now for a young physician—male or female—to establish a private practice. Salaried medicine—at work sites, public health centers, schools, and hospitals—offers an increasingly rare security of employment. For women who are mothers as well, salaried medicine also offers more convenient working conditions, especially insofar as scheduling child care is concerned.

3. BUDGETING REFORMS AND HOSPITAL COST CONTAINMENT

During the socialists' time in power from 1981 to 1986, health policies proved to be an area of great reform. However, while François Mitterrand's platform in the 1988 presidential election mentioned ten specific propositions in the general area of health care (out of 101 propositions overall), none of these was the focal point of the campaign. The socialists reformed so much in health care mainly because there was so much that needed reforming. This, in turn, was the case because of the complex, sometimes irrational, always very expensive character of the health care system. Many of the socialists' reforms—even some of those that were fought in bitter ideological terms—had their origins in previous attempts by conservative governments, especially Giscard's, to reorganize the system and to contain costs. The first major area of socialist reform—and perhaps the one area in which they enjoyed the most unmitigated success—was the budgeting reform essential to containing hospital costs.

As of November 1986, the French public hospital system was made up of 1,058 establishments: 29 regional medical centers (including 27 university teaching and research hospitals), 505 general hospitals, 98 psychiatric hospitals, 69 medium- and long-term convalescent centers, and 357 local and rural hospitals. The number of beds totalled 512,344. In the hospital sector, there were 44,000 full-time physicians (including residents in all specialties) and 4,500 part-time physicians. There were 620,000 nonmedical employees. The total budget for 1985 was 139 billion francs (see table 4.3). There were also 2,572 private hospitals in France: 1,407 acute care facilities, 814 medium-term convalescent centers, 25 long-term care hospitals, 20 cancer treatment centers, 283 mental health and drug and alcohol dependency centers, and 23 psychiatric hospitals. The number of beds totalled 209,634. Physicians practicing full- or part-time in private hospitals totalled 40,000. There were 210,000 nonmedical employees. Total budgets were 51 billion francs in 1985 (see table 4.4). The distribution of medical personnel in the French hospital system is shown in table 4.5. In the French health care system, hospital costs take up over half of all health care expenditures. The Paris hospitals alone (40 hospitals in the Ile de France region) accounted for 20 billion francs of expenditures in 1985. They treated 640,000 bed patients and employed 76,000 persons (*Le Monde*, 2 January 1985). Hospitals are thus an obvious target for state reforms.

Hospital budgeting reforms in pursuit of cost containment in this vast

TABLE 4.3

Public Hospitals in France, 1985

	Number of establishments:
29	regional hospital centers (CHRs), including 27 university medical centers (CHUs)
505	general hospitals
98	psychiatric hospital centers
69	medium- and long-term convalescent centers
_357_	local and rural hospitals (without full-time physician staff)
1,058	total public sector hospitals

Number of hospital beds (1 January 1985)
= 512,344

Number of hospital physicians:

44,000	full-time physicians, including residents
4,500	part-time physicians
18,000	temporary physicians
66,500	total hospital physicians

Number of nonmedical personnel:
= 620,000

Total budget (fiscal 1985)
= 139 billion francs
(+ 8.0 percent increase for 1985)

Source: French Ministry of Health, mimeo. (November 1986).
Notes: "CHR"—Centre hospitalier régional
"CHU"—Centre hospitalier universitaire

system show some of the characteristics of successful state policymaking in French health care. As *L'Express* put it in a June 1985 article, it turned out to be *"la grande misère des hôpitaux."* In 1983, many hospital directors thought it was a joke when a memorandum was sent out from Jean de Kervasdoué, then Director of Hospitals in the French Ministry of Social Affairs. It ordered that tap water be substituted for mineral water for inpatients (*L'Express*, 28 June–4 July 1985). But in two years, with the institution of a new prospective budgeting system, the *budget global*, French hospital spending slowed dramatically. Pencils were hard to get, vacant positions were no longer filled, physical plant expansion became a thing of the past, and

TABLE 4.4

Private Hospitals in France, 1985

Number of establishments:

1,407	acute care hospitals
814	general hospitals
25	medium- and long-term convalescent centers
20	cancer treatment centers
283	mental health and drug and alcohol dependency centers
23	private psychiatric hospital centers
2,572	total private sector hospitals

Number of hospital beds (1 January 1985)
= 209,634

Number of physicians practicing in private hospitals:
= 40,000
(all categories together)

Number of nonmedical personnel:
= 210,000

Total budget (fiscal 1985)
= 51 billion francs
(+9.3 percent increase for 1985)

Source: French Ministry of Health, mimeo. (November 1986).

reduced maintenance crews could barely keep up. The *budget global* has proven extremely effective in slowing the growth of hospital expenditures. For more than a decade, hospital expenditures had grown at annual rates of between 16 and 20 percent. In 1985 hospital expenditures grew only 3.1 percent, a pace far inferior to the rate of inflation, 6.7 percent (*Le Monde*, 26 February 1986; *Le Quotidien du Médecin*, 15 January 1986).

The retrospective per day/per bed method of financing hospitals had its origins in France during the eighteenth century (Imbert 1981). After the French Revolution, hospitals were in a disastrous financial state, in part because—being charity institutions—they depended upon the church for most of their resources. But most of the church's holdings in France had been confiscated. The Directory assigned responsibility for hospitals to local municipalities and required them to accept patients from outside their communities. These were most often soldiers or inhabitants of nearby villages

TABLE 4.5

Distribution of French Hospital Medical Personnel, 1986

In regional hospitals and university medical centers:	
University full professors (Step A), including 2,380 chiefs of service	3,400
Associate professors and laboratory or program heads	1,250
Junior hospital staff and assistant professors	4,130
Full-time senior staff, including 2,300 anesthetists	4,000
Part-time staff (all levels)	100
Temporary staff (all levels)	13,000
In general hospitals:	
Full-time staff, including 4,850 chiefs of service	9,400
Part-time staff, including 2,500 chiefs of service	4,300
Temporary staff (all levels)	5,000
Residents (all hospitals and medical centers):	21,150

Source: French Ministry of Health, mimeo. (November 1986).

where there was no hospital. The easiest way to finance this system was to fix a daily rate.

The decree of 28 March 1953 specified two categories to French hospital budgeting. The first category provided for investment monies to fund the construction of hospital facilities and the acquisitions of furnishings and medical equipment. These monies came mostly from allocations by the sickness funds—in close consultation with the Ministry of Health—and from direct subsidies by the state, decided by the Ministry of Finance in negotiations with the Ministry of Health. The second category covered personnel salaries and regular operating costs, including supplies. These were funded through the retrospective system of per bed/per day rates. At first, per bed/per day rates were equal for all services in the hospital, from pediatrics to obstetrics to all forms of surgery. An early attempt to discriminate between the different hospital costs of different illnesses and services was the decree of 29 December 1959. Its effects, however, were not significant.

Per bed/per day retrospective payment is known in the French hospital system as the *tarif journalier*. Its advantages are not insignificant, in that despite the type of illness or the character of services involved in treating it, standard bed rates avoid the real problems of evaluating and affixing a price to highly complicated and highly variable treatments—even for the same illness. Only the advent of very powerful computers has recently enabled medical technologists and economists to begin constructing rough ideal type categories of illness that can usefully discriminate among different pathologies and the services required to treat them. The definition of 468 diagnostic related groups (DRGs) in the United States, affixing a cost to the treatment of each group and using price as the prospective basis for payment for Medicare, is one of the first systems of this kind. The French also began work on an extensive statistical analysis of hospital treatment patterns and expect to combine the *budget global* with a system of *groupes homogènes de maladies* (French DRGs) in order to better adapt prospective payment to the individual character of each hospital.

The disadvantages, however, of a *tarif journalier* lie foremost in its disincentives to economize. If the hospital budget is retrospectively fixed for a succeeding year as a function of the number of patient bed days from the preceding year, hospital physicians and directors can only increase their budgets by admitting more patients and keeping them in the hospital longer (*Le Monde*, 4 January 1984). Budget increases quickly became quasi-automatic and self-perpetuating. Further, there is no rational way to calculate increased budgets on the basis of more objective factors, like treating a greater number of more expensive cases even if each case takes fewer bed days.

The socialists were by no means the first policymakers to perceive the disadvantages of the *tarif journalier* and seek a better substitute. During the preceding Giscard governments, prospective payment systems—most of them variations of the *budget global*—were experimented with in 1977 and 1978 (*Le Concours Médical*, 20 October 1979). The socialists adopted the *budget global* as a matter of general policy in the law of 19 January 1983. The decrees of 11 August 1983 and the *arrêtés* of 20 and 22 September 1983 laid out its specifics. In the new system, a sickness fund was created solely to administer hospital budgets by collecting funds for this purpose from the other funds and by assigning certain amounts to each hospital in France. The individual hospital administration would receive twelve monthly payments and could lobby during the fiscal year for extra monies from the oversight sickness fund to cover special projects or unforeseen expenditures. In fact, the oversight fund—under strict orders from the government to hold down expenditures—has been very stingy in granting these exceptions.

During the administrative and legislative process leading to the enactment of the *budget global*, there was some resistance to it, but this resistance came mostly from the hospital directors, who are the ones who deal most closely with budget matters. The Conseil supérieur des hôpitaux held a "consultation meeting" on 4 July 1983 about the *"projet de décret,"* or "tentative decree," on the proposed budgeting method. It rejected the proposed text of the decree by a vote of eight to four. Its objections were mostly those criticizing the lack of funds and the fact that too much concern was being given to cost cutting. The Syndicat national des cadres hospitaliers (SNCH), representing hospital directors, staked out a position against the "severity" of the proposed decree. To exert pressure on the ministry, it organized a letter-writing campaign to deputies in order to draw their attention to the financial consequences of the reform on public hospitals—most of which were, not so incidentally, located in assembly districts where powerful local political interests were present (*Panorama du Médecin*, 11 July 1983). Clearly the SNCH felt that its administrative lobbying had failed. All that remained was legislative lobbying. But that a parliamentary debate over methods of hospital financing could deter a government holding an absolute majority in parliament and gravely concerned about social security deficits was not clear. The final decree was published in the *Journal officiel* on 12 August 1983. It included all the main provisions of previous proposals. (*Panorama du Médecin*, 22 August 1983). The hospital directors sustained a stunning defeat.

The *budget global* was put into place, however, gradually. For its first year, 1984, it affected only the twenty-nine regional and university hospital centers. The remainder of French public hospitals were subject to it starting in 1985. Further, initially, some hospital expenditures would not be regulated by it at all, such as outside consultations or abortions. Nevertheless, by January 1987 all activities and all hospitals were funded prospectively through the *budget global*. Private hospitals, known in French as *cliniques*, however, were not covered by the *budget global*.

Hospital directors—and hospital physicians—complain more and more about the "nefarious effects" of the *budget global*—mainly because the system translates into a "shortage" of funds. "Such austerity in the financing of hospitals condemns the development and application of medical progress," the SNCH maintained in a press release. It argues that the only legitimate criteria for hospital budgeting are those of medical need, not medical economics.

Many physicians believe that increasing hospital budgets by rates far less than inflation severely cuts into the hospitals' ability to keep up and thus works to the detriment of the quality of medical care—and to more economical care that happens to require investment in new technologies. "We wanted to perform kidney transplants on some of our patients who are currently on dialysis," reported one chief of urology in a large regional hospital center. "The director of the hospital said it was out of the question given the hospital's *budget global*. Same answer when I wanted to buy a lithotripeter [that can] treat renal calcium deposits without surgical intervention."

For the 1987 budget, the Chirac Government chose to limit the growth of hospital expenditures—through the instrument of the *budget global*—at only 1.9 percent (*Panorama du Médecin*, 20 January 1987). Both hospital physicians and hospital directors were understandably outraged. The Syndicat de la médecine hospitalière (SMH) argued that "the critical threshold has been breached. . . . Mr. Balladur [minister of finance] has defined what the Chirac Government's policy for public hospitals really is: it is strangulation, nothing but strangulation." The hospital directors' association, the Syndicat national des cadres hospitaliers (SNCH), maintained that the budget was "highly unrealistic. . . . It deliberately ignores previously negotiated salary agreements and permits no technical or physical progress." But the budget passed, and the hospitals had to make do with their 1.9 percent.

4. THE REFORM OF UNDERGRADUATE AND GRADUATE MEDICAL EDUCATION

The reforms of medical education enacted by the socialist government from 1982 to 1985 experienced more mixed success than the *budget global*. The history of these reforms begins to point toward some of the general conditions of success and failure for reform in health care in France. Before these reforms, French medical students followed a seven-year curriculum before being granted the Doctor of Medicine degree. This degree permitted a student to practice general medicine immediately upon his or her registration with the Ordre des Médecins office in the locality of his or her choosing. Any student who had passed the baccalaureate examination in sciences at the conclusion of secondary school could enter the first-year class of a medical faculty.

During the first year, the curriculum was given over to the study of basic sciences, such as chemistry or biology. At the close of the first year, students wishing to continue medical school were obliged to sit a competitive comprehensive examination, called a *concours* in French. The Ministry of Education set the number of places open each year nationally for entry into second-year studies. These were apportioned locally according to the size of each medical faculty. Setting the quotas every year for the medical school *concours* was a powerful tool that the Ministry of Education used in conjunction with the health ministry to control the number of medical students trained by the system and consequently the supply of physicians. For those who succeeded in the *concours*, the second year of medical studies was also devoted to the basic sciences, in their more advanced versions. These two years together constituted the "first cycle of medical studies," and a diploma was awarded to those successfully completing it.

The "second cycle" lasted four years and was divided into two sections. The first section of the second cycle lasted for one year and its curriculum was solely devoted to a program of initiation to hospital, or clinical, functions. This was the first point at which the medical student actually felt as though he or she was studying medicine. The second section of the second cycle lasted three additional years. The curriculum emphasized a mix of pathology, therapeutics, and actual participation in hospital activities, however brief. At the close of the second section of the second cycle, the medical student had been in medical school for six years. A seventh year spent in an internship *(stage interné)* that emphasized therapeutic responsibilities was then required. At the same time a student embarked upon his or her doctoral thesis, which usually took about six months to finish, rarely more than a year. Upon completion of the internship and the doctoral thesis, the Doctor of Medicine degree was awarded. This degree could lead directly to private general practice, to employment by the state's administrative agencies as a public health officer, or to a position with a pharmaceutical company as a medical representative.

During the last year of regular medical school, students could choose to sit the national competitive examination (again called a *concours*) for admission into a residency program in one of the recognized specialties. As with any *concours*, a quota was set by the Ministry of Education setting the number of students who were permitted into the residencies. The distribution of students permitted among residencies, however, was not regulated. Further, there were actually two separate *concours* for specialty residencies. The first was for acceptance at the university hospitals (CHUs). The second was for acceptance to the regular public hospitals. The university hospitals were considered more prestigious because only they could lead eventually to a prestigious career on a university medical faculty.

The specialization residency (called an *internat* in French) usually lasted from four to five years, depending upon the specialty. Thus, seven years of medical school (after completion of secondary school studies) were required to become a general practitioner. Eleven to twelve years of schooling were required to complete both general medical education and that of a specialty. The residency often led to employment on a hospital staff—heavily weighted to specialties—or to private specialist practice. The most prestigious positions in the French medical system were reserved for those who did best in the university hospital residency programs and then worked their way up through the medical faculty system. This track was also the most difficult to succeed in, as its *concours* were not only more advanced but their quotas were also the most restricted.

While a residency was required of those who wished to enter the university system and—to a lesser extent—of those who wished to enter the hospital system, residencies were not the only way that one could become certified as a specialist for private practice. A parallel system existed, dating from the earliest postwar years, called the *Certificat d'études spécialisées* (or C.E.S.; in English, a Certificate of Specialized Studies). A C.E.S. program existed for almost every specialty for which there was also a residency program. Traditionally, the difference between the two was that the residency stressed clinical experience. Its whole duration was passed "hands on" in the hospital environment. The C.E.S., on the other hand, was classroom and examination oriented, devoted to a complex program of theoretical studies. A specialist trained on the C.E.S. track spent very little time in clinical settings.

The reforms of 1982–1985 changed medical education in France in two principal respects. First, a required residency of two years for general practitioners was established. This followed requirements of the European Community. Second, the C.E.S. track for specializing was abolished. Henceforth, all specialists would be trained through formal hospital-based residencies, while theoretical studies in these programs were expanded and reinforced. The program of medical studies established by the law of 23 December 1984 and numerous successive decrees is presented schematically in figure 4.4.

The broad outlines of these reforms in graduate medical education were first set out in the Veil law (so called after Simone Veil, then minister of health and social affairs) during Giscard's term, in particular the institution of a general medicine residency required of all future medical practitioners who did not pass into a specialization residency (*Le Monde*, 7 February 1979). This reform was required in part by the terms of the European Community protocols on medical practice. But it was also widely recognized that the quality of general practitioners in France needed to be improved. The most obvious way to do this was to require two years of additional study,

FIGURE 4.4

Organization of Medical Studies in France, 1986

Baccalaureate (average age: 18–19)	
1st Cycle—2 Years	
1st year	Basic sciences
	Competitive examination to pass into
	2nd year (60% + failure rate)
2nd year	Basic sciences
	Diploma 1st cycle medical studies
2nd Cycle—4 Years	
1st section (1 year)	
1st year	Semiology
	Initiation to hospital functions
2nd section (3 years)	
1st year	Pathology
2nd year	Therapeutics
3rd year	Participation in hospital activities
	Certificate 2nd cycle medical studies
3rd Cycle—2 to 5 Years	
General medicine residency, 2 years	Specialization residency, 4–5 years
(internat de médecine générale)	*(internat de spécialité)*
Doctor of Medicine	*Doctor of Medicine*
Private general practice	University hospital staff
State and administrative health	Public hospital staff
officers	Private specialty practice
Public health organizations	State and administrative health officers
Pharmaceutical companies	Public health organizations
	Pharmaceutical companies

Source: Adapted in part from Anne-Marie Heuzé (1985).

as had been the practice in many other countries, such as the United States or West Germany. But many parts of the Veil law were indicative rather than obligatory.

The change in residency requirements was formally adopted by the socialists in the 1982 law of medical education, in which a residency of general medicine was created and specialists were obliged to be trained solely through residencies (invalidating the C.E.S. track). The reform also conferred the title of resident on all those following the obligatory two-year program in general medicine. This provoked hysteria among the specialty residents and among conservative medical groups. Finally, the reform initially envisaged an obligatory examination at the close of second-cycle medical studies that would not only test for minimum medical competence in various subfields but would also rank all those entering the third cycle. This ranking would serve to classify students eligible for specialty residencies. And since the distribution of openings into the various specialties was to be controlled, the second-cycle exit exam would also serve to give priority to higher-ranking students when too many students chose the same specialty studies. Ideally, a great measure of additional coherency would thus eventually work its way into the demographics of medical specialties.

The National Assembly voted the medical education reform into law on 23 December 1982. Less than two months later, the longest strike ever undertaken by French medical students had begun. The movement began more or less spontaneously among the students at the university hospital center at Saint-Antoine in Paris. They were protesting the required classifying examination at the close of the second cycle. Passing this examination was to be obligatory for entering the general medicine residency and for qualifying to sit the national residency examination for the specialties. Within two weeks, the strike had spread to every medical faculty in France. It lasted ninety-six days altogether, until 20 May 1983. In an unusual display of cooperation, *all* medical student organizations of all ideological shades supported the strike (with the exception of a communist group), from the Union nationale des étudiants de France indépendante et démocratique to the Association nationale des étudiants en médecine de France. In March over ten thousand students marched in the streets of Paris. In a questionnaire distributed to medical students all over France, more than eighteen thousand responded. Ninety-four percent opposed the classifying examination. In late March, medical students occupied the entry hall of the Ministry of Health. They were "brutally evacuated" and several injured. The government finally appointed a "mediating commission" and charged it with negotiating the crisis (*Le Quotidien du Médecin*, 9 March 1983, 11 March 1983, 24 March 1983, 11 April 1983, 27 April 1983, 3 May 1983, 14 May 1983, 16 May 1984). The agreement reached by the students and the mediators called for abolishing the classifying examination and guaranteeing a certain number of residency posts in specialties and general medicine, as well as funds for stipends.

Resistance to the reforms of medical education came mainly from two quarters. First, the medical students—particularly the less talented ones who were not likely to pass into a specialty—objected to the classifying examination at the close of the second cycle, as we have seen. Previously, only those students who wanted to test for a specialty residency were required to sit an examination at this stage. Tradition was a powerful ally in opposing the institution of a new examination. The medical students in the residency for general medicine also wished to be remunerated at the same levels as their specialty peers.

Second, the medical professors and many specialists objected to the "demeaning" of the title of resident by awarding it also to those students in the two-year general medicine postgraduate program.[5] The "internat pour tous," or the "residency for everyone and no one," became the center of vicious polemic and a call to arms of the political right in the medical corps. The SNAM, for example, claimed in its white paper of 1985 that general medicine residents "are not real residents at all. They often refuse to assume the constraints and responsibilities of real residents. They should have no right to the title" (La médecine hospitalière, October 1985).

Roger Luccioni, national delegate of the Syndicat autonome des enseignants de médecine, typified the university and specialist view: "Why is their [general medicine residents'] level of remuneration the same as the real residents? Why pay those who do not pass a competitive examination the same as those who do?" (Le Quotidien du Médecin, 24 October 1984).

In early 1985, the specialty residents went on strike until Georgina Dufoix, then minister of social affairs and national solidarity, agreed to pay them more than the general medicine residents. Many chiefs of service refused to accept the general medicine residents or to assign them any duties when they arrived. A great many specialty residents refused to treat general medicine residents as peers (Panorama du Médecin, 28 January 1985). Some pointed to the general medicine residency as proof that the socialist government was intent on leveling French society as a whole.

Later, when Michèle Barzach, minister delegate for health in the 1986 Chirac government, proposed to substitute "résident" and "résidanat" in the place of "interne" and "internat" for the two-year general medicine program, the issue became the focal point of unrest among the general medicine residents who did not wish to give up their claim to a prestige title. Many general medicine residents had come to speak of themselves as real residents, arguing that "general" medicine was just as important as—if not more important than—the specialties. The revalorization of general medicine was crucial to making a go of a career as a generalist when establishing *any* private medical practice as a young physician had become extraordinarily hard to do. In any case, several unions had already been formed to represent the interests of the general medicine residents (cf. *Panorama du Médecin*, 20 March 1985).

Further demonstrating the importance of the cleavage within the medical profession between generalists and specialists, most of the medical unions representing generalists sided with the general medicine residents. They planned a series of demonstrations calling for the retraction of the government's proposal withdrawing the prestige title from general medicine students. Said one general practitioner, "Before the law of 23 December 1982 [which established the obligatory general medicine residency], general medicine was a ghetto. Neither the hospital nor the university paid it any attention. Now they want to put general medicine back into the same ghetto." Another claimed that "the only reason the government wants to reform general medical studies now is to satisfy the elitist university hospital lobby" (*Panorama du Médecin*, 28 April 1987; also *Panorama du Médecin*, 29 April 1987, 6 May 1987).

For both socialists and conservatives, the reforms of medical education have enjoyed only mixed success. The tools of control that the state enjoys, such as controlling quotas and administering all medical schools (except one) directly from Paris, enable the state to sharply influence demographics and to institute significant changes rapidly into the medical education process. But in medical education reforms, unlike the *budget global*, the state was by no means immune to the pressures of extensive and entrenched interests—medical students, medical professors, and physicians. When the National Assembly considered the reforms, it eliminated the ranking function of the exit exam as a result of these pressures, leaving distribution of specialists as uncoordinated and as poorly distributed as before.

On the other hand, one important source of fragmentation inside the medical corps—generalists versus specialists—enabled the state to stick to its reforms of the general medicine residency. Entrenched interests, when united, can effectively challenge an otherwise strong French state. But insofar as entrenched interests remain splintered within a sector, the state is provided with opportunities to demonstrate its preeminence and consolidate it.

5. THE DEPARTMENTALIZATION OF HOSPITALS

A third major reform area during this period was the reorganization of hospitals into departments. In contrast to the success of the *budget global* and the mixed success of medical education, departmentalization was—over the short term—an almost unmitigated failure.

Traditionally, French hospitals were organized into a system of fief-like services that exhibited little coherence in the range of specialties covered by an individual hospital. There was also little concern about making the best use of available funds without needless duplication and—thereby—avoiding waste. For example, it was not unusual to find two pediatric services in the same hospital. Duplication occurred in a number of hospitals and in a number of specialties. The heads of these services were the *chefs de service*. They were named by prefectural decree at the direction of the government and upon nomination of the hospital medical commission. The latter usually followed closely the recommendation of the retiring chief of service to appoint his senior assistant. The chiefs of service were named for a life term —until reaching mandatory retirement age (sixty-five years for general hospitals, seventy years for university hospital centers).

One of the major reforms of the socialist governments between 1981 and 1986 was therefore the reorganization of public hospitals into departments. The organizing principle would be the "rational" one of recognized medical specialties. Thus neurology, neurosurgery, and other subspecialties of the nervous system would be combined, for example, into one department. Two urology services would be merged into one urology department, and so on. Departments would be overseen by elected heads serving five-year terms, much as in the American academic system, in conjunction with an advisory commission. This commission would be composed of fifteen members: four senior staff physicians, four junior staff physicians, one part-time staff physician, four paramedical employees, and two nonmedical employees. The government's overt goal was to do away with "factors of rigidity" and enhance teamwork and an efficient use of resources. Many physicians favored the broad goal of using resources more efficiently, but most of them differed from the government's view of how to achieve the goal. In particular, making departments obligatory, placing them under the direction of elected heads, and abrogating the rights and responsibilities of the chiefs of services placed the government in direct opposition to the vested interests of a powerful older stratum of hospital mandarins.

The most important legal texts regarding departmentalization are the law of 3 January 1984 and the decree of 28 December 1984. The time elapsed between the two is one indication of the vociferousness of the medical corps' opposition. Edmond Hervé, secretary of state for health, originally planned to have a series of "concertation" meetings with interested parties during spring 1984. He intended to submit the final text to the Conseil supérieur des hôpitaux in June 1984, send it to the Council of State for a final legal opinion in July, and publish the decree shortly thereafter. But the facts that despite vociferous opposition a detailed implementation decree was nevertheless promulgated and that the twelve months of 1984 were full of administrative negotiations over the modalities of the decree are also signs of the government's and the administration's seriousness of purpose regarding the reform (for general versions of the departmentalization reforms, see Le Quotidien du Médecin, 16 January 1986; Le Monde, 1 January 1985).

Edmond Hervé, then secretary of state for health, defended the departmentalization reforms as part of a global effort that would permit a better approach in light of new ways of taking care of the sick. "[Departmentalization] will provide the conditions for better teamwork between complementary staffs and a heightened sense of responsibility. . . . [Furthermore,] it will achieve a better utilization of the means, techniques, and possibilities available through the participation of all hospital personnel. . . . This is not a revolution nor is it a new idea. Way back in 1976, a memorandum highlighted the importance of new coordination between hospital services" (Le Monde, 3–4 March 1985).

The hostility of the hospital medical corps was—as the Quotidien du Médecin headlined it (7 January 1985)—"quasi-general." The first departmentalization decree was issued in December 1984 and, by early January 1985, almost every hospital syndical group—except the hospital directors and the midwives—opposed it, either in its entirety or in most of its most important elements. The chiefs of service objected to both the powers of a department head over them and to the fact that their terms would no longer be for life, but subject to reappointment. Only full-time senior hospital staff would be eligible for election as department heads, and therefore both part-time and junior staff objected on grounds of discrimination. Further, both the head of department and members of the advisory commission would be chosen by election in which the various medical (and other unions) would wage electoral warfare. Almost everyone denounced the "politicization" thereby of the hospital. Nine hospital unions joined together in an unusual display of cooperation and formed the CLASH—the Comité de liaison et d'action des syndicats hospitaliers—in opposition to the reform. The opposition belied the government's wish that departmentalization be "a central element in the modernization of hospital organization, conceived pragmatically to be a flexible framework so that all actors in the life of the hospital will have great liberty to go about their tasks. The new organization will be largely the fruit of their common reflection and experience and may be reviewed at the close of a two-year period."

Bernard Debré—chief of service at Cochin Hospital (a university medical center in Paris), a Gaullist party activist, and son of former Prime Minister Michel Debré—arranged with the conservative newspaper *Le Figaro* to run a photograph of him and his staff—identities of the latter hidden by surgical masks—in an operating room. All those in the photograph wore stern expressions. The caption read "Sovietization of Our Hospitals." On the wall behind were affixed the hammer and the sickle. In the text of the article Debré lamented that "our hospitals are being transformed into popular communes where it's mediocre doctors who reign, overseen by excited syndicalists."

The departmentalization reform process was turbulent, to say the least. The law authorizing departments was voted on 3 January 1984. The original decree implementing them was published in the *Journal officiel* on 28 December 1984. (In France, laws have no effect until a decree is issued that specifies the modalities of execution. This system forces interests to attend to two largely unconnected lobbying processes, the legislative and the bureaucratic. Sometimes laws reside on the books for decades without having any effect whatsoever for want of an implementing decree.) Opposition was so swift and vehement that Dufoix and Hervé announced jointly that the original implementation timetable would be "relaxed"—so long as the final deadline of the establishment of a departmental structure in hospitals by 31 December 1987 was respected. On 26 June 1985, the government withdrew a second proposed decree from the consideration of the Conseil supérieur des hôpitaux, when it became clear that the advisory council was going to reject it *en bloc*.

By June 1985, Georgina Dufoix had personally taken over the departmentalization dossier from Edmond Hervé and announced that each hospital would be able to departmentalize as and when it wished. The new approach was called "departmentalization *à la carte.*" By September she had decided to name a neutral party—an *haut fonctionnaire* from outside the health ministry, Jean Terquem, who came to be known as "Mr. Departmentalization"—as negotiator with the hospital groups over the ultimate version of an implementation decree (*Panorama du Médecin*, 11 September 1985). On 1 October 1985, the chairmen of the medical faculty advisory commissions—four of whom sat on the Conseil supérieur des hôpitaux—announced that they would break off all relations with the secretary of state for health. Consequently, they would boycott their monthly meetings at the health ministry and would resign from the hospital advisory council (*Le Quotidien du Médecin*, 4 October 1985). In the midst of the uproar, Dufoix also tried inducing support for departments by suggesting that while opponents would certainly not be punished, those who cooperated would be rewarded with certain "inducements," such as the attribution of additional staff positions and the authorization for new equipment.

Many groups and individual hospital physicians favored the general principle of a more rational organization of hospitals. Some duplication of services had long been too flagrant to ignore. The crisis of health care expenditures and the hospitals' role in it were also obvious. The principal organization of French hospital physicians, the Syndicat national des médecins, chirurgiens, spécialistes et biologistes des hôpitaux publics (SNAM, often called the Syndicat Garbay after the name of its president, Michel Garbay)—in a representative "compromise" view—argued forcibly that (1) the department should unite only those services or other functional units responsible for similar or complementary pathologies, (2) each physician must conserve total clinical responsibility for his patients, (3) departments should be headed by a "coordinating physician" elected by his peers to a renewable term, (4) the chief of a functional unit should be selected by his peers according to criteria of professional reputation as a clinical or research physician and experience (to avoid excessive electoral politics among medical unions), (5) the department advisory council should include all medical personnel (but no nonmedical employees), (6) any departmentalization must be *strictly voluntary* and decided *internally* by each establishment, and (7) the department should never be organized for budgetary reasons but only as a function of clinical or technical characteristics (*La médecine hospitalière*, October 1985, 16–17).

Nevertheless, the final socialist decree on departmentalization still contained the following provisions, despite opposition: (1) departmentalization would be obligatory (although the timing of it would be highly flexible), (2) departments would be placed under the authority of a department head elected to a limited term and governing in conjunction with an elected council, (3) departments would be divided into "functional units," each under the authority of a "chief of unit" appointed by the department head and whose appointment could be revoked, (4) incumbent chiefs of service (the "mandarins") could claim the right to be a chief of unit, and (5) the department head would define the medical responsibilities and orientation of the department (with the advice of the governing council) and would participate in the preparation of the department's budget and in the assigning of the department's nonmedical personnel in conjunction with the hospital director.

Clearly, the socialists ceded some important points in the face of the opposition of influential elements of the hospital corps. Foremost, while departmentalization remained obligatory, its timing in individual establishments was so flexible that the immediate effectiveness of the reform was severely compromised. Second, the development of the functional units as a key aspect of the reform clearly corresponded to the current organization of services and thus preserved many of the prominent prerogatives of the traditional chief of service. But the spirit of the reform remained in force over the long term. Given the medical demographics of the hospital corps, the likelihood of an eventual evolution of hospital organization along the lines of departmentalization remain very high. The younger hospital physicians see departmentalization as a way of advancing in the hospital system. As the mandarins retire, the influence of younger age groups will have more effect. Michèle Barzach recognized this and knew that the difference was not one of political sympathies or ideological identification but rather one of generation and career concerns. The Chirac Government announced that departments would be established on a strictly voluntary basis and that the powers of the department heads would be curtailed. The government made good its promise in part with the law of 24 July 1987, which abrogated the departmentalization law of 3 January 1984 and reinstated the service as the basis of hospital organization and the chief of service as its head.

No one doubts that French hospitals will eventually be reorganized. Fiefdoms are inconsistent with the imperatives of modern hospital medicine, particularly in times of severe economic crisis in health care financing. Over the short term, the French state in this case has been rather fully defeated by united and entrenched hospital interests. But over the long term, it will almost certainly prevail, for the character of hospital interests is changing.

6. HEALTH CARE POLICYMAKING UNDER MITTERRAND

In general, much of the socialist governments' policymaking in health care from 1981 to 1986 was initially characterized by a will to disrupt entrenched interests and reform the health care system to make it more equitable. This view was epitomized by the celebrated remark of Nicole Questiaux, Mitterrand's first minister of health and social security. She said, "Je ne serai pas le ministre des comptes" (I will not be the minister of accounting). Questiaux lasted little more than a year in her post before resigning in evident frustration. The financial problem was too significant for even socialists to ignore. Questiaux was succeeded by Pierre Bérégovoy, a traditional socialist, but also a hard administrator. He said, "Je saurai compter" (I know how to count). Bérégovoy made good on his pledge by riding hard on health expenditures and seeking out areas of waste. One of his most significant accomplishments in this area was the prospective payment method for public hospitals known as the *budget global*. When Bérégovoy was called by Mitterrand to head the Ministry of Finance in the 1984–1986 Fabius Government, he was succeeded by Georgina Dufoix, another hardnosed "moderate" (read: pragmatic) socialist. She continued the program of reform in austerity.

Mitterrand made ten specific promises on health care in his 1981 platform: (1) a new emphasis on preventive health care, especially through infant and childhood care; (2) free hospital care; (3) abrogation of the *convention* method of negotiating fees; (4) promoting the position of the general practitioner in the health care system; (5) nationalizing the large pharmaceutical corporations and creating a national center for drug research and production; (6) abolishing the private sector in public hospitals; (7) negotiating with the sickness funds and local communities a substitute for per bed/per day hospital budgets; (8) developing centers of integrated health care that serve all the medical needs of a community; (9) abolishing the Ordre des Médecins and all other similar corporate bodies; (10) rationalizing the forms and levels of facilities and institutions in the hospital sector (*Le Monde*, 26 February 1986). The 1981 campaign was not fought over these pledges. They made up only ten of 101 planks in Mitterrand's platform. Many of these also were either continuations of Giscard/Barre policies or were reforms that Giscard and Barre would have approved. (An accessible summary—in French—of a wide range of policy issues in health care during socialist rule from 1981 to 1986 is found in a series run in the *Quotidien du Médecin*, 14 January, 15 January, 16 January 1986.)

The eighth plank, calling for the extensive development of "integrated health centers," is revealing of the shifts between electoral rhetoric and practical governing undergone by the socialists once in power. The Left had long envisioned these centers as the ultimate way to get quality health care distributed to the most people. These centers would employ salaried physicians, would administer comprehensive health care, combining both hospital and ambulatory functions, and would be financed by global budgets—not through fee-for-service nor through a kind of diagnostic-related group whereby the specific diseases treated during a year would determine levels of funding. Private practitioners opposed integrated health centers for economic and ideological reasons. Economically, they could be a source of stiff competition. Ideologically, they could introduce salaried medicine for ambulatory care on a widespread scale, in direct contradiction to the principles of *la médecine libérale*. The socialists voted a law in parliament authorizing a development program of the centers financed by the sickness funds. But in the period of general economic austerity beginning in 1983, more and more emphasis was placed on balancing social security's books. The law quickly became symbolic. By 1986, only one integrated health center had opened— in Saint-Nazaire on the Breton coast fifty kilometers north of Nantes. In the face of such great hostility on the part of most of the medical corps toward these centers—and as the election approached—the government quite evidently decided that a low profile was best.

Another long-standing promise of candidate Mitterrand was to abolish the Ordre des Médecins. The Order developed its poor reputation with the Left because of its overtly conservative politics during the 1960s and 1970s. Its support of conservative forces during the 1968 student and labor crisis and its virulent opposition to liberalizing abortion laws were two elements of this reputation. The Order's popularity with the left was not enhanced by the fact that it had been established first by Vichy and that it mandated membership of all physicians who wish to practice medicine in France. It thus projected a very corporatist image. For many years the Order also actively opposed the spread of integrated health centers, a concept dear to the Left (*Le Concours Médical*, 17 June 1967, 21 October 1978).

But after 1981, Mitterrand showed little interest in pursuing his grudge with the Ordre des Médecins. One reason is that the Order had changed significantly beginning in 1975. It reformed its decision-making process, opening it to more levels and more categories. At its national assembly in December 1975, the Order voted to institute regular meetings with the presidents and secretaries-general of its regional and departmental councils. A new code of ethics was also adopted that minimized its opposition to abortion and permitted physicians to perform them in accordance with the provisions of the 1975 abortion law. The leaders of the Order after 1975 were men who played politics much more discreetly and with more respect for the sentiments of the rank and file than had their predecessors.

Mitterrand's opposition to the Order also abated because his government had many other and more pressing issues on its health care agenda. Mitterrand's first secretary of health, Jack Ralite, a communist, said that reforming the Order "is not the foremost question on our minds today. There is no reason that the state should regulate all the affairs of doctors. There is no reason either that doctors should necessarily constitute a corps completely apart" (*Le Concours Médical*, 9 September 1981). Opposition to the Order became more and more symbolic. Insiders in the health ministry and in social security had never cared very much—as long as the positions of the Order on important issues such as abortion were not obstructionist. Even an organization formed by leftist physicians for the express purpose of lobbying for the suppression of the Order admitted defeat. "We thought that the Left in power would keep its promise," lamented one member (*Le Monde*, 28 January 1986), naively.

Clearly, in the face of a moderate Order, Mitterrand and the socialists had more important battles to fight, not the least being the legislative elections of March 1986. The health care policies they chose to push—hospital budgeting, medical education, hospital departmentalization, holding down expenditures—were perceived as more significant over both the short and long terms. Besides, there was no overriding surge of support *within* the medical corps for abolishing the Order. One survey showed that 66 percent of French physicians fully supported the Order in its licensing and disciplining functions, 43 percent preferred to see some modifications in the way Order officers were elected, and only 28.4 percent sought its abolition (*Impact-Médecin*, 16 March 1985, no. 134).

Mitterrand, and indeed the whole Left, also had a long-standing commitment to eliminate private beds and private consultations in public hospitals. Private beds and consultations had been instituted by the sweeping Debré reforms of 1958, which modernized the French hospital system and put into place the extensive system of university research hospitals. To recruit the best practitioners—especially to the research hospitals—specialists were permitted to devote two half-days per week to private consultations in their hospital offices and to admit a certain number of their private patients per year into the hospital beds of their services.[6] These two provisions were specifically aimed at making full-time service more financially and professionally attractive to a large corps of specialists who looked down upon the public hospital at the time. Private beds and private consultations were thus thought of as crucial to the success of the modernizing reforms.

With time, however, a certain amount of corruption set in and the Left used it to criticize generally a politically conservative medical corps. Some physicians admitted far more than the reasonable allowable number of patients. Some devoted more office time to private consultations than to their salaried duties. Some did not pay the required percentages back to the sickness funds. Further, for the Left, the whole notion of a private sector in public hospitals was offensive. The Left's view of medicine tended to emphasize salaried and total service in the public sector. The private sector represented "medicine for the rich." Upon assuming power in 1981, one of the first symbolic legislative acts voted by the socialists was the abolition of private sector activities in public hospitals.

Curiously, however, the law of 1 January 1983 did not eliminate private beds and consultations completely or immediately. Physicians could choose. Those who abandoned all private activities immediately had their retirement pensions and health care coverage increased by the sickness funds—at the government's direction. Others could continue private activities as late as 31 December 1986 (Le Monde, 7 May 1986).

The abolition of private beds and consultations became a rallying cry to conservative elements of the medical corps leading into the legislative elections of March 1986. They portrayed the private sector as an essential liberty for both physician and patient that should be protected by the public system. One of the first acts in health care of the Chirac government that emerged from the March 1986 elections was a restitution of the private sector in public hospitals. Michèle Barzach called the private sector a "sphere of liberty" (Le Monde, 27–28 April 1986; Le Quotidien de Paris, 29 April 1986). In another triumph of symbol over substance, however, the economic impact of this restitution was expected to be minimal. Even in 1981, only a little more than three thousand hospital physicians engaged in any private activities in the public hospitals. Of these, 976 were university hospital physicians. The remainder practiced in general hospitals. In Paris, in 1984, 307 practitioners accounted for forty-three thousand bed days out of a total of 10 million bed days (*Le Monde*, 7 May 1986).

One issue in Mitterrand's 1981 campaign that bridged both health care and more general economic issues was the nationalization of the pharmaceutical industry. Making good on this promise with the law of 26 October 1981, the National Assembly voted to nationalize the two largest pharmaceutical groups, Rhône-Poulenc and Péchiney-Ugine-Kuhlmann. The state also bought a 40 percent interest in a third large pharmaceutical group, Roussel-Uclaf (a subsidiary of the West German group, Roussel-Hoechst). A fourth group, Sanofi, is 50.8 percent held by state-owned Elf-Aquitaine, the petroleum conglomerate.

Socialists wanted to nationalize pharmaceutical groups as a means of "defending" consumers' interests in a crucial health care sector. Likewise— as did their conservative predecessors—the socialist governmental exerted more or less constant and direct pressure on the pricing of drugs. In 1981, the prices of prescription drugs eligible for reimbursement by the sickness funds (at various levels from 15 to 100 percent) were permitted to rise 2.5 percent, whereas inflation for the same year ran at 14 percent. In 1982, 1983, and 1984, prices of prescription drugs were permitted to rise 3 percent, 3.3 percent, and 3 percent, respectively, whereas inflation for those years ran at 9.7 percent, 9.3 percent, and 6.7 percent, respectively. Moreover, from 1982 to 1986, the number of new drugs eligible for reimbursement fell an average 35 percent annually. While the pharmaceutical industry has objected vociferously, there has been little it could do, given state dominance of the sector. Further, the Chirac Government has continued the same pharmaceutical macropolicies. Although it sold off the state's interest in Rhône-Poulenc and Péchiney as part of its privatization program, it still controlled prices. In the law of 30 July 1987, the Chirac Government completely deregulated prices for many traditionally regulated consumer goods and services. Pharmaceuticals, however, were a conspicuous exception to this deregulation. Further, for 1988, the Chirac government planned to permit the pharmaceutical industry only a 1 percent increase in drug prices (*Panorama du Médecin*, 21 December 1987). However, evidence suggests that the consequences of this ongoing state policy—besides significantly cheaper drugs—are a decrease in research and development and a loss of competitiveness in the international markets for prescription drugs to such countries as West Germany, the United States, and Japan (Wilsford 1989).

Finally, the Left came to power in 1981 espousing freedom of access to the medical education system. The principal tool for increasing access was the competitive examination at the close of the first year of medical studies. The quotas for the numbers of students accepted from this examination for passage into the second year of medical studies are set by the Ministry of Education, as we have seen. Jack Ralite announced a "pause" in the quota system in 1981. But the galloping demography that we have explored soon changed his mind. Quotas were reestablished in 1982 and progressively tightened. The number of students allowed to pass into the second year fell from 6,482 in 1982 to 4,750 in 1986. The socialists had planned an additional 6 percent decrease for 1987, which the Chirac Government implemented. Michèle Barzach, minister delegate for health, and Alain Devaquet, then minister delegate for higher education, announced that for 1987, the quotas for admission into second-year medical studies would be reduced to 4,460. Nonetheless, the medical associations were still not entirely satisfied. The CSMF, for example, still maintained that little progress in containing medical demography would take place until the second-year quotas were reduced to at least four thousand (*Panorama du Médecin*, 23 September 1986).

7. HEALTH CARE POLICYMAKING UNDER CHIRAC

Despite the usual campaign rhetoric and despite the fact that physicians as a group came back from their 1981 political defection from the conservative political cause, the principal point underlying most health care policymaking under the 1986 Chirac Government remained the control of health care expenditures. In this respect, health care policies under the conservatives resemble very closely the policies of their socialist predecessors.

The emphasis on containing health expenditures was evident at the CSMF's Congrès de la médecine libérale in Paris, held 14–15 June 1986. During the first day of the congress, Michèle Barzach, Chirac's minister delegate for health, was invited to speak. Barzach, a physician herself—a gynecologist by training and a private practitioner in Paris—had long been responsible for health policy planning for Chirac's Rally for the Republic (RPR) political party. For the first time in decades, the health minister was a physician, and seemed to be more of a physician than a politician. The medical corps was delighted at this prospect.

Yet the speech to the assembled CSMF delegates sparked no enthusiasm.

Some measures were announced and received with polite applause. Coverage of physicians by social security would be made more comprehensive—no small matter, as these physicians are almost solely self-employed. Tax advantages would be enacted, such as increasing the rates of allowable depreciation of office equipment. The Chirac government would also maintain the *numerus clausus*, or quota of medical students permitted to pass into the second year (by competitive examination), at forty-five hundred or less. But on the key question of fees, Barzach was silent. One CSMF activist noted afterward. "This has been an incredible morning. For so long we waited for a physician as health minister—someone who knew our problems, someone who spoke our language, someone who was *one of us*. She [Barzach] just gave a speech for over forty-five minutes *and didn't say anything.*" After a year and half as minister delegate for health, Barzach appeared on the televised *"L'Heure de Verité,"* a widely watched political interview program. Indicative of the medical corps' reaction to her "performance," the *Panorama du Médecin* headlined its report, "Doctors say, Michèle Barzach has forgotten us" (*Panorama du Médecin,* 7 September 1987).

Those attending the congress were also invited to a reception at the Hôtel de Ville hosted by Jacques Chirac, both prime minister of France and the mayor of Paris. During his welcoming remarks to the five hundred CSMF physicians present, he made it clear that controlling health care expenditures came before granting any increase in physician fees. Specifically, Chirac announced that physicians' fees would not be increased on the following 1 July as had been agreed by the previous socialist government. In this he demonstrated that he would continue to follow the hard austerity line practiced by his predecessors. Further—and even worse for physicians—he linked any eventual increase of fees directly to controlling the number of medical services rendered by physicians in the succeeding six months. Organized medicine objected strongly to this linkage. The assembled physicians booed, hissed, and whistled the prime minister's remarks, a prime minister they had just overwhelmingly supported in the legislative elections three months beforehand. For the medical associations, putting the onus for control of expenditures on physicians' treatment patterns ignored factors that were just as or more important, in particular, patient demand. It also questioned the medical profession's traditional claim to be the sole judges of treatment.

Subsequently, both the CSMF and the FMF agreed to cooperate as fully as reasonable in a "moderation" campaign—yet another one—undertaken by the Chirac government to control health care expenditures. But both associations made it clear that physicians should not be made the scapegoats for rising medical consumption. The CSMF physicians at the Hôtel de Ville reception in June 1986 clearly felt like scapegoats. The evolution of consumption, they thought, was in equal or greater part due to the other social partners in the sickness funds—the funds themselves, the employers, and the labor unions—and was due as well to the character of scientific and technical progress in medicine. The CSMF emphasized its opposition to "moderation" if moderation meant rationing of health care. The FMF argued that any "modernation" program should in no way interfere with the physician's freedom of diagnosis, prescription, and treatment.

At the urging of the government, the national sickness fund (the CNAMTS) "invited" the presidents of the local funds (caisses primaires), who are responsible for the admiration of reimbursements, to undertake a local evaluation of health care spending, with the cooperation of local physician groups. A campaign was then to be mounted to "sensitize" physicians, employers, and labor unions to the problems of controlling health care expenditures. Finally, a public campaign was to be mounted for the bon usage des soins (wise use of health care services). In return for their cooperation in this program, physicians would receive the support of the sickness funds at the national level for an increase in fees (Panorama du Médecin, 11 July 1986).

In December 1986, physicians were finally rewarded by the Chirac government with a modest increase in fees. The fee for a general practitioner's consultation was raised from seventy-five francs to eighty francs. It was again increased on 1 June 1987 to eighty-five francs. The specialist's consultation remained for the time being at 110 francs, but was then increased on 17 April 1987 to 118 francs and on 15 September 1987 to 125 francs. The psychiatrist's consultation remained initially at 175 francs, then increased to 185 francs and 195 francs at the same time as the specialists' fees. The negotiations over this revised schedule between the CSMF, the FMF, and the CNAMTS proceeded for several months and could only be concluded once the government had given its explicit approval. While the final results were not considered totally satisfactory by the CSMF and the FMF, their presidents and chief negotiators, Jacques Beaupère and Jean Marchand, claimed that "the rehabilitation of the [physician's] intellectual act has begun" (Panorama du Médecin, 19 December 1986). For their part, the sickness funds insisted that the agreement include language committing the medical associations to supporting campaigns for the "wise use of health care services" and controlling the growth of health care expenditures. Maurice Derlin, president of the CNAMTS, maintained that "it's not a gift to the physicians." As Barzach had also promised, the government enacted several fiscal reforms that allowed some tax advantages to private practitioners, such as faster depreciation schedules for office equipment and certain deductions for business use of personal vehicles.

In health care, it is clear that the Chirac government's policies did not diverge significantly from its socialist predecessor's. In the matter of fees and of the whole issue of controlling expenditures, the Chirac Government was just as adamant that expenditures were out of control and that one essential way of controlling them was by controlling how physicians practice medicine —at least by indirect watchdog, carrot and stick methods. In the hospital sector, the first Chirac budget accorded a mere 1.9 percent increase to hospital operations. It continued the principle of the *budget global*. The Chirac Government also continued the *numerus clausus*, decreasing the number of medical students admitted into second-year studies by 6.5 percent, just as the socialists had planned. It also depenalized Sector 2, while enhancing the fiscal advantages of practicing in Sector 1. These were reforms begun under the previous, ideologically opposing government.

Besides all these measures, perhaps the Chirac Government's most important response to the fiscal imperative in health care was the Plan Séguin, proposed in the fall of 1986 by Philippe Séguin, minister of social affairs and tutelary minister of Michèle Barzach, minister delegate for health. Séguin assumed office in March 1986 faced with projected social security budget deficits of 10 billion francs in 1987 and over 33 billion francs in 1988. Séguin developed what he termed a "rationalization plan" for curbing projected expenditures. The measures involved were to save 9.3 billion francs in 1987 alone.

Séguin believed that most of the measures he envisioned were simply rectifications of costly abuses and *laxisme* that had crept into the system. For example, a certain number of illnesses, such as diabetes, had been designated by the sickness funds as 100 percent reimbursable, "exonerated" from the usual copayments *(ticket modérateur)*. Séguin, however, planned to save 2 billion francs by having physicians distinguish between treatments and prescriptions for the actual "exonerated" illness and other charges unrelated to the exonerated illness, such as treatments for colds or flu. The ten principal measures of the Plan Séguin are shown in table 4.6

In December 1986, the Commission des comptes de la sécurité sociale

TABLE 4.6

Ten Measures of the Plan Séguin

	Savings (in millions of francs)
1. Reimbursing at 40 percent pain-relieving drugs prescribed to "exonerated" patients	3,300
2. Exoneration of copayment reserved strictly to treatment associated with the exonerated illness	2,000
3. Reform of the list of 25 exonerated illnesses and elimination of "catch-all" 26th exonerated illness	1,150
4. Eliminating franking privilege for mailing paperwork to the sickness funds	900
5. Adjusting hospital charges to the type of hospital service	500
6. "De-reimbursement" of vitamins	500
7. Eliminating all reimbursement for drugs not prescribed by a physician	500
8. Increasing hospital copayment to 25 francs per day	240
9. Eliminating 100 percent reimbursement beyond three months authorized sick leave	200
10. Extending over three months the base period for calculating daily allowances	100
TOTAL	9,390

reestimated the 1987 health care deficit at 15.7 billion francs. The Plan Séguin was put into place by the Chirac government in early 1987 and the actual deficit incurred for 1987 was only 2.3 billion. The annual rate of growth for health care expenditures fell to 5.1 percent for 1987 compared to 8.2 percent in 1986 (*Panorama du Médecin*, 30 March 1988). Total health care expenditures in 1987 constituted 7.9 percent of GDP (*Quotidien du Médecin*, 25 March 1988). But, of course, many of the Plan Séguin's measures provided for one-time-only savings.

Important symbolically, but with less practical and certainly less immediate effects than the Plan Séguin, were the Estates-General of Social Security convened by Jacques Chirac in February 1987 (*Panorama du Médecin*, 27 February 1987). In a series of local and regional meetings throughout France —not unlike those that prepared the *cahiers de doléances* before the Revolution—representatives from the local and regional sickness funds and from the departmental units of the principal medical unions, along with local political notables, such as members of the local and regional councils (*conseils*,) met to propose and discuss ways of cutting health care expenditures over the long term without sacrificing the traditional quality and comprehensive coverage of French medicine.

The national Estates-General was then convoked in Paris in April 1987 by Chirac himself. These deliberations—and all the local and regional *cahiers*—were then synthesized by a *comité de sages*, six impartial, respected "statesmen" of France, who drew up final recommendations for the government. Their final recommendations ranged from raising the alcohol and tobacco taxes to deregulating drug prices to establishing a new, autonomous National Council for Social Security. Reactions to the report were highly mixed. Even Chirac did not favor very enthusiastically the proposals to raise alcohol and tobacco taxes for two reasons: the inflationary effects of higher taxes on these two consumption goods and the opposition of powerful wine and spirits producers' groups to raising alcohol taxes.

While Michèle Barzach emphasized that the Chirac Government's health policy was centered around "the institution and reinforcement of a [neo-] liberal society" (*Panorama du Médecin*, 26 January 1987), it is clear that in health care for the conservatives, the most important problems were the same ones that obsessed the socialists: controlling expenditures, balancing deficits, ensuring that organized medicine is not too influential. The neoliberal aspects of the Chirac Government's health policies centered mainly around symbolic changes at the margins, especially the restitution of private beds in public hospitals and the contracting to private enterprise of hospital functions such as food, laundry, and maintenance services. These private-public issues have long been a focal point for polemic between the Right and the Left, but in the universe of French health care they do not involve large sums of money nor do they affect large numbers of individual physicians or patients.

8. CONCLUSION

The demographic explosion of physicians that the French state brought onto the French medical profession beginning in the latter 1960s means that younger French physicians today have a very difficult time establishing private practice. The political consequences are twofold. First, hard times have not incited young French physicians to support their medical associations and unions any more now than they ever have in the past. To the contrary, much as with labor unions in general, difficult economic periods mean that medical associations and unions—the defenders, ironically, of physicians' interests—suffer decreased support. Second, while many argue that more physicians mean greater health care expenditures, especially in a fee-for-service system like that of *la médecine libérale*, it is equally arguable that the plethora of physicians has in fact strengthened the state's hand against the medical profession insofar as fee negotiating and system reorganization are concerned. Further, it may be speculated with some certainty that in the most prominent case of the French state's failure in health care policymaking—the departmentalization of French hospitals—the state lost against a narrow, entrenched, and increasingly aged elite, the hospital chiefs of service. Too many younger physicians fight for extremely limited advancement opportunities. Eventually, this will give the state leverage against the entrenched elite to enact the proposed reorganization. As the elite ages younger cohorts will support the state's move to departmentalize hospitals.

8.1. General Rules

1. *Physicians themselves are sorely divided.* There are professional cleavages in French medicine. In particular, generalists oppose specialists. Because they suffer most from the explosion of medical demography in a system that assigns them no formal gatekeeping role over access to specialists, it is in the interests of generalists to support any potential increase in their qualifications and prestige, such as that possible through two extra years of postgraduate medical studies and through calling this program a residency in general medicine, instead of merely an internship. Further, physicians divide between generations. Older physicians support the current organization, which gives them a secure place in the medical hierarchy. They also believe sincerely that such a system assures the quality of health care. Younger physicians push for changes in organization so that their career paths— currently blocked, except in rare cases—will open up. These cleavages add to the splintering of political organizations in the French medical profession —divided ideologically and nonideologically—to severely weaken organized medicine's influence in health care policymaking. The medical corps is hypersyndicalized.

2. *The administration is generally not divided.* The political and bureaucratic direction of the French state is relatively united in its goals for the health care system. Foremost—and regardless of which political party holds power—the fiscal imperative drives policymaking. Second, all are united in a concern that the medical system deliver health care equitably and with high quality. Few policymakers or citizens are concerned with promoting or

conserving the professional prerogatives or prestige of the medical profession insofar as such support might mitigate the pursuit of overriding goals for health care. An ideology of national solidarity is one underpinning to the effective execution of the high bureaucratic mission in French health care and its reasonably successful overriding of organized medicine's resistance to change.

3. *The government can sometimes be forced to back off from proposed reforms.* While the French state gives certain tactical advantages to its politicians and bureaucrats, these policymakers are not thereby immune to outside influences. In particular, given a great deal of vociferous opposition, medical groups can sometimes win or at least gain time. This is more easily accomplished, however, in a period of approaching elections when the government will be more concerned with social peace and enhancing its policymaking record. Further, some felt that the socialists simply tried to execute too many reforms at once (Charbonneau 1983, 1984)—in part because of its absence from power for so long. Of the reforms that we have examined during the socialists' period in power, the earlier ones were more successful. "Reform overload" may have overly taxed the socialists' resources with which to fight those opposed to reform.

4. *But the state has many resources at its disposal with which to keep coming back in case of opposition.* One of these resources is a united bureaucratic corps in health care matters. Another is the clear economic imperatives to restrain health care spending.

5. The first consequence of this policymaking universe is that *the government can threaten and punish groups and entice and cajole their cooperation.* The government often thereby keeps the medical corps from ever uniting completely.

6. The second consequence is that *most projects and reforms are successfully implemented, but in modified form.*

7. *Polemic is endemic to French politics.* In health care politics, polemic characterizes the rhetoric of almost all issues at hand. Both the Right and the Left participate in it. Lurid and extreme language identify it. For example, regarding the elimination or restitution of private beds and consultations in public hospitals, Bernard Debré—professor of medicine, chief of service, RPR member of parliament, and son of the Fifth Republic's first prime minister—exclaimed in an article written for *Le Monde:*

Stop the hemorrhage! Protecting the private sector is not merely a symbol, it's an act required to save our hospitals. . . . Threatening to eliminate the private sector has incited young physicians to flee the public hospital. Five hundred posts are vacant. It will be the death of public service [in medicine] (*Le Monde*, 7 May 1986).

During socialist rule, the conservative daily *Le Figaro* characterized the reforms of graduate medical education as

the degradation of studies because quotas are despised [by the socialists], the cheapening of medical diplomas, which will henceforth lead nowhere, and the debasing of future practitioners. In every domain, reforms decreed by the Left will end in the destruction of the university (*Le Figaro*, 29 February 1984).

Pierre Canlorbe, president of the Syndicat autonome des enseignants de médecine, wrote about how the reforms would affect the university hospital centers:

In truth, they mean the death of university hospital centers (CHUs) as we now know them, created twenty-five years ago by the Debré reform. Certainly, the name CHU will not be abolished. But they will be CHUs on paper only, because the decree of 24 September 1960 that gave life to this system is almost totally abrogated by the new text. This sends us twenty-five years backwards, to the time when hospitals and medical schools ignored each other completely (*Le Figaro*, 29 February 1984).

Another article in *Le Figaro* (19 January 1984) was headed in 24-point type. 'The Whole Health Care System Is in Peril!"

These examples come from the Right, but as many or more could be found demonstrating the Left's forays into polemic. A leftist group, for example, published an article entitled "Stop the Sacking of Our Hospitals!" (*Quotidien du Médecin*, 14 February 1986). But persistent polemic keeps sides apart and favors the imposition by the government of policies that it wants. Imposing reforms high-handedly then results in more frequent and more violent contestation and in the exit tactics that so often characterize protest in French politics (Wilsford 1988a). Such tactics range from noisy walkouts from negotiations to street demonstrations and a variety of strike actions.

8.2 Change in Political Party in Power Makes Little Difference

Apart from symbolic measures—such as the restitution we have observed of the private sector in public hospitals by the Chirac Government—the political party in power makes relatively little difference in health care policymaking. We have seen, for example, that most of the reforms of medical education were first proposed during Giscard's term. Until the election of Mitterrand in 1981, the medical corps hated no politician more than Giscard's conservative prime minister, Raymond Barre. It was widely believed at the time that the election of the socialists could only lead to improvement. Jean Belot, then president of the FMF, observed that Mitterrand's platform took the position that the economic crisis should have no negative impact whatsoever on health care policy and financing (*Panorama du Médecin*, 12 May 1981). This chapter clearly shows that the socialists quickly backed away from their full commitment to uncontrolled health care spending. Their policies during five years in power came to be just as hated as the Giscard-Barre policies that preceded them. Socialist policies were also remarkably similar to Giscard-Barre policies. The socialist politicians who ruled over health care also came to be just as reviled by the medical corps as were Giscard, Barre, and Barrot.

The *journée d'action* of 30 September 1982 provides a telling example of how little had changed in the transition from Giscard-Barre to Mitterrand-Mauroy. In the words of the *Panorama du Médecin* in 1982:

The most recent preceding street demonstration of physicians was in June 1980. At that time, a conservative government [Giscard-Barre] was seeking to squeeze medico-social spending. The mechanism this government had in mind consisted in making the level of physicians' incomes depend inversely upon the level of expenditures that their treatments and prescriptions engendered in the social security system. This time [1982], a socialist government [Mitterrand-Mauroy] projects a two-faced posture: they verbally support private practitioners while at the same time asphyxiating them by not providing a minimum decent income. Both governments have been a menace to the public health (*Panorama du Médecin*, 4 October 1982).

A questionnaire administered for this study to French medical association activists during spring 1986—two months after the legislative elections of 16 March—confirm this impression: fully 58.3 percent of respondents (n = 49) believed that the political influence of medical associations does not change with the political party in power; only 35.7 percent believed that it did (n = 30). Asked whether the political influence of medical associations was greater under the socialists than under the conservatives, 61.9 percent thought it was the same (n = 52), 21.4 percent thought it was somewhat less or much less (n = 18), and 11.9 percent thought it was somewhat more or much more (n = 10). When asked if relations with the administration had changed since the socialists assumed power in 1981, in comparison with their conservative predecessors, 53.6 percent thought that relations had not changed at all (n = 45), 28.6 percent thought that they had changed some (n = 24), and 10.7 percent thought they had changed a lot (n = 9). Of those who thought relations had changed some or a lot, 70.9 percent thought they were worse (n = 22). The questionnaire referred to here may be consulted in detail in Wilsford (1987a). In another poll, 83 percent of physicians surveyed believed that a change of political party in power after the 16 March 1986 legislative elections would bring *no* changes to the relations between the medical corps and the state or the government (*Impact*, no. 164; the survey was conducted by the Cabinet Antoine Minkowski of a random sample of three hundred hospital physicians and private practitioners between 20 and 22 November 1985).

One indication that the political party in power makes little difference—at least insofar as hospitals are concerned—is the position taken by the hospital directors union, the SNCH, as the 16 March 1986 legislative elections approached. While denying any partisan political coloration, the SNCH nevertheless disagreed with Mitterrand's socialist governments on almost everything, from the strict enforcement of policies it disagreed with to the lax implementation of policies it *agreed* with. For example, the SNCH originally favored the departmentalization of hospitals, but viewed the government as having copped out of its original reform. "We were for it [departmentalization] five or six years ago," a press release noted, "but the final decree gives great leeway to individual hospitals. We will not go into battle all alone against the doctors. Instead we are going to follow their lead" (*Le Quotidien du Médecin*, 28 February 1986). But the SNCH also knew that the probable change in government would not mean the end of austerity in the hospital, with shortages in everything from supplies to personnel to investments. It did not.

The Syndicat autonome des enseignants de médecine demonstrates even more vividly that often the political party in power makes little difference—at least in a policymaking sector like health care where the fiscal imperative rules. This group participated fully in the elaboration of Chirac's health care and university reform platform prior to the March 1986 legislative elections. It has been closely identified with Chirac's RPR for many years. But six months into the 1986 Chirac Government's term, dissatisfaction was evident. The Syndicat autonome characterized Chirac's health care policies as incoherent and unacceptable. Provisions of the "reformed" reforms concerning the private sector in public hospitals, departmentalization, and advisory commission were criticized as either not differing enough from socialist policies or not responding to the need for more freedom in decision making by the medical corps. The only issue on which the Syndicat autonome expressed satisfaction was the renaming of the general medicine residency as an internship (*Combat Hospitalier et Universitaire*, September 1986).

More generally, the 1986 Chirac Government stirred up opposition in almost the same quarters as the various socialist governments from 1981 to 1986 and the Giscard-Barre governments from 1977 to 1981. "Hospitals Once Again in Crisis" headlined the *Panorama du Médecin* (14 April 1987) little more than a year after the 16 March 1986 legislative elections that had put Chirac and the conservative coalition in power. The article cited the government's proposals to reform medical education, abandon departmentalization, and revise the administrative status of hospital directors, as causes of the "agitation that reigns in the hospitals."

In medical education, the Union nationale autonome des nouveaux internes en médecine (UNANIM), which represents the new residents of general medicine, denounced the government's "will to denigrate general medicine" by abolishing the two-year "residency" in favor of a two-year "internship." "This reform is completely contrary to all the promises that have been made to the representatives of the residents," claimed a press release. Further, in addition to the loss of valuable prestige attached to the resident title, general medicine residents' salaries would also be cut. Residents in general medicine had already begun a series of strikes in various university hospital centers to protest the government's proposal. Michèle Barzach tried to placate the general medicine residents by promising that at least their salaries would remain the same as residents in specialties, even if their title was changed. As of October 1987, a year and a half after assuming office and in the face of UNANIM's fierce opposition, Barzach had still issued no implementation decrees changing the title of the general medicine residency.

As for the Chirac Government's plans to abandon departmentalization, partisans of the new organization, such as the Intersyndicale nationale des médecins hospitaliers, a coalition of hospital medical unions, reaffirmed their position supporting "a departmentalization that is flexible and voluntary [and that] permits a more collegial organization of hospital structures on the basis of fundamental principles of participation and responsibility for all practitioners." As Barzach herself was well aware, there was a great deal of support among younger hospital physicians for departmentalization, for it loosened the grip of the mandarins on hospital decision making. The younger physicians also hoped that some new career avenues might also thereby be opened. The coalition was preparing to "demonstrate its disagreement with the proposed texts."

The hospital directors, too, were dissatisfied with the Chirac Government's plans to "renege" on prior commitments regarding improvements in their administrative status. Their union, the SNCH, therefore broke off all negotiations and planned to organize a day of street demonstrations in Paris.

Finally, the presidential campaign of 1988 revealed a remarkable similarity of views about the reigning problematics of the French health care system. No party, except the National Front (FN), questioned the dominant role of the social security system in providing health care to French citizens. None questioned the role of *la médecine libérale* in this system. All agreed that balancing social security accounts—without sacrificing quality of care—was the foremost problem in health care facing any future government. The modalities for responding to this fiscal imperative differed marginally, but broad consensus (with the exception of Jean-Marie Le Pen) characterized each candidate's view of major health care system principles and problems. The fiscal imperative in French health care has supplanted prominent ideological reform movements and severely restricted the space in which any politician or bureaucrat has a *marge de manoeuvre.*

NOTES

1. The best overviews in English of the French health care system are Rodwin (1981, 1982), Lacronique (1982), and Economic Models Ltd. (1976). Caro (1969) explores the philosophical origins of the system. Hatzfeld (1963) examines the heyday of *la médecine libérale* in the 1950s and the beginning of the end of organized medicine's political influence in the battle over the decree of 12 May 1960. Rodwin in particular highlights the contradictions inherent in the combination of national health insurance and liberal medical practice. An earlier and equally excellent treatment in French of this theme is Bing (1971). Godt (1987) examines the state's incentives to act against the prerogatives of liberal practitioners in a deficit-prone system. Galant (1955) explores the politics and problems of establishing the current national health insurance system beginning with the social security ordinances of 1945 (see also *Le Monde,* 29 April, 30 April, 2 May 1980). J. P. Dumont (1981) gives one of the most thorough economic and social analyses of all three components of French social security: health care, retirement, and family allowances.

2. Other payment methods besides fee-for-service are salary, capitation, and case payment (Glaser, 1970, 25). Case payment is similar to that based on diagnostic related groups (DRGs).
3. "Tact and reasonableness" *(tacte et mésure)* long governed very loosely the upper limit of fees for physicians benefiting from the *droit de dépassement*. A Council of State opinion (decision of 19 February 1977) fixed the upper limit of "tact and reasonableness" at no more than double the scheduled convention fee. Nevertheless, the local sickness funds have final jurisdiction over what constitutes "reasonable." One of them (in Lille) suspended a Sector 2 physician for one month in 1987 for having charged 84 percent higher than the scheduled convention fee in 1984 and 75.3 percent higher in 1985. The local administrative tribunal upheld the suspension (Tribunal administratif de Lille, 12 May 1987).
4. However, there is an ongoing controversy among medical economists and state policymakers over the "multiplication" of services. Some argue that too many physicians do not keep overall expenditures down. To the contrary, physicians simply make up for lost income by increasing services. This tactic is particularly effective in a fee-for-service system. Increasing services ranges from recommending more follow-up visits to prescribing more diagnostic laboratory or x-ray tests. On the other hand, too many physicians give the state and the sickness funds more leverage in fee negotiations.
5. French terminology in graduate medical education is precisely the reverse of the American. The French *internat* is an American residency. The French *externe* of the 1950s and 1960s was an American intern (*Le Concours Médical*, 16 November 1963, 6259–62). In French, general medicine residents are called *internes*, serving the celebrated *"internat pour tous."* (Moreover, all residents are known in French as *internes*.)
6. The fees charged to patients for these private consultations were not regulated by the sickness funds but were fixed by a "direct understanding" between physician and patient. "Direct understanding" was a euphemism that permitted the physician to charge whatever he wanted. The physician was then required to pay 30 percent of the *scheduled* fee back to the sickness fund. As for beds, private patients could not occupy more than 8 percent of the bed capacity of the service. A patient admitted privately had to pay an additional 25 percent for the privilege over the fixed *tarif journalier*. This supplement was not reimbursed by the sickness funds.

REFERENCES

Bing, Jacques. 1971. "Les relations entre le corps médical et la Sécurité Sociale—ou la vaine recherche entre l'équilibre d'un régime d'assurance maladie et les principes du libéralisme." *Questions de Sécurité Sociale* 23 (10).
Bui-Dang-Ha-Doan, Jean. 1965. "Les besoins en médecins pour 1970, 1975 et 1980." *Cahiers de sociologie et de démographie médicales* 1: 5–14.

Caro, G. 1969. *La médecine en question.* Paris: Maspero.

Charbonneau, Pierre. 1983. "L'inflation des réformes: A propos de l'agitation dans les facultés de médecine." *Vie sociale,* October.

———. 1984. "Les réformes hospitalières: Leurs actualisations." *Revue de la Société de géographie commerciale* (3–4).

CNAMTS. 1985a. "Le Secteur libéral des professions de santé en 1984." *Carnets statistiques* 18 August.

———. (1985b). *La CNAMTS en quelques Chiffres.* (Paris: Caisse nationale de l'assurance maladie des travailleurs salariés).

Dumont, Jean. 1979. *Erreurs sur le mal français ou le trompe-l'œil de M. Peyrefitte.* Paris: Vernoy.

Dumont, Jean-Pierre. 1981. *La Sécurité Sociale: Toujours en chantier.* Paris: Editions Ouvrières.

Economic Models Ltd. 1976. *The French Health Care System.* London: Economic Models Ltd.

Fougères Commission. 1977. *La réforme des études médicales: Rapport au ministre de la santé et au sécretaire d'Etat aux universités.* Paris: Documentation Française.

Galant, Henry C. 1955. *Histoire politique de la sécurité sociale française, 1945–1952.* Paris: Colin.

Gallois, Pierre. 1984. "Réformes du système hospitalier." *Etudes* (March): 303–14.

Glaser, William A. 1970. *Paying the Doctor: Systems of Remuneration and Their Effects.* Baltimore: Johns Hopkins University Press.

Godt, Paul. 1987. "Confrontation, Consent, and Corporatism: State Strategies and the Medical Profession in France, Great Britain and West Germany." *Journal of Health Politics, Policy and Law* (Summer).

Hatzfeld, Henri. 1963. *Le grand tournant de la médecine libérale.* Paris: Editions Ouvrières.

Heuzé, Anne-Marie. 1985. *Panorama des études médicales, 1985–1986.* Paris: Théraplix.

Imbert, Jean. 1981. *Les hôpitaux en France.* Paris: Presses Universitaires de France.

Lacronique, Jean-François. 1982. "The French Health Care System." In *The Public/Private Mix for Health,* edited by Gordon McLachlan and Alan Maynard. London: Nuffield Provincial Hospitals Trust.

Rodwin, Victor G. 1981. "The Marriage of National Health Insurance and *la Médecine libérale.*" *Milbank Memorial Fund Quarterly/Health and Society* 59 (no. 1): 16–43.

———. 1982. "Management without Objectives: The French Health Policy Gamble." In *The Public/Private Mix for Health,* edited by Gordon McLachlan and Alan Maynard. London: Nuffield Provincial Hospitals Trust.

Wilsford, David. 1987a. "The Decline of Physicians' Political Power in France and the United States." Ph.D. diss., University of California, San Diego.

———. 1987b. "The Cohesion and Fragmentation of Organized Medicine in France and the United States." *Journal of Health Politics, Policy and Law* 12 (Fall): 481–503.

———. 1988a. "Tactical Advantages versus Administrative Heterogeneity: The Strengths and the Weaknesses of the French State." *Comparative Political Studies* 21 (April): 126–68.

———. 1988b. "The Effects of a Change in Regime Type on Strategic Position. Resources and Outcomes: The Case of Health Care Policy in the French Fourth and Fifth Republics." Paper presented to the Southern Political Science Association, November, in Atlanta.

———. 1989. "The Political Economy of the Pharmaceutical Industry in France." Paper presented to the American Political Science Association/French Conference Group, September, in Atlanta.

5

FAMILY POLICY IN FRANCE SINCE 1938

RÉMI LENOIR

It is a fact, though somewhat difficult to establish definitively, that France, along with Belgium, is the country that has accorded to the family the largest place in the ensemble of what society considers a matter of political life (Kamerman and Kahn 1978). In contrast to many nations at comparable levels of economic development, in France the family is a relevant category of political activity and administrative action.

In France, aid to families has been the object of a veritable institutionalization, as seen in the fact that, particularly after the Liberation, the family has constituted a specific object of activity in very different domains. In fact, the development of a family policy independent of other sectors of social policy has been accompanied by the creation of several institutions that give the policy its specificity, its credibility, and its effectiveness (Lenoir 1989).

First was the creation and official recognition of the National Union of Family Associations (UNAF), a body composed of a variety of groups representing the interests of the family. Second was the establishment of the National Union of Family Allowance Funds (UNCAF) as the autonomous principal manager of family benefits, separate from other organs of Social Security. Third was the establishment of the National Institute of Demographic Studies (INED), a research body totally independent of other similar institutions created at the same time, such as the National Center for Scientific Research (CNRS) and the National Institute of Statistics and Economic Studies (INSEE). The three organizations—UNAF, UNCAF, and INED—

Translations from the French by John S. Ambler.

are always consulted by the government when preparing measures of family policy; their administrative councils and their directors are part of a veritable lobby, as shown by their presentations to the numerous parliamentary commissions that succeeded one another during this period.

We must not forget to mention the formation and development of the Movement of Popular Republicans (MRP), a political party whose Catholic sympathies were publicly declared and that, as Gordon Wright has humorously written, "preaches and practices the Gospel of large families" (Wright 1948, 105). Most of the ministers responsible for family matters (Robert Prigent, Germaine Poinso-Chapuis, and Pierre Schneitter) came out of this party, which, along with the Socialist party (SFIO), was at the forefront of political affairs throughout the Fourth Republic.

Moreover, family policy has been coordinated and implemented within the framework of a ministry that predates the war and that has varied in name and responsibilities, including Ministry of the Family, Ministry of Population, and Ministry of Health and Population. Policy was also elaborated in the High Commission on Population and the Family, directly under the prime minister during the Fourth Republic. This commission brought together experts on the family from diverse disciplines—known collectively as "the wise ones"—thereby imbuing measures taken in this area with a suprapartisan legitimacy. We find another indication of the metapolitical nature, if we can call it that, of family policy in the fact that the family is specifically mentioned in the 14 October 1946 Constitution of the Fourth Republic, which reads, "The Nation assures the family the conditions necessary to its development."

It is true that the defense of the family seems to have lost some its importance in the political arena over the postwar period, as seen in the decline of the share of family benefits in the total social budget, in the changing nature of these benefits, as well as in the breakdown of the economic and political bases of familialism. Yet this decline may be nothing more than an appearance attributable to the misleading character of certain indicators, to the aging of some leaders, and, above all, to the displacement of the center of gravity of family policy, which has shifted from the status of the married woman to that of the child. Although changes in social structure have led to new language for discussing family policy, such as "categories of relationships" and "types of families," the basic social issues remain the same.

I. FAMILY POLICY AND NATIONAL CONSENSUS: THE POLITICAL ORIGINS OF FAMILY POLICY

To understand the political importance of family policy in France, it is useful to recall the struggles that gave birth to the movement for the defense of the family. At the end of the nineteenth century, France recently had been defeated by Germany, the proletarian elites had been decimated after the Paris Commune, and the Third Republic had been established by a margin of one vote. While it is true that the birth rate had fallen to such a point that at the end of the century the replenishing of the generations was no longer assured, it is less to this weak demographic growth than to a grave political crisis (latent at the end of the century and of which the Dreyfus Affair was but one manifestation) that we must attribute the rebirth of a populationist movement, which already had been in favor during the Old Regime and the Revolution!

By examining the prehistory of family policy in France, we can see that *familialisme* initially came into being at the end of the nineteenth century as a diverse grouping of philanthropical movements connected to social catholicism, a grouping that, in favoring large families, explicitly aimed at restoring a moral order founded on respect for the right to property and "natural" hierarchies, the respect for the right to determine freely how one's property will be distributed upon death, and respect for Christian values (Talmy 1967). In this period when republican institutions were attempting to consolidate and the workers' movement to reorganize, the defense of the family was one of the unifying principles of disparate efforts that had a common objective: political conservatism through a revival of morality, in which the family was both symbol and means. In short, the real issue was the way in which the family would affect social structure and the political structure to which it is bound (Ashford 1986, 252–53).

It is not by chance that in times of crisis the theme that crystalizes all opposing sides is "free choice of families against the encroachment of the State," particularly with respect to the secular school, for that school is the most visible competitor to the family as an instrument of redistribution relatively autonomous of position in the social structure. The family in this sense encapsulates a whole set of coherent attitudes that provide the basis for positions taken on education, the status of women, abortion, and inheritance, as well as on broader issues such as social security and the exercise of political authority.

But the most conservative social categories were not the only ones to defend the family, i.e., the social order that permitted them to keep their position in the social structure. At about the same time, other factions of the dominant classes, which almost could be considered antagonists of those conservative categories, also became interested in the family, particularly with respect to the role of the State in the management of civil affairs (Becchia 1986, 201–44). The leaders of this movement, which can be called "natalist" (the association to which most of them belonged was first named the National Alliance against Depopulation), were not business owners, army officers, or leaders of religious organizations, but representatives from the elite of a secular and patriotic republic, the one that in France came into power at the end of the nineteenth century, including doctors, high civil servants, statisticians, demographers, political leaders, etc. As always when the family is concerned, moral preoccupations were not absent from their program; but in place of an ethico-religious perception of the social world was substituted a vision that today would be called technocratic, one of scientific and rationalist inspiration: they sought to encourage a higher birth rate by economic and political means, thereby also strengthening the economic and military power of the nation.

The defense of the family no longer meant exclusively the restoration of a past social order in decline. For some it meant support for the transformation of the mode of reproduction of the social structure, in which familial patrimony no longer was to be the sole principle and the only objective. Henceforth the reproduction of the social structure took place more and more through systems of resource distribution guaranteed by the State (educational diplomas, social benefits, social rights, etc.).

Durkheim, who participated in the movement, remarks, "The center of gravity of moral life which once resided in the family tends more and more to displace itself." He adds, "The family becomes a secondary organ of the State" (Durkheim 1963a, 63). Underlying this movement toward a form of social reproduction that relied ever more heavily on the school system (Durkheim did not believe in the survival of inheritance), he found not only a new family and collective morality but also new principles that are the foundation of this new morality. This is one of the functions fulfilled by demography at the end of the nineteenth century, when Bertillon coined the expression "the normal family," or the family whose size permits the national population to renew itself (Vincent 1950, 253–56).

We can ask ourselves if new methods of population management in this period were not related both to new scientific definitions that, as Durkheim points out, aimed at extending scientific rationalism to human conduct, and to the establishment of an order of "social facts," as distinguished from "individual facts," as seen not only in Durkheimian sociology but also in the legal transition from the idea of fault in work-related accidents to the idea of risk (Durkheim 1963b, ix).

These new methods of managing the population, which include the development of governmental agencies, large firms, insurance plans, and mutual societies, are founded on moral principles (such as the "normal" family of Bertillon) with scientific (or statistical) backing, and on a social technology that relies on methods of statistical processing (indices, rates, etc.) and bureaucratic procedures (standardized norms, specialized officials, codified procedures, etc.).

In a system of statistical management, the issue in defining the "legitimate" family is no longer one of differentiating between "natural children" and "legitimate children," between "marriage" and "cohabitation"—distinctions that are relevant only when management of the family is a domestic and patrimonial affair. The new moral norms are less concerned with family relations themselves than with those standards, statistically established and sanctioned by law, that govern equitable distribution of the economic burden of educating and raising children among different categories of households.

In short, what are we talking about in France when we talk about the "family" in political terms? The recurring debate over immigrant families serves to remind us of the social factors at issue in family policies in France. It is obviously the social order that is in question: the principles of membership in this order, its hierarchy, and, of course, its method of perpetuation. This is sometimes forgotten when family policy experts discuss the priorities to accord to this or that type of family. Family types are always defined in biological terms (number and age of children, birth intervals) or in "social" terms (in the sense of "social cases," i.e., families with handicapped members, unmarried mothers, etc.). These categories tend to mask the basic social issues of conflict between social groups that are posed by all family policies.

At a time when the paternalistic and patrimonial mode of management of social relations was declining both in companies and in families, there was emerging a system of collective management of the family, whose method of functioning was bureaucratic, that is, a system in which the relations between individuals are instituted according to totally formalized mechanisms and legally defined categories—in short, a system where the relations are those of law. As shown by the typical example of the history of the establishment of family allowance funds from the 1930s onward, such a system presupposes an official, legally guaranteed definition of rights; socially mandated agents to recognize their validity; explicit and precise procedures; regulations specifying rates, contributions, and allocations; and, finally, normalization and standardization of eligibility requirements and schedules of payments.

II. FAMILY POLICY BEFORE THE IMPLEMENTATION OF SOCIAL SECURITY

A variety of measures favorable to large families were taken after World War I, ranging from reduced railway fares to public housing to the creation of a Central Committee for Family Allowances. Two initiatives attempted to give order and cohesion to these measures. First was the law of 11 March 1932 on family allowances. Faced with a persistent decline in the birth rate, the minister of labor, Adolphe Landry, obtained universal family allowances for all wage earners in industry and business having at least two children.

The second initiative was the Family Code, whose goal was above all to increase the birthrate. Government intervention in social relations was no longer limited to solving the problem of salary compensation, as had been the case essentially until the 1930s. In fact, as the threat of war increased, the political world became increasingly conscious of the serious problem posed by the falling birth rate. Daladier created a High Commission on Population responsible to the prime minister. Essentially, it was composed of three experts, men who were both politicians and scientists in the field of population. They were the labor minister, Adolphe Landry; M. Pernot, senator and president of the Federation of Large Families, (and future minister of the family in the last government of the Third Republic); and M. Boverat, president of the National Alliance against Depopulation. Thus we find working together in the same body representatives of the two trends that at the end of the nineteenth century had been so strongly opposed.

The advent of a family policy in France supposed a depoliticizing of the family, which was facilitated by the development of a parapublic administration in the form of the family allowance funds, specializing in the administering of family benefits, and by the emergence of the scientific discipline of demography, specifically devoted to the political management of families.

One must also add a political context in which the thought of war was never absent and that favored the strengthening of centrist forces, whether Catholic or secular.

This High Commission was the primary source of the decree-law of 29 July 1939 relating to "the Family and to the French Birth Rate," known as the Family Code. The latter favored families having at least three children, the allowance for the first child being replaced by a bonus at the time of birth. Moreover, the text anticipated the extension of family allowance distributions to the entire employed population and, within the framework of an assistance program, to families of the nonworking population. Without a doubt, these measures must be seen as a response to the fall in the birth rate, which was already apparent in 1921 but which became spectacular after 1935 as the number of deaths surpassed the number of births.

The Family Code was resolutely and explicitly natalist. It was also "familial" in that natalist measures were placed within the framework of a general policy concerning family life. First, on a material level, these measures were accompanied by provisions for financial aid to different categories of families: development of public assistance, improvement of the situation of taxpayers who have children, aid to farm families to assist them in financing and keeping farms, etc. On a moral level, certain measures were provided to check abortion, contraception publicity, immorality, and alcoholism. On a legal level, regulations dealing with adoption and the guardianship of illegitimate children were eased. As can be seen, this was a very diverse plan that, moreover, was supplemented in November by enactment of measures pertaining to foreigners, social insurance, municipal and departmental taxes, and especially inheritance and housing. A large part of these measures was drafted by a leading expert, Alfred Sauvy (Sauvy 1972, 75–85).

However, the Family Code did not question the administrative and financial structures established by the law of 11 March 1932 for management of family allowances. These structures were attacked by proponents of social security in 1945. From an administrative perspective, the Family Code represented nothing more than an effort to generalize, to coordinate, and to improve existing plans.

Few changes were made during the Vichy administration, in spite of the role played by the family in the Pétain ideology. "Too few children, too few arms, too few allies," declared Marshall Pétain on 17 June 1940, explaining to the country the reasons that led him to ask for an armistice. The Vichy government intended to make the family one of the foundations for rebuilding the country. Although most of the measures taken by Vichy to strengthen the family fell within the contours of prior policy, they were inspired by a conception of society that was radically different from that of the Third Republic: "The rights of the family prevail over the rights of the State and the individual," declared Pétain (Paxton 1973, 165).

The Vichy program on family matters limited itself to continuing prewar policy, but in a more energetic fashion. For example, with respect to return to the land, the Family Code of 1939 provided for loans to young couples, loans whose interest and repayment declined as children were born; it also stipulated that the son who remained on the farm should inherit a larger portion than his urban brothers and sisters. The Code also strengthened laws against abortion and returned to an earlier view of adoption in which the adopted child belonged entirely to his or her new family. Such measures lay within the scope of the conception of the family advocated by the new regime.

It was above all the role within society that the Vichy government intended to give the family that was the original element of the policy of this period. The family was the "cell of French life" and would replace the individual as the basic unit of social life. Consequently divorce was obviously the primary target of the Vichy regime. The law of 2 April 1941 prohibited divorce during the first three years of marriage. The government also favored heads of households with large families and penalized those that had few or no children. Fathers of large families had membership rights in numerous organizations, while a single man or one without children could not hope to have a career or to advance, particularly in the judiciary. Finally, if the mother of the family was glorified, it was on the condition that she remain at home: the law of 11 October 1940 encouraged women not to work; the law of 15 August 1941, providing primary schools for girls, manifestly preferred to keep pregnant women at home. Obviously women did not yet have the right to vote, a right they would earn in 1945.

Once judgment had been passed on the Vichy regime, representatives of Resistance organizations, trade unions, and political parties or tendencies, all grouped within the National Council of the Resistance, resolved to unite on a platform that gave an important position to family policy. This program called for the development of "solidarity toward the families of all the victims of the Hitler and Vichy terror"; "an important readjustment of wages and the guarantee of a wage level and remuneration which would assure to each worker and his family security, dignity, and the possibility of a fully human life"; and "a complete Social Security plan" (Conseil National de la Résistance 1944).

III. FAMILY POLICY AND THE INAUGURATION OF THE
FOURTH REPUBLIC (1946–1958)

Political discussion of the family and of the measures relating to it thereafter took on an ambiguous character. In contrast to familialism, which established the defense of the family as an explicit issue and a way of doing political battle—a sort of familial corporatism based on the symbolic and political instrument of the "familial vote," which was politically discredited with the fall of the Vichy government—"protection of the family" in the postwar political arena was no longer such a divisive issue. Even more than before, family policy became bureaucratized and legitimized.

Numerous indications attest to this neutralization of the social issues that family policy always raises. Debate on these issues came to be characterized by what could be called the "rhetoric of impartiality," evidenced in a tendency of all parties to avoid the most violent forms of polemics, to respect the positions of adversaries, and generally to reject a conception of debate in this area as open political conflict. This strategy of neutralization found its fulfillment in the "rhetoric of scientificity," in which opponents employed economic, demographic, and sociological arguments with increasing frequency (Bourdieu 1982, 155–59).

The fact remains that this kind of political depoliticization of family policy was not accomplished without political clashes, as for example and in particular, the administrative organization of family allocation funds. Yet the family aid programs instituted during this period almost always were passed unanimously, despite the very different importance and significance they held for the various parties.

Political Families and Family Policy

With the Liberation, France made an ambitious choice in favor of the family, because the standard of living of families just after the war was particularly low and therefore constituted a national priority. In 1946 spending on family benefits represented almost 40 percent of total social security spending. If, in the programs of the two most important leftist parties, the Communist Party (PCF) and the Socialist Party (SFIO) (parties that together drew nearly 50 percent of the vote), allusions to family policy *stricto sensu* were rare, they were very much in evidence in the Movement of Popular Republicans (MRP). In the 13 November 1945 declaration of the French Episcopate on "the human person, the family, and society," the Catholic hierarchy, which tightly controlled the political orientation of the MRP, made a distinction between "secularism," an atheistic and materialistic doctrine, and "secularity," which could be tolerated to the extent that it concerns only the autonomy of the State in its domain of temporal order. The "duties" of the State include aid to families, not only in response to their physical needs (food, hygiene, lodging) but also to their social needs (equal opportunity) and moral needs (the fight against "individualism").

It is perhaps not in the programs of political parties (particularly in this period of economic, political, and constitutional crisis) that positions are clearly revealed, for there is little mention of family policy, except in the program of the MRP. The principles and proposals of each partisan movement are better enunciated in the statements of members of parliament, involved ministers, and experts more or less affiliated with a party, as well as in journals and in the deliberations of public bodies, particularly those of the General Planning Commission.

If all politicians and experts (physicians, demographers, representatives of family associations) agreed on natalist objectives (General De Gaulle in 1945 spoke of the "12 million beautiful babies" France needed to once again become a great nation), the attention given to demographic problems and to the methods of solving them differed according to political leanings. Thus, for the Communist minister François Billoux, the State should give aid to four categories of families: the large family, young couples without children, households of refugees and deportees, and young people about to be married.

Most of the parties of the Left and of the Right, as well as the experts, shared a concern with natalist issues. However, rifts clearly emerged, less between formal political parties than between movements, regarding the preferred type of family and moral values, and the social order with which these were associated. The shared concern is evidenced by an opinion given by the Commission on Consumption and Social Modernization of the General Planning Commission, where most of the nonparliamentary formulators of social, health, and demographic policies of the Fourth Republic were grouped under the presidency of Henri Raynaud, secretary of the General Confederation of Labor.

This opinion stipulated:

It has come to the attention of the General Planning Commission that the various commissions created to study the modernization of each sector of production 1) were not well informed as to the optimum needs of French consumers, 2) through lack of sufficient information and because of the principal objective of their work, risked neglecting the human and social side of problems posed by the Plan. . . .

The Commission determined the optimum population of France and, on the basis of this number, established the essential needs of this population in order to afford it the best possible living conditions.

The optimum was fixed at 50–60 million and was justified by the following four arguments:

1) The working population of France is insufficient to satisfy labor demands for production and defense.

2) General costs to the French nation are borne by too few individuals.

3) The burden posed by the elderly population is becoming too heavy for the younger generations.

4) The French population is too small in comparison to neighboring countries (Commissariat Géneral du Plan 1947).

There followed a detailed catalogue of methods, similar to those expressed in the Family Code of 1939, designed to satisfy all parties and intended to increase the birthrate and to improve the "quality" of the population. Apart from the obligatory mention of moral considerations regarding alcoholism and abortion, the proposal consisted of measures offering direct incentives for natality (prenatal and family allowances, declining rates for taxes and public services according to the number of children, etc.); of recommendations pertaining to nursery schools and daycare; and finally, of steps to help working mothers (extension of maternity leaves, development of part-time work, and creation of a compulsory national service for women to provide mothers' helpers). A single observation attests to the marginalization of "familialists"; the commission did not consider itself qualified to take a stand on the "familial vote," which would have given each head of family a number of votes equivalent to the number of members of his family. Yet this measure found numerous supporters in the ranks of the MRP, which was in fact poorly represented on this commission.

Finally, without attributing this tendency to a particular political movement, it is important to underline the emergence in this period of a kind of ethical avant-garde, which was particularly visible in the literary and journalistic fields (Simone de Beauvoir's emblematic book, *The Second Sex*, was published in 1949 [see Lenoir 1985b, 3–47]). This avant-garde expressed itself in the political arena only in the form of a defense of women's right (indeed, their obligation!) to work and a call for necessary reforms, as shown by this excerpt from the first report of the Commission on Manpower under the General Planning Commission:

—equalization of male and female salaries for equal work;
—increased possibilities for women to obtain and to improve their professional qualifications; access to all jobs, even at the highest levels;
—replacement of the single-income allowance by an equivalent family allowance, added to the normal family allowances,
—facilities for purchase of supplies (cooperatives, etc.) accorded to working women (28).

From whom did these recommendations come? Not only from the union members of the General Confederation of Labor (CGT) but also from members of the National Council of French Employers (CNPF) and from high civil servants, for example Paul Delouvrier. We see already a sign of what in the 1950s was to become one of the issues of family policy, creating rifts between parties and especially within each of them: the professional status of women. But in 1945 the political class was much more divided over the administrative organization of the funds for family allowances than over legislation pertaining to benefits.

Administrative Organization of Funds for Family Allowances and Legislation Pertaining to Family Benefits

The ordinance of 4 October 1945, which established the new system of social security, brought radical modifications both to the administrative structure and to the financial organization of family allowance funds. It included the funds in a unified and centralized social security structure and broke the monopoly of employers over fund management. However, the new plan sought to decentralize the administration of social security and to give beneficiaries a role in its management. The institutions created to manage benefits differed from the employer compensation funds of the previous system in the following ways. The new system has regional offices that are responsible for all benefits and that impose a uniform rate of contribution fixed by the State. Above all, these offices are managed by a council made up exclusively of beneficiaries, appointed in part by employees, in part by employers, and in part by independent workers.

At the outset, the family allowance funds were not intended to be autonomous: the primary Social Security funds were to collect contributions and distribute benefits. However, with the first social security reform proposals, representatives of the existing funds called for the preservation of a special system for family allowances. The arguments were largely of a technical nature: the uniqueness and vulnerability of family interests compared to other risks covered by Social Security, etc. In fact, autonomy for the funds and the methods of appointment of administrators constituted a major political issue after the war.

On the side of the supporters of a single fund were the leftist parties, Socialist and Communist, as well as the General Confederation of Labor (CGT); on the side of the partisans of autonomy, who did not question the idea of a vast system of social protection, were the social Christians, notably the MRP, the centrists, and a portion of the Right. Likewise, strong political opposition developed around the issue of beneficiary representation. Beginning with the First Constiuent Assembly, where the Left was largely predominant, the MRP, with a relatively large representation, introduced several bills calling for revision of Social Security ordinances. The MRP held that the family allowance funds should be independent and autonomous, employers should have a preponderant role in their administration, and the representation of male heads of households on administrative councils should be increased. All of these proposals were rejected by leftist forces. As for the selection of delegates to administrative councils, the CGT and the leftist parties were against direct election by the whole body of wage earners and supported the principle of selection by appointment.

Doubtless one must see in these conflicting positions the desire of each political organization to control the new institutions whose services were not without effect on the unions. Before the war, the Left had left the field of family matters open for the Right. One must recall that, at that time, the workers' movement was very much opposed to family allowances, for two reasons: the family allowance was considered to be a salary supplement, and its management was the exclusive responsibility of employers. Hence for employers the family allowance was a way to avoid salary increases. One has only to refer back to a series of labor arbitrations in 1936 and 1937 to be convinced of this particular function of family allowances. From 1945 to 1946, there was a marked turnaround in the attitude of union organizations and leftist political groups, a change linked both to the dissociation of family allowances from salary and to the allocation of their management to representatives of beneficiaries of the compensation funds. The mode of election of members of the administrative councils of Social Security and family allowance funds was not fixed until the law of 30 October 1946, which established the principle of election of administrators by proportional representation. The Second National Constiuent Assembly, meeting on 11 June 1946, marked a slight move to the right as the MRP became the largest party. After political negotiations led by André Morice, the Communist and Socialist parties finally accepted the principle of election.

Family allowance funds were definitively granted autonomy by the law of 21 February 1949, largely as a result of pressure from family movements and of the administrative experience of the funds. The importance of separating management of family benefits from that of other social risks was no longer contested. In addition to the fact that the generalization of Social Security encountered numerous difficulties, it was clearly apparent to the majority of administrators themselves that autonomy was necessary, even more so since in the first two elections of members of the administrative councils the CGT carried the election for the Social Security funds as well as for the family allowance funds.

If autonomy of management of the funds was the subject of a political battle, the system of family benefits, relatively simple in itself, was adopted unanimously on 22 August 1946. It generally continued existing policy, but focused on basic benefits such as family allowances, single-income allowances, and maternity allowances. Besides rate increases, the essential modifications were:

—extension of family allowances to the nonworking population, subject to justification of the inability of the concerned party to work. Consequently, the law called for the payment of family benefits no longer to the head of household, but to the person having effective and permanent care of the children;
—generalization of the allowance to all families with a single income whether the children are legitimate or natural, recognized or not, whatever the nationality of the parents (Ceccaldi 1957).

Like the system of family benefits, that of family tax deductions (*quotient familial*) was also adopted easily in the law of 31 December 1945, with the only reservation expressed being that it did not give a sufficient advantage to taxpayers burdened with a family. To be sure, family policy as a fiscal matter does not date from 1945; but economic circumstances, legislative revisions, and the needs of the State had reduced family tax deductions to a minimum. Creation of the family "quotient" established a policy resolutely favorable to a growing birth rate, not only be allowing deductions for dependents but also by taxing neither income linked to the family (family allowances) nor indirect income (Social Security).

Professional Needs of Married Women and the Family Model

If, since the eve of Liberation, family policy has been above all concerned with the changing status of the married woman, it is because that which is fundamentally at stake is the mode of reproduction of the social structure. Each mode of reproduction implies a definition of the role and of the position of the woman not only within the family but throughout society.

The official recognition of a "family interest," to use the legal expression, was accompanied by the diffusion of a "family model" that justified all possible measures in favor of this "basic societal cell," according to the organistic terminology still in vogue at this time. The dominant model was still the legitimate family, of French nationality, with at least three children and in which the mother remains at home and the father is legally the "head." The "mother at home," the original name for the allowance paid to households where the woman does not work, was the principal instrument of this family doctrine, which was politically instituted under Vichy and which survived more or less until the 1960s. Thus, in 1943, the allowance to single-income families represented more than 52 percent of paid benefits, for 76 percent of mothers of two children, 88 percent of mothers of three children, and 92-98 percent of mothers of four children received this allowance. This family model and the status of the woman that is associated with it were not really questioned during the Liberation or for almost twenty years after, except with respect to political rights, with women earning the right to vote on 5 October 1944, and divorce, with the ordinance of 12 April 1945 eliminating the prohibition of divorce in the first three years of marriage.

The creation of a right to Social Security and social aid, along with the development of specialized institutions in what has come to be called the "social sector" (cf. Durand 1953a), led to the creation of a legal definition of the family different from that of civil law, partly because new objectives were being established but also because a new set of lawyers and experts addressed the problem. Two examples from the 22 August 1946 law bear witness: family benefits were no longer paid to the "head of household" but to the person having "effective and permanent care of the children"; the notion of "child in care" supplanted the notion of legitimacy and the allocation of the single-income family allowance came into general use for all children, legitimate or not, recognized or not, regardless of the parents' nationality.

IV. THE FOURTH REPUBLIC: THE SPLENDOR AND DECADENCE OF FAMILIALISM

Without a doubt we must attribute both the rapid development and the orientation of family policy under the Fourth Republic to the strategic position of the MRP in the political field at this time and also to the alliance in which the MRP was almost always a leading party.

The Golden Age of Familialism

A series of measures taken in this period had symbolic value as bearers of the familialist banner: the Medal of Honor for the French Family was upgraded in 1947 and Mother's Day was created on 29 May 1950. It was also during this eventful period (one of the Cold War, the Indochinese War, the debate over the creation of the European Defense Community, financial stabilization, and a halt in economic growth) that a proposal to divert 0.75 percent of family allowance contributions to social insurance provoked a ministerial crisis! The Pinay government was in fact dropped by the MRP on 23 December 1952, apparently for this reason, but actually because of the European Defense Community. In the name of and on behalf of the family, ad hoc groups formed to take action, for example in the passage of the law of 1 September 1948 on decontrol of rents, in which the principle of decontrol was accepted in return for compensation in the form of a housing allowance for the families of wage earners and independent workers with two or more children. In short, it can be said of family policy what Queuille reputedly said about politics in general: that it served "not to resolve problems, but to silence those who posed them."

Until the mid-1950s, the political importance of family policy was reflected in a budget that would never again claim as large as a proportion of social spending: in 1949, it made up 40 percent of Social Security expenditures against 28.8 percent in 1960. Already in the 1950s other social benefits, notably for health and old age, were growing faster than family benefits, even as the rate of payroll taxes for the family allowance programs rose from 13 percent to 16.75 percent in 1959. Even if financial resources allocated to family benefits shrank relatively, social treatment of the family continued to develop in accord with barely euphemized familialist objectives. Three measures taken during this time bear witness: creation of a housing allowance (1 September 1948); extension of the single-income allowance, originally entitled the "mother at home" allowance, to families whose head was not a wage earner; and the scaling of family allowances to the real cost of childrearing through the establishment of differing rates according to the age of the child. It is true that the index of all family benefits per child hardly increased and that the average of total benefits for each eligible child, as a percentage of gross national product per capita, fell from 21.8 percent in 1949 to 14.6 percent in 1958. The two most important benefits, financially and symbolically (the "most familialist" benefits), the single-income allowance and the family allowance, reached their highest level in 1955 (10 percent more in constant francs than in 1949), but declined thereafter, the former immediately and the latter after 1959 (Nizard 1974).

The Erosion of Family Policy

Although a few new benefits were created during this period and the family allowance funds were granted definitive autonomy, proving that the idea of a family policy was not in question, it is clear that not only the financial foundations but also the political and moral foundations of this policy were seriously shaken.

With respect to finances, family benefits found themselves in competition with the other two principal branches of Social Security, health insurance and old-age insurance, which were growing at a faster rate. Very soon, one of the great principles of 1946 was abandoned, that of indexing family benefits against average salaries. For the whole of the period, benefits rose more or less in accordance with prices and not income, which inevitably produced a surplus, since the revenue from contributions based on income necessarily increased faster than benefits at a time of rising real income.

The problem of revising benefits recurred throughout this period. On the eve of the legislative elections of 1951 (the first since the Communists had left power in 1947), an interparliamentary commission was created to study the various family benefit plans, with a view to the eventual revision of both the financing and the content of the system. Without going into the details of the report edited by Robert Prigent, former minister of population and family (MRP), it appears that all the parties were agreed on changing the basis for calculating family benefits; only the employers heard by the commission were against this measure, which would lead to a rise in employer contributions. In the parliamentary debates that followed the presentation of this report, only the minister of the budget, Edgar Faure (a radical), opposed the commission's proposal on the grounds that it would lead inevitably to a rise in the overall deficit of Social Security.

If on the question of finances one could see an opposition forming between, on the one hand, the Radical Party and certain members of the Rally of the French People (RPF), who gave priority to restoration of French financial strength over an increase in family benefits, and, on the other hand, the other parties, above all the MRP, along with the Communists and Socialists, these temporary and ambiguous alliances broke up over other issues. This was the case in two debates that concerned, respectively, the housing allowance (1948) and the allowance to the mother at home (1955), debates that crystallized opposing camps with regard to what constituted the essence of "family policy" at the time: defense of the "traditional" family.

With regard to housing, the Communists and Socialists proposed a vast program for the construction of inexpensive housing. Conversely, the MRP, which had never ceased to submit bills calling for an allowance in this area, and which was to make housing policy one of its major themes in the legislative elections of June 1951, saw the housing allowance as a component of family policy. So we read in the preamble of a bill submitted on 12 December 1946:

Large families are the ones that are most miserably housed. They are clearly disadvantaged compared to households without children and single persons not only because of a relative inferiority of resources . . . but also with regard to the structures themselves. . . . Jammed together in monstrous barracks, these families of the masses lose their taste for home and family and develop the bitter feeling that they form a class apart. . . . The consequences of such a state of affairs are serious: a drop in the birth rate, alcoholism, public immorality, death, etc.

These same principles were evidenced in the debates on the single-income allowance, which concerned the status of women in the family as well as in the labor market. The positions taken by associations can be summarized in terms of three categories. Family organizations, those that have a monopoly on the representation of families in the UNAF, and, more generally, organizations belonging to the Catholic movement (CFTC, MRP, etc.) favored legislation that would contribute to keeping the woman at home, with justifications varying according to the traditions appropriate to each movement, but all emphasizing the educative and integrational role of the mother. Conversely, secular union organizations (CGT, CGT-FO) and leftist parties defended only "equality of the right to family benefits between families where the mother works and those where she does not," that is, "replacing the single-income allowance with a complementary allowance to each mother" (CGT [Confédération générale du travail] 1953).

Both of these positions can be contrasted to a third, modernist tendency politically represented by the radicals and *mendésistes* (followers of Pierre Mendès-France) then in power (Jacques Chaban-Delmas, Jean Caillavet, Edgar Faure, etc.). This tendency reflected the point of view of economic planners and decision makers, who, given the labor shortage, had been favorable to women working ever since the Liberation. Thus, during the preparation of the Third Plan (1958–1961), the Manpower Commission under the general Planning Commission, meeting in the mid-1950s, explicitly favored an increase in numbers of working women and advocated part-time work, flexible hours, increased daycare, and, as a compromise solution between the social actors represented on this commission, the allocation of the single-income allowance neither for the nonworking mother nor for all mothers, but in accordance with the amount of time spent working.

The attitude of the National Council of French Employers (CNPF) is more ambiguous and is explained by the desire to meet manpower needs and to lessen their costs by shifting the financial burden of Social Security from payroll taxes to general taxation. The CNPF preferred allowances for children rather than for mothers, working or not, as if the "child" personified henceforth the neutral ground of social confrontations, substituting itself in a sense for the "woman." At the same moment the feminist movement, finding a cause in birth control, was transforming the issue of the social and economic status of "the woman" by placing it on the political agenda. Even the familialists were reduced to economic arguments: the language used to justify support of the mother at home, for example, was based not only on simple moral values, as was still the case in the early postwar familialist movement, but increasingly on the economic evaluation of domestic work, as suggested in the notion of the "maternal salary."

Assessment of Family Policy under the Fourth Republic

With some exceptions, legislation regarding the development of major benefits was not significantly modified under the Fourth Republic. The exceptions are the creation of the housing allowance, although this was closely linked to the great reform of 1948 that led to the freeing of rents; the creation of increases relating to the age of the child; and the creation of the mother-at-home allowance.

We must point out the importance of the housing allowance as an element of family policy during this period. This allowance was designed to give to the family the resources needed to meet the greater housing costs required by having more children. The familial character of the housing allowance was strengthened during this period and the eligibility requirements were relaxed. However, particularly in the first few years, the number of beneficiaries was very small and in the cities (rural families did not occupy housing that would qualify for the allowance), and the beneficiaries were for the most part families with relatively high incomes. This particular form of aid to families developed particularly quickly in the 1970s; the number of beneficiaries tripled, from more than 400,000 in 1959 to 1,278,000 in 1971. The percentage of beneficiaries of basic family allowances who also received a housing allowance increased steadily, from 0.9 percent in 1950 to 2.5 percent in 1953, 12 percent in 1958, 23 percent in 1963, and 34 percent in 1971 (Nizard 1974, 302).

In addition to the housing allowance, the State and local communities expanded the construction of public Moderate Rent Housing (HLM) to the point that it represented 30 percent of housing units completed in 1958 and 27 percent in 1971. To encourage investment in construction, the State subsidized private construction by offering low-interest, long-term loans. Beginning in 1953, industrial firms were required to invest 1 percent of their payroll in social housing, a policy that was continued after 1958. Finally, special home savings plans were created in 1965 and expanded in 1970.

Together these investments of public or semipublic origin played a very important role; they represented more than 50 percent of total investments in housing until the mid–1950s. And even if their share has consistently decreased since, they still constituted 32 percent of investments made from 1969 to 1971 (Magri 1977).

To avoid a restrictive definition of family policy, we must not forget to mention the growth under the Fourth Republic of regulations and services affecting family life, notably in the areas of health, housing, and schooling. We know that maternity insurance covered the costs of childbirth and a part of the loss of salary for the working mother. Medical coverage of the child and the mother is ensured primarily by a network of medical offices serving infants and toddlers. In 1960, there were 8,560 offices, which, in the best-equipped areas, served almost 60 percent of all mothers.

The only shadow in this picture, related to the still dominant though declining familialist perspective of the period toward family policy, was the number of daycare centers. The number of centers built on the initiative of local communities and various organizations with the help of the CNAF grew from 360 (12,000 cribs) in 1947 to still only 697 (31,750 cribs) in 1971! Faced with a shortage of daycare (five hundred thousand mothers with a child younger than three were working), public authorities would later look at ways to improve the system of private daycare providers (*Journal Officiel* 1971).

Before taking up the subject of the evolution of family policy under the Fifth Republic, which, in comparison with its predecessor, saw in the political arena not only the decline of the familial movement with the fall of the Popular Republicans (MRP) and the French Confederation of Christian Workers (CFDT) but also a resurgence of the natalist movement, we must point out that a separate social family law developed during this period alongside civil law, which theretofore had enjoyed exclusive competence in this domain. These two bodies of law regulated two different forms of the economy that family relationships now made necessary and that were by nature relatively independent without being exclusive. It would be incorrect to speak of the "depatrimonialization" of family law or of the decline of the function of family patrimony in determining the careers and social positions of individuals. But it is true that new forms of capital, especially economic, could be passed on only to children who had acquired the proper culture, or training. The acquisition of the required characteristics presupposed training that became progressively longer and costlier. These new forms of socialization were, among others, at the heart of the idea of the child as a social as well as an economic charge.

Social law should not be viewed as the law of proletarian and working-class families, as opposed to civil law as the law of patrimony and the bourgeoisie. The two logics underlying the two bodies of law overlap and function simultaneously. This was particularly true during the Fourth Republic, when the majority of family benefits were allocated without regard to income and when generous tax deductions for dependents were most advantageous to high-income families (Durand 1953b).

V. BEGINNINGS OF THE FIFTH REPUBLIC (1958–1969): THE DE GAULLE PRESIDENCY UNDER PRIME MINISTER MICHEL DEBRÉ (1959–1962) AND PRIME MINISTER GEORGES POMPIDOU (1962–1969)

In this period there are clear turning points that mark the beginning of changes in the orientation of family policy. They correspond to real modifications in the way in which family policy was conceived, diffused, and applied, since it is true that family policy depends, even if in small part, on the balance of power in the political arena.

A New Political and Economic Context

From the beginning of the Fifth Republic, family policy, like policy toward Europe, was an area of conflict between the Gaullists of the Union for the New Republic (UNR) and the MRP, which was represented principally by Joseph Fontanet and Paul Bacon, who headed the "social" ministries of Public Health and Labor. Faced with a policy of economic austerity (the Rueff Plan) that sought to reestablish a balanced Social Security budget through limitations on spending, and especially on family benefits, the family associations and their political lobby reacted by denouncing "the absence of a family policy" in the Fifth Republic. In 1960 the government had created a Study Commission on the Problems of the Family, headed by Robert Prigent, a recognized expert respected by the familialist movement. But in addition to discussing traditional techniques for increasing and differentiating benefits, the report submitted at the close of 1961 was devoted essentially to the single-income allowance, that is, to a redefinition of the social status of the woman.

The conflict between the familialists, represented politically by the MRP, and Michel Debré, prime minister at the time and known for his natalist views, focused essentially on two points: balancing the Social Security budget and the single-income allowance. On the first point the Prigent Commission proposed, among other things, the separation of family allowances from the social insurance budget, the transfer of benefits of a natalist character to the State budget, and the linkage of allowances to increases in the minimum wage. The prime minister, on the contrary, hoped to increase existing sources of social insurance revenue by raising the ceiling on wages subject to Social Security taxes.

As for the second point of contention, the commission, though divided (which was itself a sign of division in the familialist ranks), demanded increases in the single-income allowance, at least for low-income and single-parent families. The prime minister considered abolishing this allowance, which discouraged women from working, and in its place creating an allowance paid to young couples for the purpose of encouraging the birth of children in the first years of marriage (*Le Monde*, 3–4 September 1961). During this period, the Catholic newpaper *La Croix* continued to accuse Michel Debré of sacrificing family policy in the name of a balanced Social Security budget and in favor of a natalist policy that did not adhere to the values implied in the family model advocated by familialists, particularly keeping mothers at home (*La Croix*, 2 September 1961).

At the beginning of the Fifth Republic, as new political personnel replaced the old and the political weight of the MRP declined, it appeared that defenders of the familialist position were on the defensive and conducting a rear-guard battle, forced to adjust, at least part, in the face of the victory of those who, in the name of "modernization" or "growth"—in short, of what was called "economic democratization"—were in control of the State and, little by little, the bureaucracy, including the social agencies. One of the sources as well as one of the instruments of this new view of the world was the planning process. Thus, the Rueff-Armand Report, resulting from preparatory work for the Fourth Plan, recommended the cancellation of the single-income allowance, which was viewed by the experts as a disincentive to part-time labor. This plan made no recommendations regarding the family except for the development of child care.

This was also the period when the postwar baby-boomers entered the educational system ("the school boom") and, far more often than in the past, continued to higher education. Finally, this was also a period of growth in the number of working women, including, to the alarm of critics, married women with children. From 1962 to 1968, the increase in the proportion of women in the work force was greatest among those whose husbands were middle-level and higher-level managers (see Table 5.1). All of these indicators attest to the transformation of the economic role of the family, especially within the bourgeoisie, whose wealth henceforth was based primarily on salary, which had become the legitimate method of acquiring profits from capital (Boltanski 1982). We must also note the fall of the MRP in the November 1962 elections, when it won no more than 5.3 percent of the vote. After General de Gaulle's press conference of 15 April 1962, in which

TABLE 5.1

Evolution of the Percentage of Working Married Women between the Ages of 30 and 34, from 1962 to 1982 (according to the occupational category of husband)

	1962 [1]	1968 [2]	1982 [2]	1968 / 1962	1982 / 1968
Senior Management and Liberal Professions	25.7	34.2	63.2	1.33	1.84
Middle Level Management	36.5	45.5	70.8	1.23	1.55
White Collar Workers	37.8	43.6	67.5	1.15	1.55
Blue Collar Workers	24.5	28.9	57.3	1.18	1.98
Owners of Business and Industry	38.7	41.6	65.3	1.07	1.57
Farmers	60.3	62.5	71.3	1.03	1.14

Notes:
1. 1962 census.
2. Lery (1984).

he denounced the "fiction" of European integration, the MRP had no deputies serving on the cabinet.

Family Policy: Element of an Economic and Social Policy

As the result of changes in the political and economic arenas, family policy was no longer pursued as an end in itself, but as a means toward broader economic and social goals.

With respect to economic policy, although reference to and reverence of the "woman at home" were still obligatory concessions to familialist ideology, it was nonetheless true that in various areas of the law, the paid labor of mothers henceforth tended to be recognized and guaranteed. The reform of marriage law on 13 July 1965, for example, did away with the husband's right to oppose a separate professional activity by his wife. The single-income allowance saw its funding and its share in the family benefits system continue the decline begun in 1956; this decline accelerated after 1958 and at the end of this period, the allowance had decreased to half of what it had represented in constant francs at the beginning of the 1950s. Finally, in 1967 it was the object of a reform that sought to reduce the number of beneficiaries by establishing varying levels of benefits depending on family income and the ages of the children.

Another economic dimension of family policy was the development of the housing allowance, which was the object of an important reform in 1961 aimed at improving the structure of payments to benefit families with the most modern incomes. The share of all benefits received by low-income families doubled during this period, despite changes made in the calculation of this benefit in 1966 to slow down the rate of increase in total payments, which were doubling every three years. Public housing regulations were being reformed in the same period.

From the start of the 1960s, the sacrosanct principle of familialist policy began to be questioned publicly. This principle constituted as its essence, if not its primary goal, the granting of identical benefits without regard for family income, or the principle of "horizontal" compensation of family expenses. Several administrative reports demonstrated the social inequity of this principle and the economic reasons for changing it. It was difficult to get those who worked in this area to accept the new orientation, as witnessed by the fact that, unlike earlier plans, the preparations for the Fifth Plan (1965) included the creation of a family benefits commission. In the Fifth Plan traditional family benefits were retained, but at the price of a concession on the housing allowance, whose growth had to be slowed. But change was inescapable: the General Inspectorate of Social Affairs (1967), presided over by Pierre Laroque, and even the specialized planning commissions, ended by accepting variation in levels of family benefits according to the income of individual families (see particularly the 1969 work of the specialized group on demographic problems in preparation for the Sixth Plan).

At the same time, family policy became a less and less autonomous element of social policy. In the name of economic austerity, the powers of certain groups in the administrative councils of the Social Security system were reduced, particularly those of trade union representatives. In the face of rapid growth of 20 percent per year in payments on health claims, and to a lesser degree as a consequence of increased benefits for the elderly, the family benefits branch was made to cover expenses for which it had never previously been responsible. It was symptomatic of the relative loss of identity and of social priority of family policy in this period that tax deductions for dependents continued to grow in relation to family allowances, as the latter grew more slowly than taxable income.

As an element of "incomes policy," according to the expression of the time, family policy, always identified principally with family benefits, tended to become the instrument of a broader policy, of a "global social" policy whose scope was beginning to be transformed (Lenoir 1991)

During these twelve years it appears that what was known in the Fourth Republic as family policy, relating to the material and moral problems of the home (income, housing, patrimony, family relationships, education), was beginning to break up into several sectors, each progressively acquiring its own autonomy. Family benefits continued to be used as instruments of economic policy (income, consumption, purchasing power, etc.) or of housing policy, where the home was reduced to housing in its architectural definition. Any monopoly on the definition of family values seems to have been definitively broken during this period. The issue of family policy no longer belonged to the familials, who conceived of the family as the home. Particularly in the presidential election of 1965, the woman as a political issue began to replace, or at least take a place alongside, the family, in whose name new measures were taken to reverse the decline in the birthrate beginning in 1964.

The rise in the relevance of women's issues, publicly expressed and manifested by the feminist movement, gave this movement the opportunity in the successful battle for the legalization of contraception (the law of 28 December 1967 was voted almost unanimously) to establish its independence from traditional familial associations and other special-interest organizations accustomed to taking the lead on social problems related to the family. Similarly, the reform of marriage law in 1965, a year marked by numerous elections, resulted in part from the pressure imposed by this new lobby, which sought to increase the equality of spouses. In short, the emergence of feminism as an ideological and political force transformed the scope and process of policymaking regarding the family, particularly through the establishment of a new definition of the civil and social status of women (Lenoir 1985a).

At the same time, the political goal of family policy shifted, as shown by the evolution of measures taken in its name. Despite its progressive dilution in a changing global social aid policy, which resulted in part from the arrival of new actors in the social policy arena, family policy nonetheless was to find in natalism (the fall in the birthrate had worsened in 1972) the means of its survival as a distinct policy area.

VI. 1969–1974: PRESIDENCY OF GEORGES POMPIDOU (PRIME MINISTER, JACQUES CHABAN-DELMAS, 1969–1972)

Under Georges Pompidou we witness a very strong intensification of the effort to integrate family benefits into the global system of social transfers. All new benefits under the Chaban-Delmas Government were created essentially for the benefit of the most disadvantaged families.

All of this occurred as if ideas and programs discarded by officials in other branches of Social Security were destined to emerge in the form of family benefits, at a time when specifically family issues were losing their separate identity in the political arena. As risks like illness and old age were covered in the 1950s, the "family" became a vehicle for meeting a variety of social needs, many of them not directly related to family life.

The "Social" Vocation of Family Policy

The arrival of Jacques Chaban-Delmas as prime minister was the beginning of the rise of a new category of social affairs specialists, especially administrators (Jacques Delors, René Lenoir, etc.), and consultants (Jean-Jacques Dupeyroux), who already were rethinking the whole system of social protection. Much of the rethinking took place within the General Planning Commission, where new positions were being outlined by the reformers, many of whom later supported Socialist governments. They sought to make family benefits one element of an "active family policy," as it as then called—that is to say, a selective policy. They emphasized professional training for women, child care, and preschool instruction, with the family component of policy being diluted in a sense into the societal.

The priorities that remained in the social sector then became the aged, whose numbers were increasing and whose condition was becoming more precarious with an increase in forced retirements, single mothers, and the handicapped. In brief, as René Montjoie, general commissioner of planning, wrote, "What we have lost in our capacity to guide the economy as a whole we must regain by concentrating our means on a small number of priority programs" (*L'Expansion*, May, 1971). In social affairs, this was the time when René Lenoir called attention to the "excluded," Jacques Delors spoke of "social indicators," and the technocrats experimented with the "rationalization of budget choices" (RCB). In the area of family policy, which henceforth had a social vocation, this meant specialized benefits for certain categories of children, such as orphans and the handicapped, and for certain types of families, particularly young couples without children and families with small children. It is not surprising that President Pompidou and his "progress contracts" for the family received a cold reception at the Twenty-fifth Congress of the National Union of Family Associations (UNAF) in 1970.

In short, the families that were the beneficiaries of new social measures were the most impoverished; the distinctions in effect up to this point, particularly the occupational status of mothers, gave way, at least in part, to the criterion of income. All of the benefits created by the Chaban-Delmas government were conditional upon income. This was particularly the case with the single-income allowance and the allowance to mothers at home, both of which guaranteed a payment to families in which the wife remained at home to care for the children. The law of 3 January 1972, in addition to providing an increase for mothers at home with young children and large families, created a child-care allowance for working mothers that was to be similar to the single-income allowance.

Toward Recognition of the Rights of Mothers

At the same time, a number of actions were taken, usually by unanimous vote, to protect pregnant women and mothers, both on the labor market and in the workplace. These measures noted the "irreversible" increase of working women and the inescapable decline in the birthrate. Henceforth family policy recognized the right of mothers to work and tended to become one element in the policy of the Ministry of Labor and Employment, and no longer of the Ministry of Health and of Population, to which it nominally belonged. The law of 31 December 1971, which gave insured women who reared at least two children an increase in the period of insurance coverage credit equal to one supplementary year per child, was a sign of the still ambiguous emerging right of mothers to work.

This transition from the "woman at home" to the "mother of a family," whether at the house or at the place of work, was also seen in the evolution of civil law. After the reform of marriage law in 1965, which definitively established the right of the mother to work, the law of 6 June 1970 abolished "paternal power" and replaced it with "parental authority," which henceforth was exercised by the father and the mother. The law of 3 January 1972, which accorded the illegitimate child a status equal to that of the legitimate child, for the first time gave the mother the possibility of removing the presumption of paternity from her spouse, a necessary and ultimate step in the development of parental egalitarianism before the law. It is clear that this progression in the legal status of mothers was inseparable from the evolution of the rights of illegitimate children and children of adultery, particularly in matters of inheritance, where this distinction was still in effect. What was in question was still the legal redefinition of the family and its place in the system of social reproduction, as this changed in interaction with the evolution of patrimonial structure and the household economy.

Nevertheless an old tension, indeed a contradiction, appeared between the competence of the "family" (and therefore of the mother) and that of the "woman." We see this clearly at the end of the Fourth Legislature (1972–1973), when the problem of abortion became an increasingly acute issue. Even if differences of opinion on family matters did not completely follow party lines, especially on the Right, and if party positions were not clearly expressed in electoral programs, except perhaps for the former Popular Republicans, nonetheless the nature and intensity of sensitivity on this issue varied by party group. The Left, mobilized by an alliance based on a Common Program that defended family policy and supported equality of women, won the majority of votes on the first ballot of the March 1973 elections, but lost the majority of seats to the Right in the runoffs. On the eve of the elections for the Fifth Legislature (1973–1978), the Independent Republicans around Valéry Giscard d'Estaing attempted to check the rising tide of demands, particularly from feminists, by adopting them as their own, at the risk of alienating both their own electorate and their Gaullist allies (and rivals). The Independent Republicans were moving toward a posture that combined moral liberalism with economic conservatism.

To be sure, before a meeting of candidates of the conservative majority in Provins on 7 January 1973, the Gaullist prime minister, Pierre Messmer, developed several of the same themes proposed by the Independent Republicans: reform of the 1920 law that outlawed abortion, creation of two thousand daycare centers, aid for home child care, etc. All were measures previously advocated by the Left's Common Program. Pierre Messmer here joined with Michel Poniatowski, minister of health and an ally of Valéry Giscard d'Estaing, who hoped, in vain, for a vote on abortion before the elections.

VII. 1974–1981: PRESIDENCY OF VALLERY GISCARD D'ESTAING

In the field of family policy, the seven-year term of Valéry Giscard d'Estaing was characterized both by a continuation of developments initiated at the beginning of the 1970s and by the outline of new policy orientations: experimentation with the idea of the negative tax; extension of the right to benefits to the whole population; a search for a neutral posture on the question of women in the work force; and higher priority to large families. But this policy developed in a very tense political climate in which there were confrontations not only between parties of the Left and of the Right, but also between opposing tendencies within these movements.

1974–1976: The Chirac Government

This was a period of worsening divisions among leading actors in the field of family policy. As a consequence of the differentiation, if not of "family institutions" then at least of those institutions that represent the family, one began to hear of "multiple families," "different family models," and "the end of the family."

Family Policy and "Social Assistance" Policy. There was a continuation of the policy of using social assistance to the "family" (in the double sense of a group of related persons and as a group of agencies specializing in family matters) as a mechanism for general public assistance. The policy of social assistance to low-income families was intensified and diversified, as exemplified by the school allowance (law of 14 July 1974) and the allowance to handicapped adults (law of 30 June 1975). New measures were taken to protect working mothers, including protection of pregnant women and new mothers against dismissal and the extension of the insurance coverage bonus from one to two years per child for mothers who cease working.

1975 was also the year of the woman, the year of the creation of the Secretariat of State on the Condition of Women, headed by Françoise Giroud—the year, hence, in which a clearer political and institutional distinction was drawn between the realm of the family and that of the condition of women.

The legal status of the family increasingly was shaped by the emergence of a policy that regarded "the woman" as an appropriate object of governmental action, both with regard to employment, with the law of 11 July 1975 prohibiting discrimination in hiring on the basis of pregnancy, sex, or marital status, and with respect to birth control. A law passed in 1975 authorized abortion, although the majority of deputies from the governing majority voted against it. It was only thanks to the support of opposition deputies that this reform was adopted. Even those majority deputies who supported the bill did so on condition that the government establish a more rigorous family policy. It was in this setting that the first negative tax was created, an idea that had been popularized in the works of Louis Stoléru and Christian Stoffaes. A minimum guaranteed income for single parents was passed unanimously on 9 July 1976. The new divorce law of 11 July 1975 is further evidence of a legal redefinition of the distinction between the realm of the woman and that of the family. Later governments further strengthened this distinction. The 1975 divorce law was passed with a large majority, but without the support of almost a third of the deputies of the Right!

1976–1981: The Raymond Barre Government

This period was marked by a deepening of the economic crisis, an intensification of political conflict, and a high level of social tension. Given financial constraints, both the mechanisms of the social benefit system (such as the various retirement plans) and its institutions (such as the hospital system) became almost immune to modification, except within the limits built into the system itself.

The Irresistible Decline of Family Benefits. Under the government led by Raymond Barre, the financial resources dedicated to family benefits continued to decline as a proportion of all social expenditures, but at a slower rate than in the preceding period. Between 1970 and 1978, expenditures for family benefits grew at an annual rate of only 12.5 percent, compared to 18 percent for sickness, 18.9 percent for old age, and 41.5 percent for unemployment. The monthly base on which allowances were calculated continued to increase less rapidly than per capita salary (10.2 percent compared with 13.1 percent). However, it must be noted that the relative decline of financial aid to families in this period was partly offset by a strong increase in social aid to children (18.5 percent per year) and by an important increase in tax deductions for children (15.8 percent). The fact remains that family benefits as a proportion of all social benefits fell from 21.2 percent in 1970 to 14.7 percent in 1980, partly as a result of the reduction of the rate of payroll taxes earmarked for family benefits from 11.5 percent to 9 percent. Family policy had a serious financial effect only on small households with high incomes and large families with modest incomes. However, for this second category of families, the contribution of family benefits was far from negligible, either in absolute value or as a percentage of total income. In 1978, family benefits represented more than 50 percent of the income of families with at least four children under the age of ten and in which the husband was an industrial worker. If corresponding tax reductions are included, all family benefits amounted to 63 percent of the worker's salary. A senior manager with the same type of family received family benefits totaling 22 percent of his salary, of which 14.1 percent was in the form of tax deductions, for a net gain of 27,970 francs, or more than the net gain of 22,280 for the worker.

The Disenchantment of the Ideological World. The French birthrate became one of the most frequent themes in political debate in this period, which was marked by electoral setbacks for the government parties and by their efforts to regain a lost constituency, particularly traditionalist women. The optimistic and modernist vision of the social world, of which one version was expressed by the language of women's liberation, in effect gave way, in ruling circles, to a disenchanted representation of the future, where the family appeared as a refuge, a place of intimacy and profound values (in the sense in which this term is used in "La France profonde"). Gone was the era of great liberating struggles; the ideological mood was one that tended more toward security than toward liberty. Work on reform of the Family Code was halted in favor of reform of the penal code. The Veil Law authorizing abortion was discreetly extended by the law of 31 December 1979, which was accepted even more reluctantly than the initial law.

In short, the ideological climate favored the mother more than the woman. Attitudes were also shifting with respect to the educational rights of young working parents, who were finding that their work prevented them from receiving the instruction that they needed in order to succeed at school. This problem had been foreseen in the law of 12 July 1977, which created a "parental education leave."

The plight of unskilled workers, whose limited educational achievements left them in a weak position in a period of rising unemployment, together with the market-oriented policies chosen by Raymond Barre to deal with this problem, contributed to a revival of familialist thinking. And yet existing family policy as a whole tended to favor two-income families. The law of 12 July 1977 merged the single-income allowance and the child-care allowance into a new "complementary family allowance," but failed to achieve its objective of neutrality with respect to working mothers. Special tax benefits for single-income households were far too small to compensate for the contribution made to the total household revenue by a second income, which averaged 70 percent of the principal income.

New policies established in this period sought to favor households with one income over those with two. The criterion that seems to have dominated family policy in this period was family resources. With the law of 4 July 1975, family benefits ceased to be salary supplements, as they had been considered from the beginning, since the requirement that at least one of the two parents be employed was dropped. Similarly, the expression "woman at home" was no longer used, being replaced by "mother of a family." Thereafter it was a question of a "minimum family income," according to the title of the allowance created by the law of 17 July 1980, an allowance of varying size that brought the income of three-child families up to an established minimum. Although women were no longer required to stay out of the work force in order to establish eligibility for most family benefits, the new criterion for eligibility, household income, implied that the woman could only claim maximum benefits by renouncing the idea of working. From the perspective of women's liberation this was a step backward, for it sought to check the "irresistible" increase in working women by encouraging them to stay at home in a period of high unemployment and by reinventing a social demand by women for part-time work, which permitted the conciliation of an occupational career with the "job" of raising children (laws of 1980 and 1981).

The concept of the "large family" continued to be used to defend family interests. It was, to be sure, reduced in size by the realities of the times to three children, the "golden number" of demographics, a number that assured the biological renewal of the generations. Family policy at this time was marked by a return to this priority, less natalist than familialist. An entire concept of the family was at stake. "Large" was the adjective that summarized all the characteristics of the traditional family structure: with three children, women did not work, did not divorce, did not spend, etc.; everything was done "as a family"—meals, leisure activities, etc.

Family policy during the seven-year term of Valéry Giscard d'Estaing was characterized by measures that sought to favor families with three or more children and that found their ideological justification in demographic trends in the country. In fact, after 1963 the trend in fertility rates reversed itself and France experienced another demographic decline. The French fecundity rate, while remaining higher than in most industrialized countries, dropped from 2.90 in 1964 to less than 2.0 after 1975. In 1976 women were having on average only 1.6 children during their period of fertility, whereas the number necessary for the renewal of the generations is 2.1. This demographic decline cannot be attributed to a refusal to have children, for 90 percent of couples had a least one child. Although there was some decline in two-child families, 80–90 percent of the overall reduction in fertility was the result of a decrease in the number of women having three or more children.

The increasing reticence of families to have a third child can be explained in part by the reduction in living standard brought on by its arrival. The third child was costly in several ways: first, it often forced the family to seek larger accommodations; second, the cost of the third child was added to the cost of the first two; but most of all, it almost inevitably forced the mother to leave her job. Faced with mounting expenses, the household found its available funds considerably diminished.

Priority to Large Families. In the fall of 1979 the government's desire to prioritize aid to families with three children was clearly affirmed, but several measures taken beginning in 1977, as well as the Blois Program of January 1978, had already announced this new tendency. The law of 12 July 1977, which created the complementary family allowance, established "three children" as one of the alternative criteria for eligibility. The schedule for personal housing assistance established in 1978 favored families with three children. The rate of family allowances for three children increased from 37 percent to 41 percent of base salary between 1 January 1978 and 1 July 1979, while the rate for two children went up only a single point in the same period.

Presented to the National Assembly during the debate on family policy in November 1979, most of the following measures took effect in July 1980. An increase of 3 percent per year in the purchasing power of family allowances was guaranteed to families with three or more children, double the increase guaranteed to families with two children. Postnatal allowances for the third child were increased, raising the total of all benefits for the birth of this child to ten thousand francs, or the famous million old francs. Maternity leave for the third child was extended to twenty-six weeks, instead of the sixteen allowed for the first two children; the old-age insurance benefit for mothers was extended to include women raising three children; a family income supplement was created to guarantee a minimum income for families with three children; and, finally, the 1981 finance law granted a supplementary deduction to taxpayers with three dependent children.

A new status for "mothers of large families" was developed along the lines of these measures. Whether she "worked" or not, the activity of the mother at home was thereafter classed as work, as seen in the fact that the mother of a large family benefited from similar social protection to that enjoyed by the working woman in the case of loss of spouse, illness, old age, or even job training.

In contrast to the parties of the Left, which attempted in the next legislature to rebalance the distribution of aid among different types of families and assure a greater neutrality regarding working women by creating daycare facilities for small children, the parties of the Right were opposed to what was then called "the collectivism of the cradles." To be sure, on the eve of the 1978 legislative elections, the delegates for women's action of the parties of the Right did not oppose the creation of daycare centers, especially company centers and minicenters. Stress was laid above all on traditional methods that permitted mothers to stay at home with their children, since it was a question of "not penalizing those households with children." This was the watchword. And yet the policy followed under the direction of the conservative parties continued to be unfavorable to these families, particularly in the field of housing, but also with regard to certain family benefits. Thus the creation of means-tested allowances and the transformation of the single-income allowance and the mother-at-home allowance did not give priority status to large families. As observed by the High Commission on Population, in the period 1971–1977 the proportion of families benefiting from the supplementary family allowance/mother-at-home allowance (and from the later increment in this benefit) increased less among families with three children than among those with one; the child-care allowance benefited 10 percent of families with one child, but only 1.68 percent of those with two; and, finally, the proportion of beneficiaries of the housing allowance more than doubled for childless couples and for families with one child, while it fell for families with three children! These were perverse and unintended consequences of the policy of the government in power.

Despite the declared familialist orientation of the leadership, collective facilities directly serving working mothers continued to grow during this period by non-negligible proportions, though still insufficient to satisfy needs. This was particularly true of those who provided maternal and infant care between 1970 and 1979: in addition to the number of full-time doctors, which tripled, and the number of pediatric nurses, which doubled, the various forms of collective infant child care multiplied, in particular the number of daycare centers. The capacity of community nurseries doubled, that of family nurseries increased almost tenfold, and the number of mother's helpers rose by 77 percent.

In conclusion, family policy during the seven-year administration of Giscard d'Estaing was marked by five principal orientations: the generalization of family benefits as the result of the elimination of restrictions on employment; an effort at simplification through the substitution of the complementary family allowance for several other benefits; the creation of the single-parent allowance; a rationalization of housing assistance; and incentives to encourage women to work part-time.

VIII. PRESIDENT OF THE REPUBLIC, FRANÇOIS MITTERRAND (1981–1988): PRIME MINISTERS, PIERRE MAUROY (1981–1984) AND LAURENT FABIUS (1984–1986)

The arrival of the Left in power in 1981 constituted a type of sociological experiment to determine the influence of specifically political factors on the evolution of family policy. This was a particularly appropriate occasion to examine such relationships since the Left had announced its preferences, although not without some inconsistencies, with respect both to family policy and to the models of family life that should be encouraged. It was apparent that the "family" constituted a category of political action, perhaps more than ever, as *Le Monde* indicated in an article titled "The Courting of the Family" (24 November 1981). Precise policy guidelines in this field had been defined during the electoral campaign, and, when the new government was formed, a secretary of state for the family (Georgina Dufoix) was named under the minister for social affairs and national solidarity.

The major components of the Socialist policy were a massive increase of approximately 25 percent in family benefits; strong rejection of any "interventionist" policy aimed at favoring one "family model" (e.g., based on the number of children) over another; placement of a ceiling on tax deductions for dependents; social assistance to maintain the child in his or her milieu of origin; housing assistance in the form of "family contracts"; and development of facilities like contract nurseries.

As shown by government statements and even more concretely by the division of labor among ministries, the categories of government intervention had not changed. Everything concerning "aid to the family" was under the jurisdiction of the secretary of state for the family: the protection of the condition of women—momentarily combined with the family under Monique Pelletier—was assigned to the Ministry for the Rights of Women (Yvette Roudy). As for family law, it remained the monopoly of the minister of justice (Robert Badinter). It is clear that these divisions followed the lines of existing institutions, pressure groups, and areas of specialization (administrative, legal, scientific, etc.), which survived political changes and weakened their effects.

"The Child" and Family Policy

Although in 1982 the economic situation forced a review of the policy of increasing family benefits, the objective of policy in this area remained the same: the equalization of rights, whatever the status of the children. Changes in civil law followed the same objective.

Rebalancing of Aid among Families of Different Size. This objective is explicitly contrary to that of preceding governments. It follows from the government's announced desire not to favor any particular family model. All measures that sought to distinguish clearly between the advantages due to families with fewer than three children and those with three or more were called into question, with the result that from 1980 to 1984 purchasing power increased by 34.5 percent for families with two children aged three or more, as opposed to an increase of only 7.5 percent for those with three children. In order to limit benefits to high-income families with large families, the budget of 1982 limited the allowable tax benefits per child to seventy-five hundred francs.

The devaluation of the franc on 13 June 1982, accompanied by a freeze of prices and wages, led to a series of economy measures, including the reduction of family benefits by approximately 13 billion francs. Among these economy measures we find the reduction by half of the postnatal allowance for the third child. Finally, the law of 4 January 1985 also contributed to the rebalancing of aid to the family by combining the prenatal allowance, the postnatal allowance, and complementary family allowances into a single allowance to small children, payable for each child in the family under three years of age, without any test for family income until the infant's third month. This allowance continues until the child reaches three years of age for the great majority of families (80 percent), whose income is below the allowable ceiling, which is the same as for the complementary family allowance.

Continuation of the Assimilation of the Different Legal Categories of Children. Another manifestation of the primacy of "the child" as the target of political action in favor of families was the law of 25 June 1982, which allowed extralegal proofs of natural parenthood, thereby giving the child additional means of establishing his or her filiation. In the same manner children were the primary object of the law of 6 June 1984 "relating to the rights of families in their relations with the agencies charged with protecting the family and the child, and to the status of wards of the State." The objective of this law in effect was to make adoption easier and more rapid and to facilitate the maintenance of contact between families and those of their children whom they turn over to the State for care.

This at least apparent interest in the child was manifested as well in many studies, meetings, reports, and commentaries, including the "Research and Families" colloquium in 1983, the creation of the Institute of Childhood and the Family in 1984, and the colloquium on "Procreation: Genetics and the Family" in 1985. However, as shown by the parallel evolution of the law relating to parental authority, or the management of joint property, this preeminence of the child can be fully understood only when placed in the context of the vast transformation of family law that began more than twenty years ago.

Facilities for Children. Despite the economic problems confronted by the Mauroy and Fabius governments from 1981 to 1986, a special effort was made to accommodate children outside the home, this being a specific characteristic of the family policy of the French Left. Hence thirty-five thousand nurseries were created. Alongside "collective" nurseries, one saw a rapid increase in the number of "family nurseries," "mininurseries," and "parental nurseries." Finally, daycare centers and recreation centers, partially subsidized by the family allowance funds, also were created in large numbers, although always insufficient in relation to the rapidly increasing demand in this area, taking into account the continuing growth in the number of working women.

Twenty "family contract" programs sought, without great success, to facilitate housing construction and improvement, taking into account the welfare of families. Moreover, new tax measures were approved, such as deductions for child care and for home remodeling, which favored families with children.

Transformation of Marriage Relationships and Parental Responsibilities

It appeared that little by little what formerly had been combined was being disassociated: the conjugal relationship and parenthood. It is well known that during this period the number of unmarried couples living together greatly increased and the number of divorces was constantly growing. Even more than these developments, which were known and recognized because they were registered in the law and in statistics, family relationships as a whole were being transformed in all areas of daily life, both in relationships between spouses and in those between children and parents. In brief, the whole "family" relationship was modified, a relationship that the law, for its part, contributed to changing, if only by giving these transformations its own force: the officialization and legitimization of established facts. On the one hand one sees a progression toward legal equalization of the spouses under marriage law, in the management of the property of minors, and even with respect to family name; on the other hand, perhaps because it lacked the power to do so by and through marriage, legislation continued to reinforce the ties and obligations of parenthood, particularly in cases of unmarried parents and divorce.

Legal Equalization of the Spouses. The law of 13 July 1965 left standing some traces of the old dependence of the wife on her husband: the latter was still the sole administrator of joint property (with the exception of "reserved property"); common property was liable for the payment of his debts, while those of his wife could be claimed only against her own property and reserved property; and, finally, he retained major legal responsibility for managing the property of the children. During this period, the category of reserved property was abolished. Henceforth the debts of each spouse could be claimed against all community property, but this could be used as collateral for a loan or for bail only with agreement by both spouses. The major role of the father in the legal administration of the property of children was abolished, etc. With respect to family names, the system adopted by the deputies only authorized a practice that was increasingly widespread in the highest social echelons and that consisted of using the hyphenated names of both spouses for themselves and for their children, for example in school enrollment.

Reinforcement of Parental Obligations. Two measures illustrate the tendency of the law to reinforce the permanence of the "parental couple." On the one hand parental authority seemed to undergo a radical evolution during this period if one judges by the decisions of the Court of Appeals of 11 March 1983 and 7 May 1984, giving divorcing parents the right to joint custody, and by similar legislation that allowed joint custody over illegitimate children when both parents recognized them. (Previously the mother had been given sole custody.) On the other hand the law of 2 December 1984, which replaced the allowance for orphans with a family support allowance, empowered family allowance funds to aid in the recovery of child support when a parent fails to pay.

The Revival of Natalism. Such measures, demonstrating the adaptation of the law to new forms of conjugal union and disunion and to their effects upon the condition of children, fit within a family policy that once again became resolutely natalist, indeed familialist, as a result of measures adopted following the report of Evelyne Sullerot to the Economic and Social Council on filling the gaps in tax law favoring unmarried over married couples. Certainly the new policy emphasis on large families was not as marked as in the governments preceding the arrival of the Left in power. The change in policy resulted from the wishes of the president of the republic, who was aided by the High Commission on Population and especially by the relevant specialized committee of the Ninth Plan (1985–1988), which persuaded the government and the parliament to adopt a "priority program" "in order to ensure an environment favorable to the family and to the birthrate."

In pursuance of these goals, a parental education fund was created by the law of 4 January 1985, providing for payments to each person who stops working or reduces hours of work as the result of the birth of any child beyond the first two, for which the parent(s) is responsible. Among other similar measures, the allowable income for recipients of the young child allowance was increased on 1 July 1984 for families with three children or more.

This new allowance was the object of lively criticism from certain members of the Socialist Party, who saw in it a first step toward the "maternal salary," the bête noire of the feminists, who were well represented in the Socialist Party. This point of view is exemplified in an article by Véronique Neiertz on the 3 January 1985 issue of *Le Monde*, where she writes, "A maternal salary would be an insult to all those without resources, an insult to all workers, an insult to all women who combine motherhood with a profession. . . . There are two ways of making motherhood compatible with a career: create more flexible working hours for everyone and expand child care for small children. If the number of social benefits is to be increased, let us look rather toward a guaranteed minimum income for everyone." These are prescient comments in view of the arrival in 1988 of the Minimum Insertion Income (RMI) for job seekers, whose impact on family policy no doubt will be very important.

The history of family policy since 1981 is characterized, at the very least, by a certain continuity. This cannot be attributed simply to the search for ways of halting demographic decline. It must be seen, rather, as the result of enduring institutions, of social forces institutionalized in the form of bureaucratic organisms and management mechanisms, of associations whose representatives and interests are virtually immovable, of modes of representation that are virtually immune to the effects of specifically political action. Without doubt political life—at least its calendar and its rhythms—is not without influence on decision making, which often is preceded by lengthy preparation and negotiation until such time as the issue mobilizes political forces and culminates in official action.

To be sure, there was evidence of the arrival on the scene of new actors in the field of family policy, particularly the feminist movements, now converted into "responsible" actors in the double sense of the word, with representatives within the political parties (particularly the Socialist Party), in the Ministry of the Rights of Women, in research centers, and elsewhere. The law of 31 December 1982, which provided partial reimbursement for the expenses of abortion, produced a long polemic between leaders of the parties of the Right, notably Jacques Chirac, and spokspersons in the field for the Left, particularly Yvette Roudy. Other measures sought to reduce the penalties on families with working mothers, as in the law of 1 July 1984, which substantially increased the income ceiling for two-income families receiving the young child allowance.

But beyond these cleavages that divided political parties, unions, and associations and that go back to definitions of the role and condition of the woman, the familialist consensus triumphed, paradoxically reinforced by political competition, out of which emerged a unanimity of opinion in favor, if not of the "family," at least of "the child." With some coming and going, family policy is returning to the essential task of aiding new families and large families, but with a revised symbolic focus. "The child," like previously the "family," is only a word on which everyone can agree, for it is the geometrical point at which all conceptions intersect. The interest of the child obviously is not the same according to all social classes, nor is the interest in having children. As shown for example in the 1984 demonstrations in favor of private schools, the way in which children are treated is an issue in political and social conflict! Yet the child who is the object of family policy incarnates a vision of a natural, nonconflictual world, a vision that henceforth constitutes the profound unconscious of all collective action in this field. This would not be the least of the contributions of family policy to the forms that political struggle takes in France, at least the struggle for opinion and elections. And on this market, the family is still a sure value!

REFERENCES

Ashford, Douglas E. 1986, *The Emergence of the Welfare States.* New York: Blackwell.

Becchia, Alain. 1986. "Les Milieux parlementaires et la dépopulation de 1900 à 1914." *Communications* 44: 201–44.

Boltanski, Luc. 1982. *Les Cadres: La formation d'un groupe social.* Paris: Editions de Minuit.

Bourdieu, Pierre. 1982. *Ce que parler veut dire.* Paris: Fayard.

Ceccaldi, Dominique. 1957. *Histoire des prestations familiales en France.* Paris: Uncaf.

Commissariat Général du Plan de Modernisation et d'Equipement, Commission de la Consommation et de la Modernisation Sociale. 1947. *Rapport.* Paris.

Confédération Génerale du Travail. 1953. 29th cong., June.

Conseil National de la Résistance. 1944. *Les Jours heureux.* Brochure published 15 March 1944.

Durand, Paul. 1953a. *La politique contemporaine de sécurité sociale.* Paris: Dalloz.

———. 1953b. "Les Équivoques de la redistribution de revenu par la Sécurité Sociale." *Droit Social* 16: 292–98.

Durkheim, Emile. 1963a. *L'Éducation morale.* Paris: PUF.

———. 1963b. *Les Règles de la méthode sociologique.* Paris: PUF.

Journal Officiel, Lois et décrets. 1971. November 11, 11145–46.

Kamerman, Sheila B., and A. J. Kahn, eds. 1978. *Family Policy.* New York: Columbia University Press.

Laroque, Pierre. 1986. *La Politique familiale en France depuis 1945.* Paris: Documentation Française.

Lenoir, Rémi. 1985a. "L'Effondrement des bases sociales du familialisme." *Actes de la Recherche en Sciences Sociales* 57–58: 69–88.

———. 1985b. "Tranformations du familialisme et reconversions morales." *Actes de la Recherche en Sciences Sociales* 59: 3–47.

———. 1989. "Problèmes sociaux, problèmes sociologiques." In *Initiation à la pratique sociologique,* edited by Patrick Champagne, Rémi Lenoir, Louis Pinto, and Dominique Merllié. Paris: Bordas, Dunod.

———. 1991. *Famille et politique.* Paris: Editions de Minuit.

Lery, A. 1984. "Les Actives de 1982 n'ont pas moins d'enfants que celles de 1968." *Economie et Statistique* 171–172 (November–December): 29.

Magri, Suzanna. 1977. *Logement et reproduction de l'exploitation; Les politiques étatiques du logement en France (1947–1972).* Paris: C.S.U.

Nizard, Alain. 1974. "Politique et législation démographique." *Population* 29 (special number): 285–326.

Paxton, Robert O. 1973. *La France de Vichy, 1940–1944.* Paris: Seuil.

Sauvy, Alfred. 1972. *De P. Reynaud à Charles de Gaulle.* Paris: Casterman.

Talmy, Robert, 1967. *Histoire du mouvement familial en France (1896–1939).* 2 vols. Paris: Uncaf.

Vincent, Paul. 1950. "La Famille normale." *Population* 5: 253–56.

Wright, Gordon. 1948. *The Reshaping of French Democracy.* New York: Reynal and Hitchcock.

6

FRENCH HOUSING POLICIES IN THE EIGHTIES: COMPLEXITY, CONTINUITY, AND IDEOLOGY

NATHAN H. SCHWARTZ

I. INTRODUCTION

This paper examines the development of housing policy in France with a particular emphasis on the period from 1981, when François Mitterrand was elected to his first term as president of the Republic, through the period of "cohabitation" (1986–1988), when Prime Minister Jacques Chirac led a government of the Center and Right, through the announcement of the second budget (September 1989) of the Socialist government that took office in 1988 when Mitterrand won his second term as president.* It is a particularly interesting period, for at its outset, a socialist party long excluded from power came to office with the hopes of bringing more social justice and equality to France after years of conservative leadership. The Chirac Government that followed was overtly committed to the market ideas espoused by Margaret Thatcher and Ronald Reagan, in clear opposition to the ideals of the previous socialist government, as well as representing a change in emphasis from earlier right-wing governments. The Socialist government that followed Chirac, tempered by its previous electoral failure, faced the conflict between its ideological goals and its concern to govern France in a way that would preserve its grip on office. This paper examines the way in which the goals of these governments affected housing policy, but also the way that the

Support for this research was provided by the Alexander von Humboldt Foundation and the University of Louisville. Translations from French are my own.

TABLE 6.1

Distribution of Housing Tenures in France: 1982

Type of Tenure	Number (in thousands of housing units)	Percentage
Owner-occupied	9,928	50.7
Rented—HLM	2,644	13.5
Rented—Other	5,389	27.5
Free Housing	1,629	8.3

Source: Direction de la Construction 1986, 10.

structure of housing policy affected the way these governments went about seeking their goals.

II. THE CONFIGURATION OF FRENCH HOUSING POLICY

One useful indicator of the operation of housing policy is the distribution of housing tenures—typically in terms of owner occupation, rental in the private sector, and rental in the public sector. These categories often reflect a whole set of public policies differentiated by tenure, and, as Rex and Moore (1967) have persuasively argued, tenure often predicts the political forces at work. However, relative to public policy, it is important to understand the ambiguity of these categorizations. As in the case with British and American housing policy, French housing policy is extremely complex, and state action shapes and subsidizes virtually all forms of tenure.

Figures for the basic French housing tenures are shown in table 6.1. As in both Britain and the United States, in France those people who own or are buying their own homes are a majority of the population. HLM housing (Habitations à loyer modéré) is subsidized housing offered at moderate rent and owned and managed by HLM associations—this is the French equivalent to American "public housing" and British "council housing." At 13.5 percent of the total, HLM housing represents a much larger proportion of French housing than is the case with public housing in the United States (1.6 percent), but represents a smaller share of total housing than British public housing (27 percent). Accounting for slightly more than one-quarter of French housing, rental housing in the private sector is smaller than the United States's 32 percent, but much larger than Britain's 11 percent (U.S. Department of Commerce 1982, 751, 760; Central Statistical Office 1989).

To describe French housing policy, we will first examine the history of French housing policy from the end of World War II to the election of François Mitterrand as president, then examine the direct subsidies provided to build or obtain housing, the subsidies provided to housing through the tax system, the special forms of finance that provide funding to housing, and rent regulation.

The Development of Postwar French Housing Policy

Current French housing policy is best understood in the context of its history since the end of World War II. At the end of the war, France faced an enormous housing shortage as almost 20 percent of the prewar housing stock had been destroyed or severely damaged, while at the same time an increasing birthrate and a large influx of refugees swelled the demand for housing (Pearsall 1984, 9).

While the French government lacked the financial means directly to promote massive new construction, in the period from the end of the war to the early 1950s, a set of measures was adopted that regulated and promoted housing activity short of the direct creation of housing. Termed the "pillars" of French housing policy by Duclaud-Williams (1978), these measures continue by and large today, often in highly modified form. The first pillar is the 1948 Rent Act, which controlled the rents of pre–1948 housing in the attempt to keep the available housing affordable; the issue of whether rents should be controlled became an important point of difference between the governments of the Right and the Left during the 1980s. The second pillar was what Duclaud-Williams terms the "intermediate" or "semipublic" sector of housing, established in the law of 21 July 1950, which set up a private bank, the Crédit foncier de France (CFF), to provide loans and subsidies for house construction. Duclaud-Williams (1978, 18) says of the nominally private Crédit foncier that "its directors and governor are appointed by the Minister of Finance and it serves in fact as the government's errand boy in the field of housing finance." Furthermore, while its funds come from public issues, it is up to the minister of finance to approve them, giving the government powerful control over CFF activity (Duclaud-Williams 1978, 18). The third pillar of French housing policy is the HLM movement (Habitations à loyer modéré), organizations that provide "social" housing for rent and sale; these organizations were reestablished in their prewar form by the law of 3 September 1947 (Duclaud-Williams 1978, 19). Funding for the

HLM organizations activities comes from low-interest loans and other subsidies. All three pillars involve the French state in the provision of housing and the regulation of the housing market, but at one remove.

From the early 1950s to the mid–1970s, a financially stronger French government encouraged massive amounts of new construction. A first phase of this period was from the mid–1950s to the mid–1960s, when the French government subsidized the building of most new housing through subsidies to the social housing agencies, the HLM organizations, to construct rental housing, and through the provision of subsidies and subsidized loans to individuals for the purchase of new housing (Pearsall 1984, 13; Conseil Économique et Social 1989, 21–22). In a second phase lasting from the mid–1960s to the mid–1970s, the French state could no longer afford to provide so much direct subvention. The emphasis now shifted to the use of private finance to provide the funds for housing construction (Conseil Économique et Social 1989, 22). One measure adopted in this period, the so-called *débudgétisation* (debudgetization) of 1966, involved ending the French treasury's role as lender to the HLMs; that function was transferred to the Caisse des dépôts et consignations (CDC—the national bank in charge of financing local government) (Conseil Économique et Social 1989, 41). A second measure, adopted in 1973, removed from the budget the specification of the number of housing units to be financed by the national government, so that unexpected price increases in housing would not be a drain on the budget (Conseil Économique et Social 1989, 41).

In a literal sense, Pearsall's (1984, 9) characterization of this period as "the rise of the private sector" is accurate, but fails to convey the continuing and expanding role of government. The "conversion" to private sector sources of finance was accompanied by new governmental measures to provide direct incentives to the private sector to invest in housing. The government also restructured the financial system, providing specialized circuits of finance in order to insure that capital for housing would be available on a continuous basis. Such measures, more fully discussed in the next section of this chapter, included tax breaks for special savings accounts whose capital was to be invested in housing (Livret A); special housing savings accounts that gave both tax breaks and subsidies to depositors using their savings to finance house purchase *(épargne logement)*; the creation of specialized financial institutions to raise and distribute capital for housing (CDC, CFF); as well as a tax on employers of more than ten employees whose proceeds were also devoted to housing (1 percent funds). The private sector did gain a new role in the provision of housing, but these developments hardly represent a disengagement of the French state from housing policy.

Record numbers of houses were built in this period; the Economic and Social Council (Conseil Économique et Social 1989, 22) has noted that in the period from 1970 to 1975, the rate of French housing construction, relative to the number of inhabitants, set new international records. At the same time, as Pearsall (1984, 10) has noted,

Crude output was emphasized however, at the expense of quality, and many dwellings were constructed at standards and in locations unacceptable today.

With rising incomes during the 1970s this issue of quality became more important. The French began to feel cramped in comparison to their neighbors; in 1973, the average useable size of a new housing unit in France was 73 square meters (786 square feet) compared to 85 square meters (915 square feet) in West Germany and 124 square meters (1335 square feet) in Denmark (Conseil Économique et Social 1989, 23).

In response to the call of government commissions for policy to improve the quality of the French habitat, a major new housing act was adopted in 1977. This legislation, which structured much of policy in the 1980s, had three major aims. The first was to encourage home ownership as the preferred means to stimulate the production of new housing and the improvement of older housing. The second aim was to improve the quality of rental housing, both by encouraging new construction and by improving existing units. The third was to reduce the general aid given directly for the production or renovation of housing (aide à la pierre) and to replace it with new forms of aid for families that could not afford the new (and higher) rents or mortgage payments (Conseil Économique et Social 1989, 23). On its face, this third goal was to target aid directly to those most in need, without engaging the state in financing those who could afford to pay their own way.

Direct Subsidies to Housing

There are basically two forms of direct government subsidies to housing. The first offers subsidies for the construction or acquisition of housing units (aide à la pierre), with the aid based primarily on the cost of building a new unit or acquiring an existing unit of housing. The second goes directly to individuals to help them pay rent or buy a house (aide à la personne), with the subsidy based on a family's income and the cost of housing. Prior to 1977,

TABLE 6.2

Subsidies to Housing Units and Individuals (in millions of francs)

	1981	1982	1983	1984	1985
Subsidies to housing units (includes, but not limited to, PLA and PAP)	20,638	24,618	23,614	21,549	13,144
Subsidies to individuals (includes, but not limited to, APL, AL, AFL)	2,641	4,750	7,494	10,431	13,520

Source: Direction de la Construction 1986, 18, 26.

French housing policy stressed *aide à la pierre*, but with the 1977 housing law (Law No. 77-1 of 3 January 1977), the emphasis switched to *aide à la personne*, a trend also evident in British and American housing policy (Schwartz 1987a). The rationale behind this shift is that while subsidies for the construction of housing increase the supply of housing, it is very difficult to insure that the beneficiaries are those most in need; more direct subsidies to needy individuals are seen as more effective. The shift from an emphasis on aid to construction and acquisition of housing to providing aid directly to individuals can be seen in table 6.2. From that table it can be seen that while the subsidies tied to particular housing units (and directed to developers and/or HLM associations) fell 46 percent from 1982 to 1985, the subsidies to individuals rose fivefold from 1981 to 1985. Similarly, while in 1981 subsidies to individuals accounted for only 11 percent of the subsidies to housing units, by 1985 subsidies to individuals had outstripped the subsidies to housing units (table 6.2).

In terms of the aid to housing units, there are two categories of subsidy. One category of subsidies is for rental housing: the PLA program (*prêts locatifs aidés*) provides low-interest loans for the construction of rental housing available for those under certain income limits. In theory these loans are available to public and private developers, but in fact, given the low return on investment in this type of housing under current economic conditions, very little PLA money has been used by the private sector. Most of the construction under the PLA program has been used by HLM associations, the semipublic organizations that build and manage social housing. There are over a thousand of these organizations, and they tend to be very closely tied to local government; it is not unusual for the board of directors to be headed by the local mayor, with other key positions being filled by important local politicians.

The other category of subsidies for housing units is for owner occupation, in their current form also a legacy of the 1977 reworking of housing policy. One such program is the PAP program (*prêts aidés pour l'accession à la propriété*), which provides low-interest loans for the purchase of housing by people falling below certain income limits. In addition to the PAP program, there is one type of housing loan (*prêts conventionnés*) that is made by regular banks that get a small government subsidy to lower the interest rate to a level between the market rate and the much lower rate of the PAP loans. There is also a set of direct subsidies in which the government provides subsidized loans for the rehabilitation of housing (PALULOS).

The major program providing subsidies directly to individuals is the APL program (*l'aide personnalisée au logement*), which was created in 1977. Benefits are a housing allowance based on family situation and available resources, and they require that the beneficiaries live in units of housing meeting certain standards (Heugas-Darraspen 1985, 55–66). One important aspect of the housing allowance program (APL) is that it can be used not only by renters but also by those buying their own homes. Indeed, in 1985, almost 790,000 French families received housing allowances (APL) as owner occupiers, compared to 625,000 families receiving housing allowances as renters. Thus French direct subsidies benefit not only renters but also home-owners. In addition, there are two older programs of direct subsidies to individuals, the *allocation logement familiale* (AL) and the *allocation logement sociale* (ALS), which provide subsidies to families in special circumstances, including the retired and handicapped (Pearsall 1984, 12).

Tax Subsidies to Housing

In addition to the direct subsidies mentioned above, a major housing subsidy is provided by French tax law that allows some of the costs of housing to be deducted from taxes. While there exist tax provisions to encourage investment in rental housing, provisions encouraging home ownership are particularly numerous. For example, as in many other countries, including the United States and Great Britain, French tax law gives special treatment to mortgage interest: for the first five years of a home mortgage, income tax may

TABLE 6.3

Selected Tax Measures Favoring Owner-Occupation (Figures are in millions of francs and represent revenue not collected because of tax provisions)

	1981	1982	1983	1984
Tax Provision				
Deductions from taxable income for main residence (including energy-saving expenditure and building upkeep)	580	645	1,125	1,350
Deductions from taxable income for interest on loans for main residence	6,240	6,560	7,010	7,279
Exemption of interest and bonus payments on home-ownership savings plans and accounts	2,660	3,000	3,360	3,750

Source: Ministère de l'Equipement, du Logement, de l'Aménagement du Territoire et des Transports.

be reduced by 25 percent of the interest paid up to a ceiling of nine thousand francs, plus fifteen hundred francs per dependent.

In addition, owner-occupiers living in new housing financed by subsidized loans are exempted from property tax for ten years from the date of completion of the home. Furthermore, there are housing savings plans subsidized by the government that provide bonuses to savers meeting certain conditions; the interest and bonuses are also tax-free. Moreover, there are tax deductions for owner-occupiers on part of the cost of making a home more energy efficient, making major repairs, and undertaking restoration work. Lastly, the capital gains resulting from the sale of one's primary residence are also tax-free.

The cost of these deductions is very high. A selection of the possible housing deductions is contained in table 6.3. The cost runs into billions of francs per year. For purposes of comparison to other forms of housing aid, the average cost per year of the measures in table 6.3 for home ownership is 10.93 billion francs. That is more than the average of the direct subsidies for building rental housing, which over the same period averaged 9.9 billion francs per year (Direction de la Construction 1986, 18), and far exceeds subsidies aiding individuals to rent housing, which averaged 2.5 billion francs in the same period (Direction de la Construction 1986, 26). When the direct subsidies for building housing for owner occupation and the housing allowance (APL) for individuals buying housing (both costing the government more than the comparable subsidies for renters) are added to the tax measures that subsidize home ownership, it becomes clear that the subsidies for home ownership are enormous.

Special Avenues of Finance

In his study of French economic policy making, John Zysman suggested that one of the keys to French economic development may not have been its use of planning so much as the control over finance exercised by the planners (Zysman 1983, 99–169). French housing policy is also marked by distinctive arrangements in the realm of finance. In most western industrial countries, housing is greatly affected by the operation of finance markets. It is routine to hear of upturns or downturns in housing construction resulting from changing conditions in financial markets as interest rates rise or fall and as housing competes with other forms of investment for financial resources. Government subsidy policy does not always get around this problem. For example, in the United States many federal subsidies for the production of low-income housing were based on interest-rate subsidies and loan guarantees; these subsidies were not always enough to overcome high interest rates or shortages of available capital (as was the case in the late 1970s).

One of the distinctive aspects of the French case has been the creation of special sources of capital for the finance of housing largely insulated from competition in financial markets; when the mechanisms used to implement these policies function as intended, the finance of housing in France is less affected by the fluctuations in general finance markets than is the case in other countries. These special channels of finance include special tax-free savings accounts that, along with government subsidies, provided low-interest loans for the building of social rental housing and for home construction for low-income families; tax-free savings accounts that receive an additional government bonus when used to purchase housing; and funds raised by a tax on large employers that provides funds for the construction of housing.

One special source of funds for housing is tax-free savings accounts, called "A Accounts" (Livret A). A Accounts pay interest at a rate at or below the inflation rate, which is substantially below the market interest rate. Despite their low return, these accounts have been popular because they are exempt from taxation. Thus the resources in the A Accounts are a source of low-interest money for housing. The money from these accounts, along with a subsidy from the government to lower the interest rate even more, is used to subsidize housing activity by the HLM associations. Before 1977, these loans to HLMs were called "HLM loans" *(prêt HLM)*. In 1977, these moneys were divided into three different loan programs, all assisting the creation of housing through the HLM associations, including loans for construction of social rental housing (PLA—*prêt locatif aidé*), for construction of homes to be purchased by people with incomes below certain limits (PAP—*prêt d'accession à la propriété*), as well as for the rehabilitation of social housing (PALULOS—*prime à l'amélioration des logements à usage locatif et à occupation sociale*) (Conseil Économique et Social 1989, 41–44).

These loan programs make significant amounts of funds available at below market interest rates. For example, in the spring of 1987, the rate of subsidy was 12 percent of the overall value of the loans for the building of social rental housing; the interest rate possible under these arrangements was 4.9 percent, a great contrast to market rates for home loans of 9.5 percent to 10 percent. Furthermore, the government has been willing to give mortgages of up to thirty-nine years, a much longer period than is available in the private market.

The raising and administration of these loans funded by Account A is handled by a government bank, the Caisse des dépôts et consignations (CDC). The recent role of the CDC in housing has been an expansion of its role relative to government agencies and its subsidiary banks. From 1966 to 1986, the actual administration of CDC housing loans was the responsibility of an offshoot of the CDC, the Caisse des prêts aux habitations à loyer modéré (CPHLM). In 1986 the CPHLM was renamed the Caisse de garantie du logement (CGLS); at that time it ceded the ability to grant loans to the CDC, but The CGLS retained the function of administering the loans it had made and also gained the ability to guarantee subsidized loans to recipients when they could not get guarantees from other government agencies (a guarantee is normally necessary to be eligible for a subsidized loan). While overtly the CGLS has a smaller role relative to the CDC than it did in its earlier incarnation as the CPHLM, its role is still quite large: the portfolio of loans under its administration was 266 billion francs in 1986 (CDC 1987).

When it was given the responsibility for providing HLMs loans for building social rental housing (PLA) and housing for purchase by lower-income families (PAP) in 1986, the Caisse des dépôts et consignations (CDC) gained a power that the old CPHLM did not have—the authority to make the decision whether a particular recipient could receive the loan. The CPHLM had been bound to accept the decision of the Ministry of Housing about whether the recipient qualified for a loan. In that regard, the moving of the loan-approval function to the CDC also strengthened its standing as a bank, albeit one that had special sources for its operation. In 1986, the CDC was able to draw upon 34.7 billion francs in funds from the A Accounts (Livret A) for housing and 4 billion francs in subsidies from the state. In the same year, it granted 26.9 billion francs in PLA loans for rental housing, 7.7 billion in PAP subsidized loans for home ownership, and 4.1 billion in loans for rehabilitation (CDC 1987). As an aside, it is important to note that the A Accounts funds (Livret A) are not exactly free to the government; the cost of exempting A Accounts from taxation was 3 billion francs in 1984. It is important to note that in budget terms this is money not collected, not direct expenditure; in other countries such tax breaks are considerably less vulnerable to change than direct expenditures (Schwartz 1987B).

An important related institution is the Crédit foncier de France (CFF), nominally a private bank, but, as noted earlier, very much controlled in important aspects by the French treasury. Until 1977 the Crédit foncier made CFF loans (*prêt Crédit foncier*) to home buyers who fell below certain income limits. The funds for this Crédit foncier activity came from funds raised in the financial market, with government subsidies to keep interest rates low. In the major revision of housing policy in 1977, the CFF loans were superseded by loans for lower-income families to purchase housing (PLA—*prêt locatif aidé*), but unlike loans of the same name given by the CDC to the HLM associations to aid lower-income people in purchasing housing, these CFF loans go directly to families for home purchase (Conseil Économique et Social 1989, 41–44).

For the purposes of this discussion, the importance of the CFF is that it has taken an increasing role in the management and provision of finance for housing, a role insulated from the general financial market. In 1983, a single pool of funds for low-interest loans for lower-income families to purchase housing (PAP) was created within the Crédit foncier (CFF), merging all funds for this end; from this point on the CDC brought its funds for this PAP program into this pool. Both banks continued to make their loans separately, but the initial funds were merged. The second development, in 1985, was designed to improve the stability of the system; both banks would improve the supply of funds for the loans for lower-income home ownership (PAP) by bringing into the pool excess funds from their retirement savings accounts as well as funds from mortgages that had already been paid off (Conseil Économique et Social 1989, 44).

This developing relationship between the CFF and the CDC signals several important aspects of French policy in this area. The first is that policy arrangements often get quite complicated, in this case creating a joint pool for funds while preserving the separate roles for the distribution of funds for both banks. The second aspect is that while the administrative complexity of the system grew, that complexity seems to have increased the flexibility of policy change; by creating a common pool of funds for the subsidized loan programs for home ownership, the government seems to have given itself the possibility of making greater changes in the balance of loans granted by the CDC to HLMs and by the CFF to individuals than would be possible when each bank had only its own pool of funds. A third aspect is the commitment of policy makers to preserving potential sources of funding by allowing both banks to draw on funds raised from special savings accounts for retirement. The banks were allowed to put funds from these retirement accounts that were not immediately needed to pay retirement benefits into the pool for housing loans—thus increasing the amount of money available to these funds.

French policy has created another form of finance insulated from the general financial market, that of special housing savings accounts. There are two different kinds of special housing savings account, the *plan d'épargne logement* (PEL) and the *compte d'épargne logement* (CEL). Both offer government-provided bonuses (based on the interest earned), exemption from tax on the interest and bonus, and an additional partial loan at a low interest rate if the specified amounts of money are saved on a regular basis and the savings are used for the purchase of a residence (Pearsall 1984, 26; Heugas-Darraspen 1985, 91–100). The plans differ in the amounts to be deposited, the minimum period of deposit, and the terms of the loan available. Assuming that most people will use this money for housing, the effect of the housing savings accounts is to reserve a certain amount of funds for use in housing. Table 6.4 shows the number of such accounts and plans and the amount of funds they contain; in 1985, with almost 12 million such accounts and 313 billion francs on deposit, they provided a large reserve of personal savings earmarked for housing.

Another source of housing finance insulated from the finance market are the funds contributed by employers for housing. Since 1953, all employers with more than ten employees must contribute just under 1 percent of total wages for housing construction; in exchange they have the right to nominate their workers for priority in the housing built, whether for rent or for sale

TABLE 6.4

Housing Savings Accounts and Plans

	1978	1979	1980	1981	1982	1983	1984	1985
Number of housing savings accounts and plans (in thousands of accounts)	6,110	6,886	7,468	7,862	8,459	9,513	10,503	11,985
Total amount on deposit in the accounts and plans (in billions of francs)	130.8	160.2	170.1	184.5	200.9	222.8	253.5	313.8

Source: Direction de la Construction 1986, 33.

(Pearsall 1984, 19). Some large firms administer these "1 percent funds" themselves, but most firms make their contributions to organizations founded to administer such funds, the most common type being Comités interprofessionels du logement (CILs).

While, as Pearsall (1984, 118–19) suggests, the government does not have much control over the types of housing that the CILs invest in, it is nevertheless clear that the 1 percent funds represent another source of housing finance earmarked for housing, insulated from pressures in the general financial markets. Table 6.5 shows recent levels of the 1 percent funds. In comparison to the subsidies for housing units and individuals, shown in table 6.2, the 1 percent monies can be seen to represent a substantial part of the funds available for housing. And these funds are important because they are available for housing regardless of the general state of financial markets.

TABLE 6.5

Employer Investment in Housing (in millions of francs)

	1981	1982	1983	1984	1985
Direct investments	730	783	833	954	1,078
Investments through collecting organizations (including CILs)	5,691	6,483	7,281	7,904	8,276
TOTAL employer investments	6,421	7,266	8,114	8,858	9,354

Source: Direction de la Construction 1986, 29.

Rent Control

Rent controls of one type or another have been an important feature in modern French housing policy, dating from 1914 (Pearsall 1984, 11–12). In the period since World War II, important rent controls included the 1948 Rent Act, which controlled initially over 6 million units of housing built before 1948. The number of units covered under the provisions of the 1948 act declined to less than seven hundred thousand by the mid–1980s because changes in tenants resulted in decontrol under the act, and ministerial decree removed other pre–1948 dwellings from control (Pearsall 1984, 11–12). But the rents of many housing units built with state subsidies fall under government control as well; for example, the rents for most of HLM housing are regulated by the government.

Redistributive Effects of Housing

One of the important ways that housing policy can be evaluated is in its distributive effects: who gets what. A recent study by the French National Center for Scientific Research (CNRS) explored this question, examining the impact of the housing allowances, subsidized loans, tax provisions, and subsidized bank loans on the French distribution of income (Cornuel 1989). In terms of the general redistributive effect of French housing programs, the study found that government aids to renters tended to be redistributive in an absolute sense, that is, the poor tended to benefit more than the rich (Cornuel 1989, 11). The aids to homeowners affected the general distribution of wealth by making a small contribution to "relative" redistribution: that is, richer people tended to receive a smaller percentage of their income in aid than poorer people, even though it is possible that richer people received a greater absolute amount of aid (Cornuel 1989, 11).

When looking at the impact of government aids to renters alone (not the whole population), the picture changes somewhat. The CNRS study found that within the group of renters, richer renters tended to benefit more from housing aide than poorer renters (Cornuel 1989, 11). While aid to renters is, in overall terms, redistributive, many renters at the bottom of the income scale do not receive the subsidies, a problem that began to be addressed seriously in the second half of the 1980s and is discussed later in this chapter. On the other hand, within the group of homeowners, the aid received tended to favor poorer homeowners (Cornuel 1989, 11). It is important to remember that homeowners as a group are richer than renters.

With regard to more specific government aids for renters, the most redistributive program was the housing allowance program (APL), followed in order by the programs that provided subsidies for the construction of housing units *(aide à la pierre)* (Cornuel 1989, 10). The housing allowance program was also the most redistributive program for homeowners, followed by the subsidized loan programs funded from A Accounts and government subsidies (PAP), the various tax deductions, and loans from the Crédit foncier de France; the tax-free savings accounts that received a subsidy from the government when the saver used the proceeds to buy a house are the least redistributive aid (Cornuel 1989, 10). The findings of the study seem to support the basic policy orientation emerging from the 1977 reforms that suggested that direct aid to individuals, tailored to their income, as in the housing allowance program, would do the better job of delivering benefits to poorer people than the earlier programs that emphasized subsidies for the construction of housing units, such as the PAP program.

III. MITTERRAND I: LEFT HOPES AND ECONOMIC CONSTRAINT

In May 1981, the Socialist François Mitterrand was elected president of France. In the subsequent legislative elections (June 1981), his party won 285 out of 491 seats in the National Assembly and went on to form a government including four ministers from the French Communist Party. The ascension of the Socialist Party to governmental power was grounded in a history of promises of broad change, as Doreen Collins (1987, 84) has noted:

The policy statements from the *Common Program* [1972] to the *110 propositions* contained a major emphasis upon the need for change in order that French society might incorporate more fully the themes of social justice, social equality and openness with the aim of establishing a new balance in relationships between public authorities, public authorities and individuals, and between individuals themselves.

As Sonia Mazey (1987, 3–4) has noted, "The keyword of the socialist programme was *le changement*," and upon taking power "the newly-elected government . . . embarked upon its radical programme with enthusiasm." Housing, along with concern with communal facilities, was part of this program.

The major piece of housing legislation adopted by the Socialist government was the law of 22 June 1982 (No. 82-526), known as the Quilliot Law
after the housing minister who introduced it. The law began with "General
Principles," which included the sweeping statement "Le droit à l'habitat est
un droit fondamental"—the right to habitat is a fundamental right. After
this sweeping assertion of a new right, the Quilliot Law actually focuses on
the relations of landlords and tenants; one critic has asserted that while the
opening stresses a general right and expresses the interest of the state in the
issue, the content of the law represents the granting of privileges to one
particular group, renters (Boubli 1985, 9–11).

The provisions of the Quilliot Law called for a radical restructuring of the
relation of tenants and landlord in the determination of rents. The law was
to apply to all tenants, in both private housing and in social (HLM) housing,
with the exception of tenants in housing still under the law of 1948. Within
the term of a lease, the annual rent increase was to be determined by the
annual increase in the cost-of-building index published by the National
Institute for Statistics and Economic Studies (INSEE), although the government could limit increases to 80 percent of the index. The rent increase for
a lease renewal or a new lease were to be negotiated each year by the
organizations of renters and landlords within the framework of a national
commission on rents (Commission nationale des rapports locatifs); the incentive for the parties to reach agreement was that in the event of deadlock, the
government would set the rate. A higher increase could be sought when
renovation work had been done on the dwelling.

One of the key provisions of the new law specified when landlords had the
right to set rents outside the framework of rent control. Under the Quilliot
Law, landlords had the right to set any rent they wished for new dwellings,
dwellings that were no longer covered by the law of 1948, dwellings that had
been vacant for eighteen months or more, and dwellings that were unoccu-
pied because of a court decision (as in the case where a tenant had not met
his or her obligations) (Cancellieri 1986, 127–128). The law also gave
tenants the right to renew their leasees, except in situations where the
landlord needed the dwelling for personal use or for the use of his or her
children.

Many argue that the Quilliot Law had the undesirable effect of constrict-
ing the rental market by encouraging landlords either to hold their properties
off the market entirely rather than face rent regulation and the tenant's rights
to lease renewal, or to hold a vacant property off the market for eighteen

months in order to set the initial rent level where they pleased, or to avoid the entire issue of rent and tenant regulation by selling their holdings to new owner-occupiers (Boubli 1985, 7–8, 16–17; Tuppen 1988, 167, 174). As Boubli argues, the basic right of habitat accorded by the Quilliot Law implied greater access, while the provisions of the law have operated to limit access to rental housing (Boubli 1985, 7–8).

Further expansion of government's role in the housing market was precluded by the worsening of the economic situation in France:

1982 brought a U-turn in economic strategy and the introduction of austerity measures which were further extended in 1983: benefits were cut, taxes were increased . . . there were problems, delays and trimming (Mazey 1987, 3–4).

The French government suddenly decided it did not have money to spend; the great expense of creating housing could be expected to dampen the possibilities for major housing initiatives.

But the problems of the French economy did not pose barriers simply to new programs; they also caused real problems for existing programs. The upswing of inflation in 1981 caused real problems for people seeking to buy housing. In 1981 the interest rates on unassisted housing mortgages rose from a rate of 9–10 percent to 16 percent (maintaining a real interest rate of 6–7 percent); the interest rates for subsidized loans for home purchase (PAP) also rose, reducing the affordability of housing for many people (Conseil Économique et Social 1989, 34). But the cessation of inflation and the deflation that started in 1984 also created real problems; the income of many people stagnated or fell, making it increasingly difficult for them to meet their mortgage payments. One estimate is that in the period from 1981 to 1984, there could have been nine hundred thousand families in difficulty (Conseil Économique et Social 1989, 35).

One factor accentuating the mortgage payment problem was that, not so long before, it had been quite easy to get large loans (relative to income), based on the assumption that incomes would continue to rise. Figures provided in the 1989 report of the Economic and Social Committee (Conseil Économique et Social 1989, annex 11) show that the average revenue of families obtaining loans dropped in this period, while at the same time the cost of a dwelling was increasing much faster than incomes. In the same set of figures, one finds that the average family earning two times the French minimum wage (SMIC—*salaire minimum interprofessionel de croissance*), or less, and making mortgage payments, was spending 42 percent of its income on housing, before the calculation of housing allowances (APL). Even after figuring in the housing allowance (APL), the same family was spending 28 percent of its income on housing. Another factor accentuating this problem of repayment was that many of the subsidized mortgages were graduated, with payments rising by 4 percent per year, based on the earlier assumption that incomes would rise over time (Tuppen 1988, 173). In 1986 and 1987 the French government had to reduce the progressivity and lengthen the payment period of many subsidized loans (PAP) and low-interest bank loans (*prêts conventionnés*) to keep the mortgage payment problem from becoming a disaster (Conseil Économique et Social 1989, 35).

These economic problems were also reflected in the rapidly growing cost of personalized financial aids given to renters and homeowners. Table 6.2 shows that between 1981 and 1986, the cost of personalized housing aid grew by almost 400 percent! The 1977 housing reforms had emphasized direct aid to individuals over aid to units of housing, in the double expectation that direct aid would target the people most in need as well as save the government money in the long run. The assumption was that over time, with growth in the economy, fewer and fewer people would qualify for (or need) the housing allowances, resulting in a reduction in the cost of the program (Conseil Économique et Social 1989, 42). In fact, with stagnating incomes and relatively high levels of unemployment, few recipients lost their need and eligibility for housing allowances (APL), and even more people qualified for aid. Faced with this problem, beginning in 1982 the Mitterrand government stopped trying to keep the payment level for housing allowances in line with the cost of living in order to reduce somewhat its growth.

Following the radical restructuring of landlord-tenant relations and rent determinations of the Quilliot Law, succeeding housing policy of the Socialist government was considerably more conservative in tone, consistent with the more conservative economic policies characteristic of the second half of its tenure in office. For example, to reduce some of the disincentives to landlords stemming from the Quilliot Law, three measures were adopted to moderate its effects: first, landlords could raise rents when a dwelling was improved; second, upon a change of tenants, landlords could ask for a rent increase if the old rent was deemed low in comparison to rents in comparable dwellings; and third, the entire increase in the cost-of-construction index was to be used as the basis for yearly rent increases during the term of a lease, the government giving up the option to lower the figure to 80 percent of the index.

The government also adopted measures that made clear its continuing support for home-ownership programs. While this support is often seen as a non-Left position, one finds support for such measures among the large parties of the Left in countries like the Federal Republic of Germany and Britain. While ideologues may prefer some form of collective ownership, it is clear that many individuals see home ownership as an important form of personal control over their environment and vote accordingly. In addition, the government gave HLM organizations the right to sell units of their rental stock to tenants (Tuppen 1988, 167–68). This may not represent so much an encouragement for home ownership as one way of allowing financially strapped HLM organizations to raise money to pay debts and to rehabilitate existing stock.

The government adopted other measures designed to aid the home-building industry, which was in a pronounced downturn, as is frequently the case in times of economic difficulty, with the accompanying implications for employment. The 1985 measure, "the Plan for Relaunching Building and Public Works" *(le plan du relance du bâtiment et des travaux publics)* offered lower interest rates for those borrowing money under the subsidized mortgage program (PAP), as well as increased tax relief for home buyers to stimulate the industry (Tuppen 1988, 175). In 1983 and 1985, measures were also adopted to insure that a larger and more certain pool of money was available for the PAP program (assisted loans for house purchase), as noted earlier (Conseil Économique et Social 1989, 44).

IV. CHIRAC: IMPLEMENTING THE VISION OF *"LIBERALISME"*

The government of Jacques Chirac came to power in March 1986 with the intention of reforming French society, bringing an ideological vision similar to that of Margaret Thatcher and Ronald Reagan, a vision in which the private sector is generally seen as being more effective than the state in achieving the good society. Economic resurgence was to be provided by the newly unleashed forces of individual activity and energy working through the market. The new government portrayed the future it intended for France, treating television viewers to one commercial featuring formula cars giving their all on the race track (of the market?) and another with a powerful stallion regaining the wilderness to roam (in liberty?).

For the government of Jacques Chirac, housing policy was one of the major items on the agenda. The philosophy of "deregulation" and the use of markets were key themes for the major piece of housing legislation introduced at the end of 1986 by the minister of housing, Pierre Méhaignerie (Law No. 86-1290 of 23 December 1986). While the overt content of the Méhaignerie Law deals with decontrol of rents, the government assumed that this deregulation would stimulate investment in housing. This increased investment would lead to growth in the supply of housing, which in turn would act to keep rents moderate. Hence this law freeing rents from regulation carried the title of "Investment in Rental Housing" (investissement locatif).

The most important section of the legislation deals with the issue of liberating controls on rents (Title 1). The aim of the legislation was to decontrol rents totally, by phases, calling for complete "freedom of rents" (liberté de loyers) in agglomerations of more than a million in 1995, in less populated areas in 1991. Vacant rental housing qualified for immediate decontrol. While landlords could charge whatever rent they wished on housing that had been vacant, it is important to note that the law still limited the ability of landlords to dispossess sitting tenants, except in cases where the owners were selling the property (in which case the tenant had the right to match any offer) or where the owners could show that they needed the housing for themselves.

The arrangements for the transition period from the then current arrangements to complete decontrol of rents for sitting tenants are complex. For most lease renewals, the law stipulates that landlords can lawfully ask for rent increases that are consistent with the rents for comparable housing in the neighborhood, as reported in the last three years. Any increases are to be imposed by thirds—one-third each year of the three-year lease mandated by law during the period of transition. If the landlord and tenant cannot agree on a rent, the dispute is to be taken to a departmental committee of conciliation (une commission de conciliation)—also set up by the new Méhaignerie Law (Article 24). In these rent disputes, the commission of conciliation (including equal numbers of representatives of landlord organizations and tenant organizations) had the authority to decide what the rent will be. Similar transition arrangements (including an appeals process) will be applied to housing covered by the 1948 housing law—with the exception that the aged, handicapped, and poor can maintain their rent levels and their tenancy (Le Monde, 15 January 1987, 22).

The immediate reaction to the new law was not particularly favorable. Le Monde reported that tenants and their associations were very worried about the likelihood of great rent increases, particularly in the Paris region, and felt that the new law conferred excessive power on landlords. Landlord associations expressed discontent with what they perceived as an overly lengthy period of transition to the new arrangements (*Le Monde*, 15 January 1987, 1,2). Later sections of this chapter will examine the government's response to problems with their policy and the negative reactions to the new law.

The Méhaignerie Law has another section that is of particular interest here: Title 2 of the law sets out conditions under which units of HLMs may be sold to tenants. This is an interesting parallel to the policy of Margaret Thatcher's government to encourage the sale of council (public) housing to tenants. But there is a critical difference between the two. The British legislation requires local governments to sell to tenants who wish to buy their unit of council housing. Local governments may not refuse to sell. In contrast, the French legislation does not require the HLM organizations to sell to interested tenants; furthermore, there is no special funding or financial provision for such sales, so that HLM associations, constrained by law not to run deficits, are likely to consider such sales only when the return on such sales outweighs the benefits of retaining ownership.

The other major element of the Chirac Government's housing policy is contained in the 1987 budget. The minister of housing, Pierre Méhaignerie, started his housing budget speech with a refrain that is quite familiar to those who have looked at social budgets in Reagan's America or Thatcher's Britain (Méhaignerie 1987, 2):

As you know, the new government is engaged in a policy of economic stabilization and stimulation of private initiative, which assumes fewer taxes, smaller budget deficits, and thus less public spending.

The budget proposals put heavy emphasis on increasing incentives to the private sector to increase housing supply; three different tax breaks were introduced for the construction of housing for owner-occupiers and renters. The estimated annual cost of these tax incentives was between 2 and 2.5 billion francs ($330 to $420 million); the government argued that these measures would increase the number of new housing units each year for owner occupation by twenty thousand and the number of rental units by fifteen thousand above the number that would otherwise be constructed (Méhaignerie 1986, 3–4).

In 1987, further to encourage private sector activity, Méhaignerie proposed new tax benefits worth 700 million francs to encourage the use of undeveloped land for housing (*Le Monde*, 7 October 1987, 1). The government hoped that these tax provisions would increase private investment in housing, which in 1985 accounted for only 32,500 new units. The immediate effect of these measures to encourage private sector building was very positive: in his budget message of 1987 the minister of housing was able to announce that in the first half of the year there had been an increase of 7.5 percent in the number of building permits and an increase of 4 percent of dwellings whose construction was started in this period (Méhaignerie 1987, 4). For the whole of 1987, the number of new dwellings begun represented an increase of 4.9 percent over 1986, rising to a total of 310,000 units (*Le Monde*, 23 January 1988, 24). It is important to note that this increase was heavily biased against construction based on subsidized loans; in the first nine months of 1987, the number of housing construction permits for units built with unsubsidized loans increased by 23.3 percent, while permits for units with subsidized loans fell by 15 percent (*Le Monde*, 27 November 1989, 43). Thus, if the new tax breaks were responsible for the increase in building, they were heavily favoring people with higher incomes who did not qualify for or need subsidized loans.

With regard to aid for direct housing subsidies, the government expressed the dream of most budgeters in hard times: "Thus it is not the time to slow down the effort: it is necessary to have much more housing for less money" (Méhaignerie 1986, 4). The government went on to detail its plans, which would, in general, maintain the level of subsidized housing construction, but at a lower cost. In terms of rental housing, the government's budget authorized sixty-five thousand units under the PLA program (*prêts locatifs aidés:* subsidized loans for the construction of rental housing) and ten thousand units under the PLI program (*prêts locatifs intermédiaires*—subsidized loans for the construction of middle-income rental housing in high-density areas), which represents a slight increase over the last budget (Méhaignerie 1986, fiche no. 9). In the PAP program (*prêts aidés pour l'accession à la propriété*), which provides subsidized loans for home purchase, the government proposed a budget level of one hundred thousand units, and a decrease of ten thousand over the previous year (Méhaignerie 1986, fiche no. 9; UNFOHLM 1987, 21).

The "budgetary magic" is that the cost of maintaining these programs at 1986 levels dropped in the 1987 budget: the authorization requested for rental subsidies was 4,788 billion francs ($798 million) in 1986, dropping to 1,796 billion francs ($300 million) in 1987, while the bill for the home-loan subsidy program dropped from 6,833 billion francs ($1.14 billion) in 1986 to 1,044 billion francs ($174 million) (*Le Moniteur*, 26 September 1986, 43). The minister explained (Méhaignerie 1986, 5):

Some people are going to ask how the state's housing program will be maintained at the level of 1986 when the authorization inscribed in the law of finance is 5,673 billion francs, a reduction of 57 percent!

The explanation is simple—economies have been realized in the programs since 1986 thanks to the fall in interest rates and we have reutilized the money thus available, rather than using new budget authority.

Simply put, in 1986 the cost of providing interest rate subsidies dropped because interest rates dropped; some of the budget was thus available to be used in 1987. The government could provide the same number of new subsidies at a much lower cost. This sort of budgeting is nice, allowing the government to have its cake and eat it too—keeping program levels high while reducing costs. Under somewhat different circumstances the Reagan administration played similar games in its first years, deferring expenditures and then using the funds appropriated earlier to claim that new appropriations were unnecessary (Schwartz 1984, 158).

With respect to the loan program for the rehabilitation of HLM and other social rental housing, PALULOS (*primes à l'amélioration de logements à usage locatif et à occupation sociale*), the government argued in its 1987 budget that it was maintaining the previous level of rehabilitation at about 140,000 units (Méhaignerie 1986, fische no. 10). However, one analysis of these figures has suggested that the overall budget for this program was being reduced and that maintenance of the volume of units receiving these loans was being achieved by reducing the grant included in the loan from, on average, 30 percent to 20 percent of the loan (*Le Moniteur*, 26 September 1986, 44). At the same time, the budget tripled the allocation for loans to low-income homeowners to undertake rehabilitation (PAH—*prime à l'amélioration de l'habitat*) (Méhaignerie 1986, fiche no. 10). The budget for the PALULOS program was set at 1.29 billion francs ($215 million) while the PAH program was to receive 440 million france ($73 million). While the budget for rehabilitation of social rental housing (PALULOS) still was greater than that for aiding rehabilitation of housing owned by low-income families, the trend was clearly toward increasing the relative share of these funds allocated to homeowners.

The 1987 budget maintained the levels of many housing programs while cutting outlays, thanks to the "budget magic" of carry-over surpluses from previous years and favorable interest rates that kept the necessary level of subsidy for a new unit of housing stable. But with the surpluses gone, the 1988 budget made it clear that the Chirac government was more concerned to reduce budget deficits than to increase budget authorizations in order to maintain housing program levels. The statement of Pierre Méhaignerie, minister of housing, for the 1988 budget noted that the increase for the construction of social housing (PLA) and the social housing rehabilitation program (PALULOS) together would only be 2 percent more than the 1987 budget (Méhaignerie 1987, 5). One interesting step taken in the 1988 budget was to make the funds for the construction of social housing and the program for housing rehabilitation "fungible"; the departments have the option of deciding what proportions of the total of PLA and PALULOS programs would be spent on new social rented housing or rehabilitation of the existing social housing stock (Méhaignerie 1987, 5). This gives departments more flexibility in dealing with their varying needs for rehabilitation and new construction of social housing. This fungibility, however, made it very difficult to predict how many new units would be built and how many would be rehabilitated; Méhaignerie's statement shed no light on his budget's likely effect on the social rental housing stock.

With regard to the PAP program, which provided subsidized loans for lower-income people, the 1988 budget signaled a 10 percent reduction, from one hundred thousand to ninety thousand loans; the government argued that the decline was justified by a drop in demand and increasing use of other types of loans (Méhaignerie 1987, 5). While the volume of new PAP loans was dropping, early in 1988 the government announced measures to assist people having problems paying back their loans, including a dampening of the progressivity of the loans, a concomitant lengthening of the loan period, and some immediate aid for borrowers already stretched beyond their means (Le Monde, 27 January 1988, 38).

Perhaps the biggest money issue the government faced in the 1987 budget was the cost of the housing allowance, the housing allowance program (APL —l'aide personnalisée au logement). The government noted that the budgetary costs of this program had risen from 1981 to 1986 at an average annual rate of close to 30 percent per year, with the 1986 budgetary cost amounting to 9.3 billion francs ($1.55 billion) compared to the 1981 figure of 2.375 billion francs ($396 million) (Méhaignerie 1986, 10–11). The minister's budget address called for an increase in the effectiveness of the program and restraint of its cost increases (Méhaignerie 1986, 10–11). In fact, the 1987 budget only increased the funding for the housing allowance program (APL) by 16 percent, to 10.3 billion francs, by changing the indices used to calculate the level of benefits (Méhaignerie 1986, 10–11).

Overall, the 1987 housing budget showed an increase of 1.8 percent over the 1986 budget (Méhaignerie 1986, 5), but given the 16 percent rise in the housing allowance program (APL), it is clear that major cuts had been made in funding other programs. Even the housing allowance program, because of changes in the index for determining benefits, provided reduced benefit levels for many recipients.

In the 1988 housing budget, there was also a strong concern with the housing allowance program. The budget showed an increase of 15.6 percent for the 1988 housing allowance program and for a new program, the *allocation logement* (discussed below). Pierre Méhaignerie's statement on the budget noted that it was important to set social priorities, but that at the same time savings had to be realized (Méhaignerie 1987, 6–7). The 15.6 percent increase reflected savings; without the adoption of a new scale for the housing allowance program that reduced benefits, the proposed budget would have been 1 billion francs, or about 5 percent higher (*Le Monde*, 19 September 1987).

Earlier in the year, the Chirac Government had introduced its scheme to replace the housing allowance program with a new program designated simply "Housing Allowance" (*allocation logement*, or AL). In principle the AL was to eliminate a major flaw in the housing allowance program, the restriction of benefits to people living in specified types of housing, be it new social rental housing (PLA), new housing purchased with a subsidized loan (PAP and *prêts conventionnés*), or social housing rehabilitated with subsidy (PALULOS) (Conseil Économique et Social 1989, 42). This, of course, left out poor people who live in other sorts of housing, such as private rental housing. The new Housing Allowance was to overcome this exclusion by being based only on family income, with no reference to housing type. To be gradually extended over four years to all those eligible, such a benefit would constitute *le bouclage*, or the closing of the circle of aid to include everyone in need (*Le Monde*, 19 September 1989; Méhaignerie 1987, 6–7). While the principle of the Housing Allowance appealed to many on the Right and the Left, there was criticism of its aid level. To critics, the new policy was more an attempt to save money, through lower rates of support, than a genuine attempt to aid all those in need. One member of the government's majority in the National Assembly, Jean Tiberi, identified by

Le Monde as the "grand patron" of housing in Paris, derisively termed the new program "the little APL," claiming that it provided too little aid to recipients and would slow the improvement of housing (*Le Monde*, 6 November 1989, 7).

A set of bureaucrats, interest-group representatives, and researchers interviewed in France during the spring of 1987 agreed that the government was likely to try to address the problem of funding home ownership in the housing allowance program (APL). At this point, the housing allowance could be obtained not only for renting but also for buying housing. In fact, in 1987, housing allowance beneficiaries included more families buying homes than renting; approximately 940,000 families buying housing receive housing allowances, compared to 860,000 families who rent their housing (Direction de la Construction 1988, 26). Some of those interviewed perceived that the government would try to prevent very poor people from receiving subsidies for home ownership, feeling that it was more appropriate (and cheaper) to provide subsidies for them to rent than to buy.

The Morning After: Making Policy Stick

The adoption of the 1987 budget and the Méhaignerie Law marked only the beginning of new housing policy controversies for the Chirac Government. Some of the problems they faced in the first half of 1987 were the direct results of the new measures; others had been developing for some time. This section of this chapter examines three of those problems and the political response of the government. In examining the initial policy responses to those problems, it will become evident that the government did not move consistently toward a liberal ideal but rather sought to gain acceptance of its decisions by minimizing their consequences. In contrast to the actions of the Reagan and Thatcher Governments in their first days, the evidence is that the Chirac Government was unwilling to forge ahead regardless of the political consequences.

The unwillingness of the Chirac Government to glorify the "pain" necessary to get back on a truly "liberal" track is not a complete surprise. Margaret Thatcher, as prime minister, and Ronald Reagan, as president, were both at the top of their respective political systems; Jacques Chirac, as prime minister, was not. Chirac wanted to become president of the French Republic. But during most of the first half of 1987, with the presidential election only one year away, the polls consistently had him running well behind other potential candidates, including President François Mitterrand and Michel Rocard on the Left, as well as behind Raymond Barre, former prime minister and a member of Chirac's parliamentary majority. With the economy in doldrums and with rising unemployment, Chirac clearly did not want to inflict too much pain in the name of "liberalism."

One of the first housing controversies that the Chirac Government faced in the new year centered on the new rents being asked as the result of the implementation of the Méhaignerie Law. Reports of landlords demanding rent increases of from 40 percent to 150 percent (to be spread over three years) caused, as Le Monde (6 February 1987, 1) reported, great disquiet among renters. The response of the housing minister, Pierre Méhaignerie, was rather curious for a self-professed believer in the market: he publicly called on landlords to limit rent increases to no more than 5 percent per year and suggested to tenants that they should refuse to sign any lease that seemed unreasonable and then take their landlord to a departmental committee of conciliation to gain juridical resolution of the issue (Le Monde, 12 February 1987, 24). This response hardly calmed those who feared that rents would rise radically after the transition period ended in 1995 (1991 outside of the Paris, Lyon, and Marseille regions).

The controversy over the new policy on rent control flared up again in early summer. A tenants' organization, the Confédération générale du logement (CGL), released a survey of 150 rent demands made by landlords in the Paris region for the renewal of leases. The survey found that, on average, the demands represented increases of 68 percent (Le Monde 23 June 1987, 43). The prime minister, during a television interview, attacked the report, claiming it constituted "misinformation" and attacking the press for their coverage of the report (Le Monde, 25 June 1987). His response clearly indicated the sensitivity of the government to the issue, as well as an unwillingness to consider that the result of freeing rents might be unpopular rent increases.

In fact, increases in the initial days of the Méhaignerie Law appear to have averaged far less than 68 percent. Indeed, the problem of rapidly increasing rents seemed, in general, to be a problem mainly in the largest cities, especially Paris. The estimates for Paris suggested that renters were paying on average 7 percent higher rents for renewed leases, which, when added to the increases in the cost-of-construction index, meant that actual increases were on the order of 10 percent, while the rents on renovated dwellings were considerably higher (Le Monde, 29 January 1988, 27). The larger problem in Paris was reflected in the greater numbers of renters and landlords seeking arbitration from the "commissions de conciliation"; in many areas outside Paris fewer than 1 percent of leases were being taken to the commissions, while in Paris it was 4 percent (Le Monde, 16 September 1987, 42). Adding to the problem was the complexity of the system; one French news magazine argued that no one understood the situation and that government ads on the subject were not ameliorating the problem (L'Evénement du jeudi, 8–14 October 1987, 18). In any event, these developments were hardly likely to placate many tenants, especially in the Paris region.

Another major housing policy issue was the financial situation of the HLM associations. For many of these HLM associations, the rents they receive have been inadequate for them to pay off their loans while maintaining and renovating their housing units. One key to their financial situation is the rents that they are allowed to charge; government decisions had held rents at levels that were inadequate for HLMs to remain solvent. Under the Quilliot Law, from 1982 to 1985, the HLM associations had negotiated rent rises with representatives of tenants within the national commission on rents. The new Méhaignerie Law authorized the HLM associations to raise rents twice a year (in January and July), each time by up to 10 percent, subject to the approval of the prefect. However, well before the July 1987 rent increases, Méhaignerie sent a circular to the prefects, calling on them to approve July rent increases by the HLMs only in exceptional circumstances. His reasoning was that rent increases by the HLMs would pose a real danger to the government's war against inflation (Le Monde, 22 May 1987, 30).

The HLM associations responded to the prospect of no rent increases with real dismay, fearing that many associations, already in real financial difficulty, would see their position worsen. In this context, it is important to understand the very real political power of the HLM associations. In addition to their national peak association, UNFOHLM (Union nationale des fédérations d'organismes d'HLM), they also have close ties to the political parties of both the Left and the Right, for traditionally many of their tenants were not the poorest of the poor, but civil servants (even though this has changed somewhat). The political power of the HLM associations, while normally manifested in government willingness to negotiate with them before promulgating policy, has also been manifest from time to time in the ability of the HLM associations to beat down government policy; Duclaud-Williams (1978, 133–35) has documented cases in the 1950s and 1960s in which the HLMs were able to quash or simply ignore announced government policy, and

Pearsall (1984, 41) has found a similar case in the 1980s in which the Mitterrand government had to withdraw policies that would have altered the way HLM associations managed their housing stock.

But the desire of the HLMs to raise rents raised other problems for the government. If HLM rents were to increase, this was likely to exacerbate the unhappiness of HLM tenants with the government, since many tenants were already facing the likelihood of losing some portion of their benefits under the new criteria for housing allowances (the APL program). Hence the government could not easily bow to HLM association pressure on rents without incurring the wrath of HLM tenants. The government's response to this dilemma was to propose 300 million francs in special aid to help HLMs pay off debts from building in the period 1978–1984, when interest rates were very high. This program was explicitly justified as an aid to help HLM associations that would be adversely affected by the freeze in rents in July (*Le Monde*, 27 May 1987, 36). By the end of June 1987, the HLMs were still fighting with the government to allow them some kind of "moderate" rent increase. In this instance the government clearly wanted to avoid a confrontation with either the HLM associations or their tenants. Even in a period of tight resources, the government was willing to use additional resources (the special subsidies to help the HLMs pay off debt) to avoid the conflict, nor was the conflict used as an opportunity to prove the "liberal" credentials of the government by bashing the HLM associations or tenants.

The budget for 1988 did not give the HLM organizations relief. The new provisions allowing for the fungibility of subsidized loans potentially gave the organizations more flexibility in their decisions over whether to build new units or renovate old ones. However, the declining levels of aid for housing allowance (APL) recipients, and the relatively low levels of aid in the new AL program, were seen as putting more pressure on HLM organizations to sell some of their housing stock to finance rehabilitation and new construction, since tenants would not be able to afford the rent levels necessary to finance such work (*Le Monde*, 19 September 1987). This pressure on the HLM organizations was intensified when the minister of housing sent a circular to prefects asking them to reject all HLM rent increases that averaged more than 1 percent (*Le Monde*, 6 November 1987, 32). His reasoning was that the HLMs had already been granted new rent increases to cover certain operating expenses, could freely fix the rents of vacant apartments, and had seen their debt reduced by 50 million francs (*Le Monde*, 6 November 1987, 32). These events surrounding the 1988 budget parallel the first year of the

Chirac Government, in which housing policy was characterized by a championing of free rents, an attempt to avoid antagonizing tenants in the HLM sector, and an effort to keep the HLM organizations at least minimally solvent.

The government faced another housing policy problem due to the success of the privatization of state-owned enterprises. The Chirac Government had come to office committed to the sale of state-owned enterprises and to encouraging ordinary citizens to become stockholders in these enterprises. In Chirac's first year in office, many firms were privatized. The public was offered shares at very advantageous prices in enterprises, including a bank (Paribas), a national television channel (TF1), and a glass and building materials firm (Saint-Gobain). The public responded enthusiastically to these offerings. But at the same time, it became evident that some of this investment in now-private industry was at the expense of deposits in A Accounts (Livret A). In other words, people were putting money into stocks and abandoning the traditional "investment" in the tax-free accounts that provided the low-interest funds with which the Caisse des dépôts et consignations (CDC) financed housing loans. It was estimated that the funds available to the CDC dropped from 58 billion francs at the end of 1985 to 43.7 billion francs at the end of 1986, a fall of almost 25 percent (*Le Monde*, 11 June 1987, 37).

While this drop in the A Account deposits (Livret A) could have been used to justify shrinking the subsidized housing program (including the subsidized loans for home ownership), the government announced its intentions to stop the erosion of the A Accounts system. One step taken was to increase the ceiling on the size of such accounts, providing depositors with the potential to shelter more savings from tax in the A Accounts. The other measure was to provide an incentive to the savings banks to push more aggressively the A Accounts by providing a bonus to those banks whose A Accounts totaled more in 1987 than in 1986.

As it turned out, the A Accounts were saved by the October 1987 stock-market crash. While the crash of the Paris Bourse, following on the heels of the New York stockmarket plunge, may have dimmed the faith of small investors in "liberalism," certainly it sent many of them scurrying back to A Accounts in search of a safe investment. In fact, in October and November of 1987, the amount of money on deposit in A Accounts increased more than in the first eleven months of the year combined (*Le Monde*, 15 December 1987, 42), meaning that there was a net withdrawal in the first nine months, with the balance shifting heavily toward deposits in October and November. By the end of 1987, the state of the A Account was again satisfactory (*Le Monde*, 23 January 1988, 26).

The period between the appearance of the problem with the A Account and the stockmarket crash does demonstrate that the government was not interested in allowing this special form of finance to erode. As in the other cases discussed above, the government wished to implement *"libéralisme"* but was hesitant to disrupt the basic institutional forces in housing in order to gain rapid radical change.

There still remain two other potential threats to A Accounts presented by the opening of financial borders in the European Economic Community (EEC). One fear is that financial integration will lead to French savings going elsewhere in the EEC in search of a better return (*Le Monde*, 24 February 1989, 36). This "emigration" of capital would deprive the A Accounts of deposits, as did the Paris Bourse before its crash. A second fear about A Accounts concerns changes in the structure of taxation. At present, the A Accounts are attractive to many depositers despite low interest rates, because they are free of the high rates of tax on investment. As France lowers its tax rates to harmonize with other EEC nations, it is feared that A Accounts will become less attractive (*Le Monde*, June 22, 1989; Conseil Économique et Social 1989, 46).

Two additional housing policy initiatives undertaken by the Chirac Government bear mention. The first was a reorganization of the management of the 1 percent funds, which in 1987 were actually collecting a levy of 0.77 percent of the salaries paid by large employers in order to provide funds for loans for home purchase and for the construction of rental housing. The government set up a new central agency, with broad representation from the unions, members of the smaller agencies that collected and administered the funds, and employers. Part of the goal was to insure that all the funds were actually used for housing (as opposed to investments whose connection to housing was dubious) and to direct more of the funds toward social housing and housing for immigrant workers (*Le Monde*, 22 September 1987, 45; 11 November 1987, 36). Sweetening the reform for the employers was the reduction of the levy by another 0.05 percent to 0.72 percent in 1988. Here the government seemed to be hoping again to have its cake and eat it too: to gain more efficient use of the funds for groups in need, while using the increase in efficiency to reduce the level of the tax. This initiative is one of the few that seemed aimed at making new resources available for the construction of housing for groups in need. The aim of the second initiative was to make more land available for building. To this end the government offered new tax breaks and announced the sale of some government property in Paris (*Le Monde*, 7 October 1987, 1; 20 October 1987, 20).

V. MITTERRAND II—BACKING INTO A HOUSING POLICY?

On 8 May 1988, François Mitterrand was reelected president of France. This election marked the end of the government of Jacques Chirac, replaced by a Socialist government directed by Prime Minister Michel Rocard. The new government was confirmed in office by legislative elections in June 1988. At the outset, this new Socialist government seemed to avoid the housing issue and showed little interest in immediate repeal of initiatives of the Chirac government. In late May, after the presidential election, economic figures were published showing rising inflation in April, attributed in part to rent increases. Other figures appeared showing a one-year rise of 16 percent in the cost of purchasing an apartment in Paris (*Le Monde*, 20 May 1988, 37; 29–30 May 1988, 15). Despite calls for abolishing the Méhaignerie Law and controlling rents, the new minister of housing, Maurice Faure, said that he did not think that it was a good idea constantly to change housing laws, although he did think that something would have to be done to prevent excessive rent increases (*Le Monde*, 24 May 1988, 17).

Over the summer of 1988, there was debate within the Socialist party (PS) group in the National Assembly over whether to seek a complete repeal of the Méhaignerie Law or to support revisions of the law. The government appeared caught in a bind. It wanted to prevent excessive rent hikes but was not inclined to take on the opposition and the landlords, who were already unhappy about the slow timetable for implementing the Méhaignerie Law (*Le Monde*, 12 November 1988). Apparently the specter of the Quilliot Law still haunted a government eager not to be accused of making the same mistake twice.

The introduction of the budget in September was not the occasion for any grand statements about changing the Méhaignerie Law or introducing new housing policy. In his budget statement, Maurice Faure, the minister responsible for housing, went to great pains to argue that his new budget represented a smaller annual increase than the last budget, yet provided a genuine increase in funds for housing (Faure 1988, 2, 6). His statement, rather more chatty and witty than is normal in such documents, also went to great lengths to indicate where the magic of budget balances left over from the previous year would be used to maintain or increase program levels without raising costs (without implying that such "magic" was anything more than temporary good fortune). The statement also argues that revisions in the form of budgeting adopted by the Chirac Government were leading to the appearance of rising expenditures, while the actual funds for new activity were in fact decreasing, as in the case of the program of subsidized loans for lower-income people (PAP) in 1989. His basic argument was that the 1989 budget was a transition budget, because many of the provisions for housing aid were being reviewed with an eye to large-scale change. He noted that Mitterrand had given him the task of elaborating a great "social housing project" that was to be oriented not only to construction but to the whole issue of urbanism and the revitalization of central cities and decaying suburbs (Faure 1988, 8–9).

The 1989 housing budget included further steps to ameliorate the situation of those people still having difficulty repaying subsidized loans (PAP) whose payback rate normally increased by 4 percent per year. The government had decided that there would be no increase in 1989 and that from 1990, the rate of payback would be no more than 2.65 percent per year (the expected inflation rate). The alteration would cost the government 600 million francs (Faure 1988, 9). He also announced that the actual contribution for the 1 percent funds was fixed at 0.72 percent, with 0.62 percent going to the 1 percent fund organizations, the other 0.10 percent going to fund part of the housing allowance program (APL) that is normally supported by the budget. That use of 1 percent money for the APL meant that the budget showed a 1 billion franc decline in the cost to the budget for the housing allowance program; Faure pointed out that with the 1 percent money and other funds being transferred to the housing allowance program, the overall cost of the housing allowance program had gone up by 2 billion francs (Faure 1988, 10–13). The problem of the housing allowance program's increasing costs had yet to find an answer.

In November 1988, the Socialist party group in the Assembly presented the government with a set of proposals for dealing with the housing problem. While these proposals stopped short of abolishing the Méhaignerie Law, they certainly departed from its spirit. Among their proposals was the call to make the transition features of the Méhaignerie Law permanent—that is to say, most rents would not be free but would be set by negotiation between landlord and tenant and subject to arbitration by conciliation committees, with rent increases being based on comparable rents in the area. In partial response, a law dealing with rents was adopted; the law of 13 January 1989 called for spreading out rent increases exceeding 10 percent over six years and required that all proposals from landlords to increase rents had to include proof that there were comparable rents in the neighborhood.

Later in the spring of 1989, the Socialist party group in the National Assembly was put under pressure by Faure to abandon its direct opposition to the Méhaignerie Law. However, at the same time, reports of rapidly rising rents in Paris led the party group to propose a law dealing with that problem (*Le Monde*, 31 March 1989, 13). In April, the new minister of housing, Louis Besson, announced that measures were being prepared to deal with the situation (*Le Monde*, 7 April 1989, 25).

Ultimately, the Socialist group in the National Assembly put forward a bill on rent control, with the government frantically trying to convince the opposition not to vote against the bill and to avoid creating the wrong "psychological" effect on landlords and the housing market; the government did not want to be seen as adopting another Quilliot Law (*Le Monde*, 20 June 1989, 43). Perhaps the most controversial part of the bill was a provision allowing the government to issue a decree prohibiting excessive rent increases. In the hope of gaining opposition support, the government succeeded in amending the legislation to limit any single decree to a specific geographic area. In addition, the minister of housing promised that if the opposition voted for the legislation, he would never make use of the power of decree (*Le Monde*, 20 June 1989, 43). They didn't, so he did.

On 29 June 1989, the new law governing the relations between landlords and tenants was adopted. The major provisions of the law made the transitional arrangement of the Méhaignerie Law permanent; subject to exceptions, rent increases are not under the control of the landlord. To gain a rent increase, the landlord must show proof of comparable rents in the area. If the tenant and landlord cannot come to agreement, the rent will be set by a commission of conciliation. Landlords are free from this system when they are renting a new dwelling, a dwelling that has just been brought up to certain standards, a dwelling being rented for the first time, or a dwelling on which work with a cost of more than one year's rent has been completed within the last six months. The law allows the government to issue a decree to limit rent increases in a particular area where the market is considered "abnormal." Such decrees have effect for one year. Many other provisions of the Méhaignerie Law were left unchanged, including those governing forms of contract, notice to quit, and the use of the cost-of-construction index to set annual rent increases during the term of a lease (*Le Monde,* 1 July 1989, 1, 24).

On 29 August 1989, the government used its new power of decree in the Paris region, limiting rent increases to the level of increases in the cost of construction. The decree applies mainly to renewals of leases and to rentals of unrenovated dwellings. The decree has many exceptions, including one that allows landlords whose rents are undervalued to seek higher rents (*Le Monde,* 30 August 1989, 1).

With preparations underway for the 1990 budget, it was already clear in June that housing was becoming a key government issue. President Mitterrand, in an address to the annual congress of HLM organizations, said that housing was one of the gravest inequalities dividing the French people and that, after education, it should be a priority of government. He added that he would watch to assure that the evolution of the budget reflected that priority (*Le Monde,* 6 June 1989, 28). Then, in late July, the Council of Ministers announced that social housing construction would be increased and that more land in city centers would be made available by releasing government land for building (*Le Monde,* 28 July 1989, 8). In early August, the government announced it had put housing on the list of its priorities (*Le Monde,* 3 August 1989, 1, 16).

In a further round of announcements in August 1989, prefiguring the 1990 budget, the government committed itself to maintaining the purchasing power of the housing allowance (APL), the first time since 1982 that the housing allowance was not going to be eroded by inflation (*Le Monde,* 30 August 1989, 37). It was also announced that housing aid would increase by 8 percent over 1989, with personalized aid being extended to another group of people previously excluded from the housing allowance. The government did note that after this expansion of the coverage of the housing allowance, there would still be about four hundred thousand people, mainly single people from twenty-five to sixty-five years of age and couples without children living in private rental housing, who needed to be included before *le bouclage* was complete, before everyone in need qualified for assistance (*Le Monde,* 30 August 1989, 37). The formal announcement of the budget for housing added to previous policy announcements that the rehabilitation of rental housing would be accelerated to two hundred thousand units a year (requiring a 25 percent increase in funding), that the number of new social rental housing units started would increase by ten thousand to sixty-five thousand units, and that a new PAP subsidized loan for housing purchase (*PAP rénovés*) for home buying would cover a larger portion of the total loan, thus lightening the cost for the recipients by lessening the need for higher-priced complementary loans (*Le Monde*, 2 September 1989, 21).

VI. CONCLUSION

Continuities and Change in French Housing Policy

The three governments examined here, the two Socialist governments under the presidency of François Mitterrand (1981–1986 and 1988–present) and the liberal government of Prime Minister Jacques Chirac (1986–1988), all seem to represent breaks with the past. The Socialist governments have attempted to change the outlook and policies of years of conservative rule; the Chirac Government was committed not only to undoing Socialist measures but also to bringing into French politics a new spirit of market liberalism that was alien to many of the reflexes of the French Right. Yet the examination of its housing policies reveals many continuities between these governments, as well as with their predecessors. The continuities reflect how entrenched these policies are both in French policy and politics. Their complexity makes it difficult to consider far-reaching changes, and the political support for many of these policies makes almost any change seem far-reaching, at least in terms of the potential political pain it would engender. This section of this chapter will look not only at those continuities but also at the differences between the policies of these governments. The differences are important; over time they can drastically change the shape of housing policy and the interests that surround it.

One of the simplest bases for policy comparison is the extent of change effectuated by these different governments. In terms of the provision of housing, the first period of Socialist governance, "Mitterrand I," is not marked by strong increases in government provision of direct aid to housing, which is partly attributable to problems in the French economy and to limited budgets. The government not only felt that it lacked the money to do more; it was also facing rapidly increasing budgets for the existing housing allowance program (APL), as well as the increasing problem of the many home buyers who could no longer afford the payments on their subsidized mortgages. These problems dominated the policy making of housing provision under Mitterrand I (rent control will be discussed below). In fact, the decoupling of the housing allowances (APL) from the cost of living index, which resulted in deterioration of the real value of those allowances, was initiated in this period as one of the attempts to deal with this crisis.

The Chirac Government was overtly committed to market strategies, but apart from its hope that over the long term the liberation of rents from rent controls would create a boom in the creation of new rental housing, its overall approach to providing housing market subsidies does not represent a great break with previous policies. It is true that it did provide more encouragement for private sector building, which under existing economic conditions led to great increases in private house building and declines in building for social rental housing. Over an extended period, that differential could have weakened the social rental housing sector (HLMs) vis à vis other sectors of the housing market, but the Chirac Government was not in power long enough, nor did it take decisive enough action, to bring about an immediate decline in the role or political power of HLM organizations.

The second period of Socialist government under the presidency of François Mitterrand, "Mitterrand II," started with a real hesitancy to take on new burdens, as reflected in the government's first budget. However, by the second budget, housing had become a priority, worthy of more spending, as evidenced not only in increases in aid for many programs but also in the commitment to maintain the purchasing power of benefits under the housing allowance program (APL). What accounts for the change? One report was that the president of the Republic had decided that the economic crisis was over and that it was time to consider dividing some of the new wealth. The prime minister did not wish to be seen as being outflanked on the Left by the president, so more money was allocated to social housing, among other programs (Le Monde, 29 August 1989, 1). Increased expenditures for social housing over time could strengthen the HLM organizations and allied political forces in this sector. However, beyond that, the second budget does not propose programs that will fundamentally restructure the institutions of French housing policy. In that sense, if the period of prosperity is short lived, and social housing budgets are cut back, French housing policy and the politics around it may continue to look very much the same as today.

An analysis simply of "how much" does not help us understand the qualitative changes that these different regimes may have been trying to accomplish. In retrospect, the first Mitterrand Government's major attempt to transform French housing policy was through the Quilliot Law, which represented an attempt to bring the government into the arena of housing through the use of corporatist bargaining to set rent levels. However, the belief that this would stifle the financial return on rental property, plus generally unfavorable market conditions for investment in rental property (high interest rates), led to increased shortages of rental housing. The response to this problem in Mitterrand I and II was not to change the operation of the market or to effect a fundamental change in the form of housing aid, but in Mitterrand I to backpedal on the implementation of the law and in Mitterrand II to try to avoid any impression that the Quilliot Law was being revived. Although the landlords and their allies who opposed the Quilliot Law are hardly allies of the Socialists, the policies of Mitterrand II (to date) do not represent a challenge to those forces, but an acceptance of their role in the market.

The Chirac Government followed Mitterrand I's Quilliot Law with its own rent decontrol law, based on the belief that housing problems could be solved by "going to the market." But the lengthy and very complex transition arrangements of the Méhaignerie Law speak to the desire, at least in the short run, to avoid a possible political backlash. The Chirac Government's willingness to stifle rent increases in the financially ailing HLM sector, in contradiction to its ideological bent, speaks to its vain hope to remain in political power. What is interesting also is its overt attempt, through its new program of personalized housing aid (*allocation logement*) to actually extend housing aid to a larger segment of lower-income inhabitants. As noted earlier, critics saw this new policy as not simply the extension of aid to more people, but as an attempt to implement a system of aid that would be less generous to each individual receiving aid and hence offer better control over costs than the ever more expensive housing allowance program (APL). But it also signaled that there was no assumption that the market could provide for everyone and that the government's aim was not the complete disengagement of the French state from housing policy.

Mitterrand II, from 1988 to the present, is a very interesting study in using existing structures that are overtly hostile to your goals to pursue your goals. In the attempt to avoid comparisons to the Quilliot Law, but to contain rent increases, the Rocard Government has chosen to make permanent the transition arrangements of the Méhaignerie Law. Politically, it is clear that the government is hoping that the French Right will hesitate to criticize its own creation. On its own, this action does not seem to preview a major revision of the institutions of French housing policy. It is clear that the government intends to spend more money on social housing and would like housing policy to be better integrated into the goal structure of urban policy. But it is unclear whether this is simply a "fair weather strategy," to be followed when the budget is growing and to be abandoned in the lean years, or whether it will result in institutional changes that can sustain the improvement of housing conditions in bad times. The government is very sensitive to the political power of those who would oppose new policy; new proposals may well attempt to "add" new features or programs to existing policies rather than challenge the basic structure of current arrangements.

French Housing Policy in Comparative Perspective

This final section of this chapter will compare the French case to the cases of the United States and Britain. In looking at policy in the 1980s in the United States and Britain, one is looking primarily at the Reagan and Thatcher administrations. Both Reagan and Thatcher strongly advocated widening the role of the market at the expense of that of the state, very much the overt position taken by Jacques Chirac, very much in opposition to that of François Mitterrand. Does that mean that Chirac's policy would have moved France in a direction similar to that of Britain and the United States, or that Mitterrand's policies represent moves in the other direction? Those questions will be examined in terms of the content of housing policy and the politics being constructed around housing. (Much of the analysis of the American and British data is drawn from my earlier comparisons of British and American housing policy; see Schwartz 1987a and 1987b.)

One trend in housing policy, evident in both Britain and the United States, has been a movement to provide housing by subsidizing the private sector rather than the public sector. In both countries, the trend began well before the advent of Reagan and Thatcher, but in both of these cases, the leaders have furthered that trend. In the United States, the trend began with the 1959 Housing Act, which provided subsidies to nonprofit groups to provide housing for the elderly and the handicapped; the 1968 Housing and Urban Development Act, which provided mortgage subsidies for low-income people to buy housing; and the 1974 Housing Act, which provided subsidies for the creation of housing in the private sector. The Reagan administration went one step further in its housing voucher plan, which provides recipients with set amounts of aid to supplement their own resources in finding housing in the private housing sector.

The British, having built a large amount of council housing since World

War II, began moving away from the public sector in the 1974 Housing Act, which provided aid to nongovernmental "voluntary housing associations" to provide subsidized housing to those in need. Under Margaret Thatcher the move to the private sector has been actively pursued at the direct expense of the public sector; local authorities are required to sell council housing to sitting tenants who wish to buy—approximately eight hundred thousand units out of a total of 7 million council housing units have been sold. Before the 1987 British national election, the Thatcher Government proposed that all council housing should be moved from the public sector into the hands of private management; if implemented, this would radically shift the public-private balance in British housing policy.

In the French case, it is harder to ascertain the public-private balance. In principle, private sector firms can apply for the same subsidies that HLM associations use to build low-income housing, but current economic conditions have made such investment largely unprofitable. On the other hand, the subsidized loans for home purchase by lower-income people benefit the private sector directly. The housing allowance programs (APL) for rental housing can be used in certain parts of the private sector market (this should increase further under current policy). The APL housing allowances may also be used for home purchase. In this sense, the policies of both the Chirac and the Mitterrand Governments do not represent much of a shift in policy, since the private sector already enjoys a large share of the subsidy programs.

Another trend in both Britain and the United States has been a movement toward subsidizing people rather than units of housing. Again, this trend predates Reagan and Thatcher, but continued with the Reagan housing voucher program and the Thatcher policy of "fair rents" (which assumes that council housing is rented at market rates and that eligible families will receive subsidies to pay those rents). This trend is clearly evident in France, as discussed in the earlier section of this chapter on the configuration of French housing policy in the shift from *aide à la pierre* to *aide à la personne*. However, there is a major difference between the American program and the French and British programs. In the American program, only a limited number of vouchers are available regardless of the number of eligible, while in the British and French programs, all those eligible are entitled to aid. Thus the American program creates differences among people on the basis of their place in line when the vouchers were handed out. In addition, the political costs of cutting programs would seem different: in Britain and

France, a cut in funding affects equally a large group of people with potential political clout. In the United States, since the number of people that would be affected by a program cut is much smaller and certainly does not represent all those in need of aid (even by the program's standards), recipients' objections to cuts might well be seen as complaints from an especially privileged group of the poor.

Another trend, particularly evident under Reagan and Thatcher, has been massive cuts in government expenditures for housing. But in neither country has there been a significant move to cut the tax breaks given to owner-occupiers. In both countries, the result has been that the tax breaks for home ownership cost their governments more than the "direct subsidies" for rental housing (Schwartz 1987a). What has developed in both the United States and Great Britain is a stark bifurcation between aids for the poor (usually for rental housing) and aids for home ownership; the former are funded with direct expenditures that are subject to cuts in every budget crisis, while the latter are funded by "off-budget" tax subsidies that are not part of the budget process and that keep growing in cost. As noted earlier, the shape of future housing budgets in France is unclear. Much of the aid for home ownership comes from the same programs that fund rental housing, such as subsidized loans from the Caisse des dépôts et consignations (CDC) or the housing allowance program (APL). While the Chirac and Mitterrand Governments have balanced the private and social housing sectors somewhat differently, the structure of the programs, relative to the funding process, do not automatically favor home ownership.

Despite all their other similarities, there is a great divergence between the Reagan and Thatcher Governments in terms of the institutional changes they have wrought in housing policy. The Reagan policies have pushed American housing policy toward dependence on the market; the voucher program assumes that recipients seek housing in the private rental market from ordinary profit-seeking landlords. In the British case, the shift away from the public sector has not been simply a shift to the private housing market, but to some extent has also been characterized by the use of specialized institutions, such as voluntary housing associations, to provide housing. Thus while the American case represents an attempt to deinstitutionalize housing policy, the British case represents the use of alternative housing institutions, supported by government subsidy, in addition to the use of the market. In political terms, the British case keeps more institutions involved in the politics around the policy, while American policy seems to be reducing the institutions that might play a political role in the making of policy (see Schwartz 1987b).

Certainly the actions of the French governments examined here have done little to alter the basic configuration of institutions and the politics around housing. As described earlier, the responses of the three French governments to various policy problems, certainly since the Quilliot Law, seem to have recognized the importance of existing institutions, interest groups, and policy arrangements. In addition, important special state-sponsored avenues of finance provide a rich network of institutions on which much of the French housing market depends. Any attempt by the government to eliminate these arrangements or to integrate them into the general finance market could well leave the government facing the opposition not only of renters and HLM associations but also of homeowners and businesses dependent on them.

The complexity of French housing policy could easily lead to the conclusion that the system must be an impediment to change. Certainly a complex set of institutions and political interests is involved in the creation and implementation of housing policy. However, it is also clear from the preceding analysis that different governments with different policy orientations have been able to pursue their goals within this complex general framework. The changes made have certainly altered the balance among different parts of the housing policy system as well as details of the administration of housing policy. At the same time, the general framework and the political forces involved have remained much the same. And certainly in comparison to British and American policy of the period, French policy makers have had a much richer set of options open to them (as well as accompanying political constraints).

The complexity of the French system might better be seen as providing a wealth of opportunities and possibilities for policy makers, as well a set of institutions through which policy goals could be implemented. For example, the ability of the French system to provide a protected channel of financial resources for housing is a great advantage for policy makers, providing a degree of certainty about available resources, at some remove from the pressures of general financial markets and, to a lesser extent, from budgetary exigencies. The ability of the government to obtain some of the 1 percent funds from employers to provide resources for more general housing needs as their own need to provide housing for their workers declines speaks to the ability of policy makers to alter the function of existing policy forms as conditions change. The ability of policy makers to adjust the relation between major financial institutions, as in the case of the CFF and CDC mentioned earlier, speaks to an ability to "fine-tune" the system to provide more flexibility in the allocation of resources among different programs (in this case the funds available for subsidized home loans for individuals and through the HLM associations).

Of course, the French housing policy system has distinct limits. Should the "europeanization" of finance as part of the 1992 reforms in the European Economic Community cause investors to desert A Accounts (Livret A), it is not clear that the rest of the system will be able to compensate. A radical restructuring may be extremely difficult, as none of the institutional components of the system, with their associated political interests, can be easily abandoned. Whether this complexity constitutes opportunity or constraint will be judged in terms of the ability of governments to pursue their policy preferences and the capability of the system to produce desirable outputs. In the decade of the 1980s, the ability of different French governments to pursue distinctly different goals within the same set of policy institutions speaks to the potential of complexity as an asset in policy making.

REFERENCES

Boubli, Bernard. 1985. *Le Logement*. Paris: Presses Universitaires de France.
Cancellieri, Anne, Jean Foscoso, Jean Lemoine, Maurice Mahaut, and Robert Paoli. 1986. *Maîtrise d'ouvrage du logement social en France*. Paris: Economica.
CDC (La Caisse des Dépôts et Consignations). 1987. *La Caisse des Dépôts et Consignations: Banque du Logement Social*. Paris: CDC.
Central Statistical Office, Government Statistical Service (United Kingdom). 1989. *Social Trends No. 19: 1989 Edition*. London: H.M.S.O.
Collins, Doreen. 1987. A More Equal Society? Social Policy under the Socialists. In *Mitterrand's France*, edited by Sonia Mazey and Michael Newman. London: Croom Helm. 81–102.
Conseil Économique et Social. 1989. *Le Bilan et perspective d'évolution du logement en France: Séances des 9 et 10 mai 1989*. Paris: Direction des Journaux Officiels.
Cornuel, Didier. 1989. Les Effets redistributifs des aides au logement. *Les Cahiers de l'Habitat* no. 8 (September 1989): 9–12.
Direction de la Construction, Ministère de l'Equipement, du Logement, de l'Aménagement du Territoire et des Transports. 1986. *Statistiques et études gén-*

érales: *Données économiques et financières sur le logement: n°132.* Paris: Documentation française.

―――. 1988. *Statistiques et études générales: Données économiaques et financières sur le logement: n°144.* Paris: Documentation française.

Duclaud-Williams, Roger H. 1978. *The Politics of Housing in Britain and France.* London: Heineman

Euro-Construct. 1986. *L'emploi et la réhabilitation du logement en Europe.* Luxembourg: Office des publications officielles des communautés européennes.

Faure, Maurice. 22 September 1988. *Allocution de Monsieur Maurice Faure à la presse du project du budget 1989.* Paris: Ministère de l'Equipement et du Logement.

France. 1986. *Loi n°86-1290 du 23 décembre 1986. Investissement locatif; accession à la propriété de logements sociaux; développement de l'offre foncière. N°1509-II.* Paris: Journal Officiel de la République Française.

Heugas-Darraspen, Henri. 1985. *Le Logement en France et son financement* (Notes et Etudes documentaires, n°4794). Paris: Documentation française.

Holmes, Peter. 1987. Broken Dreams: Economic Policy in Mitterrand's France. In *Mitterrand's France*, edited by Sonia Mazey and Michael Newman. London: Croom Helm. 33–55.

Mazey, Sonia. 1987. Introduction. In *Mitterrand's France*, edited by Sonia Mazey and Michael Newman. London: Croom Helm. 1–6.

Méhaignerie, Pierre. 25 September 1986. *Discours de M. Pierre Méhaignerie sur le budget.* Paris: Ministère de l'Equipement, du Logement, de l'Aménagement du Territoire et des Transports.

―――. 18 September 1987. *Discours de M. Pierre Méhaignerie sur le Budget.* Paris: Ministère de l'Equipement, du Logement, de l'Aménagement du Territoire et des Transports.

Pearsall, Jon. 1984. France. In *Housing in Europe*, edited by Martin Wynn. New York: St. Martin's. 9–54.

Rex, John, and Robert Moore. 1967. *Race, Community, and Conflict: A Study of Sparkbrook.* London: Oxford University Press.

Schwartz, Nathan H. 1984. Reagan's Housing Policies. In *The Attack on the Welfare State*, edited by Anthony Champagne and Edward Harpham. Prospect Heights IL: Waveland Press.

―――. 1987a. Housing Policy in Great Britain and the United States: Converging Trends, Divergent Futures. In *Contemporary Political Economy: Anglo-American Policy Comparisons*, edited by Jerold L. Waltman and Donley T. Studlar. Jackson MS: University Press of Mississippi.

―――. 1987b. The Relation of Politics to the Instruments of Housing Policy. In *Between State and Market: Housing in the Post-Industrial Era*, edited by L. J. Lundqvist and B. Turner. Stockholm: Almqvist & Wiksell.

Tuppen, John. 1988. *France under Recession, 1981–1986.* Albany NY: State University of New York Press.

UNFOHLM (Union Nationale des Fédérations d'Organismes d'HLM). 1987. *48e Congrès National HLM: aide-mémoire statistique.* Paris: UNFOHLM.

United States Department of Commerce. Bureau of the Census. 1982. *Statistical Abstract of the United States: 1982–83*. Washington: Government Printing Office.

Zysman, John. 1983. *Governments, Markets, and Growth*. Ithaca NY: Cornell University Press.

7

DEMOCRACY AND SOCIAL POLICIES:
THE EXAMPLE OF FRANCE

BRUNO JOBERT

To reconcile democracy and effective government constitutes one of the great challenges of our times. How can the law of the majority be prevented from leading to an indefinite expansion of the State for the purpose of establishing actual equality proportional to political equality? Both the theories and the practice of democracy have sketched out different solutions to this problem.

For the elitist democratic theorists (e.g., Sartori 1987), too much democracy and too much social mobilization risk killing democracy. This excessive participation can only lead to new demands that overload the State, which becomes bloated and blocks the dynamism of the society. Hence democracy is viable in the long term only when regulated by an external element: the elites to which the masses agree to defer. The depoliticization of the citizen and his relative apathy thus are held to be the necessary conditions for the existence of a democracy that is pluralistic and mildly interventionist.

In contrast, theories of social democracy (often presented under the misleading term *neocorporatism*) tend to show that democracy can be compatible with strong social mobilization if the latter is channeled by social organizations that are strong and capable of imposing discipline on their troops (e.g., Lehmbruch 1984). Some contemporary comparativists have attempted to classify the different states according to their approximation to one or the other of these types, on a scale running from corporatism to elitist pluralism. One logical hypothesis would be to establish a correlation between the

TABLE 7.1

Social Expenditures of OECD Countries, 1981
(in % of GDP)

		Lembruch Corporatism Scale
Belgium	37.6	average
Holland	36.1	high
Sweden	33.4	high
Denmark	33.3	average
Germany	31.5	average
France	29.5	off scale or low
Italy	29.1	low
Ireland	28.4	average
Austria	27.7	high
Norway	27.1	high
Finland	25.0	average
United Kingdom	23.7	low
Canada	21.5	low
United States	20.8	low
New Zealand	19.6	low
Australia	18.8	low
Japan	17.5	off scale
Switzerland	14.9	average
Greece	13.4	unrated

Sources: OECD 1985. p. 21; and Lehmbruch 1984.

position of states on this scale and the level of development of social policies. The more advanced the incorporation of the wage-earning class as a collective actor, the higher social expenditures should be. However, this hypothesis is not supported by the evidence. As shown in table 7.1, the level of social expenditure of countries like France and Italy is fully comparable to that of the social democratic states.

How can we explain this paradoxical situation of a political system that presents both numerous characteristics of the welfare state and a weak overall involvement of workers' organizations in the definition of social and economic strategies? This is what we would like to study here, focusing upon the experience of the Fifth Republic. Obviously this problem cannot be treated without a brief historical perspective, with which this chapter will begin.

I. THE WELFARE STATE AND BALANCED LIBERALISM

When the Fourth Republic attempted after 1945 to provide France with a complete system of social protection, her modernizing elites had to challenge certain of the fundamental elements of the conceptions of social order that had marked almost a half-century of French history (Kuisel 1981). This social order seemed to be founded on three pillars: the maintenance of stabilizing social categories, differential treatment of wage earners, and the public service.

The Third Republic long was haunted by the Commune, by fear of a brutal confrontation between the owning classes and the working classes. In order to avoid it, the Republic contributed heavily to organizing the survival of buffer social categories whose attachment to personal property seemed to guarantee prudence and wisdom. These efforts were not without results: the proportion of the working population that lived in rural areas declined very slowly, remaining at almost 40 percent in 1946. The French industrial network was less concentrated than that of Germany or of Britain, while French distribution systems remained archaic (Sellier 1984, 23).

This same concern with avoiding a massive confrontation between classes is seen again in the differential treatment of wage earners. Large-scale industrial organization, with all that it implies in bureaucracy and gigantism, seemed foreign to the French genius. The latter expressed itself better in the supposed humanity of the individual relationship between the owner of a small business and his worker, both well integrated in small cities that were themselves surrounded by countryside peacefully worked by small farm owners. The policy of social protection appears truly necessary only in situations where the network of loyalties and personal bonds have been torn: in large urban areas and in large firms. In fact, in the social domain, the active social policies of large firms (steel, mines, railroads) contrast sharply with the slowness and reticence of other sectors of French society. The contrast between sectors where labor plays a strategic role and those dependent on unskilled labor, and that between organized and unorganized sectors, define the social criteria of inclusion in or exclusion from social policies. These policies proceeded rather by accretion of partial social compromises, by sedimentation, than by general measures applicable to all workers (Hatzfeld 1971).

Built on the notion of equality of opportunity, the public service constituted the indispensable counterweight to this model of social order founded on differentiation and heterogeneity. Supported by the prevailing scientism of the beginning of the century, it was characterized by a preference for conferring management of public activities on competent professions believed to command the scientific knowledge and the methods appropriate to each of the great social problems (Pisier-Kouchner 1983).

Here we have outlined the basic elements of corporatism *à la française: protectionist corporatism* of buffer professions that expect the State to guarantee the conditions of their survival; *corporatism of workers* of the major industrial occupations, analyzed in a masterly fashion by D. Ségrestin (1984); *republican corporatism* of the major professions of the *public service*, of which teachers' unions form the most complete model.

Corporatism, which has been so maligned by recent essayists, thus appears to be a basic element of the republican state. Durkheim elaborated the theory of such a state at the beginning of the twentieth century:

A society composed of an infinite number of unorganized individuals, that a hypertrophied State is forced to oppress and contain, constitutes a veritable sociological monstrosity. . . . A nation can be maintained only if, between the State and the individual, there is intercalated a whole series of secondary groups near enough to the individuals to attract them strongly in their sphere of action and drag them, in this way, into the general torrent of social life. . . . [O]ccupational groups are suited to fill this role and that is their destiny (Durkheim 1964, 28).

Yet this model of corporatism has been only partially applied; the search for cohesion through differentiation and heterogeneity could only inhibit the formation of a global social compromise between large unions and employers' associations. The social movements of the Popular Front demonstrated the extreme weakness of employers' associations at the cross-sectoral level (Ehrmann 1957). The growth of the protective French state proceeded by sedimentation, by successive accretion of "partial social compromises" (Delorme and André 1983).

II. THE FOURTH REPUBLIC: THE DIFFICULT IMPLEMENTATION OF A NEW MODEL OF SOCIAL DEVELOPMENT

The conversion of French society to growth and modernization beginning with the Fourth Republic called into question some of the principles of the social order of the period that was ending; it implied a restructuring of the mediation network that supported the old order.

On the one hand, the policy of growth and modernization finally launched was not easily reconciled with the precarious preservation of buffer social categories. The opening of borders in 1958 and the modernization of the economy raised a new problem: that of managing the rapid decline or the restructuring of backward sectors.

On the other hand the differential treatment of wage earners, who were only partially institutionalized, turned out in two ways to lead to an impasse. First, the experience of the war and of the Resistance opened the way for new social and political demands: democratic citizenship, once reconquered, henceforth included a social dimension, embodied in the program for generalizing Social Security. Second, the opening of borders and the modernization that began with the first economic plans called for new social arrangements to accompany economic changes. The emerging economy was hardly compatible with the very partial institutional representation of wage earners and their leaders in the social and economic life of the country.

The period of the Fourth Republic was marked both by the resistance of the old mediation networks and by the beginning of changes that would bear their full fruit in the Fifth Republic. This dual and seemingly contradictory movement was fostered by the dissociation of state administration from the elected bodies of government, a trend that characterized the Fourth Republic (Birnbaum 1977).

On the one hand members of parliament appeared as the preferred target of interest groups with the largest memberships. The vulnerability of members of Parliament was reinforced by the divisions among them and by the weak structure of their parties. On the other hand, within the executive branch and in institutions relatively free from legislative pressure, another system of mediation developed, one that proved to be more directly focused on the implementation of policies of growth and social modernization.

The modernizing elite of high civil servants that took the controls of financial institutions such as the Directorate of the Treasury, the Social and Economic Development Fund, and the Planning Commission very quickly understood that it could be a true pressure group for growth only on two conditions: that this growth be accompanied by social modernization; and that there develop a new mediation network between this elite, based in the state administration, and society, providing the elite with a solid social rooting. The social preoccupations of the high clerks of the State (such as François Bloch-Lainé or Pierre Laroque) are witness to the first condition. The policy of social dialogue begun by the plans demonstrates the importance of the second. The constantly reaffirmed concern with naming *intuitu personnae* the members of the planning commissions associated with this tripartite dialogue demonstrates the desire of its conceivers to avoid being trapped in a dialogue with established organizations and to select in all sectors of society those individuals best suited to discussing and transmitting their message (Jobert 1981).

The ambiguous record of social policy under the Fourth Republic reflects the contradictory pressures of these two systems of decision making. The Fourth Republic established the foundations of a new social order. The creation of Social Security gave a new dimension to democratic citizenship. All opinion polls taken in the past thirty years attest to the importance of this event for French society. The acquisition of social rights, particularly coverage of social risks, is perceived by French citizens as an achievement whose importance can be compared only to the establishment of universal suffrage (Schnapper, Brody, and Kastoryano 1986). However, the implementation of these principles encountered grave difficulties.

Plans to expand coverage of Social Security became bogged down; hospital reform marked time; the question of social coverage of ambulatory medical care found no satisfactory solution; the spirit of renewal of the first years of the Fourth Republic was broken by the political imbroglios of the late republic.

III. THE FIFTH REPUBLIC: A POLITICAL AND SOCIAL NEW DEAL

The political, economic, and institutional new deal of the Fifth Republic demonstrably modified the rules regulating social competition. The social categories threatened by modernization saw their margin of maneuver reduced by a triple mechanism. The decline of Parliament deprived powerful pressure groups such as the General Confederation of Small and Medium Firms (CGPME) of a channel of privileged access to political decision making. The reinforcement of the executive was less favorable to groups with large memberships than to organizations whose leaders relate most easily to their partners in the high civil service. The existence of a strong nationalist and conservative party surrounding the president of the republic (De Gaulle) also limited their margin of maneuver. It was increasingly difficult to play one faction or one party against another. The more politics became bipolarized and the more declining social categories found themselves attached to one camp, the less effective the threat of defection became. Finally, the great turning point represented by the opening of borders acted as a powerful constraint imposing reason on these groups. Moreover, through struggling mightily to achieve a European agricultural policy favorable to French farmers, the government was able to win over the largest and noisiest fraction of these categories.

However, the narrowing of the political space open to these social categories does not imply their silent euthanasia. The closing of the political scene perhaps provoked the decline of the CGPME of M. Gingembre, but it also set off the explosions of anger of the Information and Defense Committee— National Union of Independent Workers (CID-UNATI) of Gérard Nicoud (Berger 1981).

The second element of this social new deal is found in the new support offered by the most diverse sectors of society for the "mystique of growth" advocated by a modernizing elite largely from the high civil service.

According to the rhetoric of the period, economic growth can avoid turning social struggle into a zero-sum game. What is important is that everyone contribute in a harmonious fashion to the production of as large a cake as possible. The social struggle should concern only how the surplus is to be divided. The unstated premise of this ideology is no doubt the acceptance of a certain level of inflation as a general anesthetic, making less visible and hence less painful the reallocation of resources and the new inequalities resulting from growth (Zysman 1983).

The most important intellectual debate seemed to pit the defenders of tradition within each group or social class against what came to be called the "living forces" *(forces vives)* of the new France. This is the period when the "young farmers" took control of the National Federation of Farmers (FNSEA), when the "young employers" (later the "young managers of firms") opposed their elders in the National Council of French Employers (CNPF), and when the new intellectual weight of the French Democratic Confederation of Labor (CFDT) was being affirmed within the world of wage earners and unions.

The major change concerned the attitude of employers, who were completely marginalized in the early postwar period. Their organizations initially were very reticent about the modernization plans issuing from the state administration. The National Council of French Employers (CNPF) was a weak and divided organization. But the demands of modernization induced the leaders of large modernizing firms to revive and consolidate the organization of employers to their advantage (Sellier 1984, 4).

The opening of borders foreseen by the Treaty of Rome (1957) induced a change in the attitude of employers, who took the initiative in engaging the unions in collective negotiations to restore unemployment insurance with equally shared financing. Employers partially abandoned their visceral anti-unionism in order to avoid the imposition by the State of a more elaborate program.

This impetus for modernization would not have gained such scope had it not been nourished by intense intellectual activity within the State. On the margins of parties and institutions there appeared a multitude of clubs and intellectual circles that intended to bring French public life into the modern era.

IV. A MODEL OF NEOCORPORATIST INSPIRATION

At the beginning of the Fifth Republic, the planning process, sanctified by General de Gaulle as a "burning obligation," became the point of convergence of these "living forces" that sought to extract France from the moroseness of a failed decolonization and to lay out new plans for the future of French society. In fact, in this period of triumphant Gaullism, the plan became the preferred instrument for affirming the supremacy of politics over the blind mechanisms of the economy. The Fourth Plan affirmed that "the opportunity must be seized for accomplishing a great, lasting work to assure that men will live better." The Plan conceived of this great work primarily in terms of an acceleration of industrial growth, but in the service of a new model of consumption. In contrast to a consumers' society of the American type, oriented toward futile consumption that creates its own unrest, the Fourth Plan presumed to offer another style of life, made richer and more communal through emphasis on public programs and facilities. It was felt necessary to "put the increasing abundance, which is beginning, at the service of a less one-sided view of man."

In order to achieve relative control over social development, the Fourth Plan, with the support of the "living forces" of the nation, intended to achieve a social consensus founded upon a rational dialogue. The two central objectives of the Fourth Plan, industrial growth and orientation of lifestyle, each implied a reasoned agreement among social partners, both to reorient the benefits of growth toward a new model of consumption and to control the evolution of nominal incomes in order to avoid a dangerous inflation in this period of opening borders.

The model of social development that the "living forces" of the nation proposed to the nation thus appears to be the sociodemocratic model that later was conceptualized by the neocorporatists with its three central elements:

—dynamic economic growth
—parallel development of the major social services
—rational dialogue among the social partners guaranteeing control over nominal incomes and thereby maintaining the competitiveness of the national economy.

This new model of reference constituted the common language for political elites of the Fifth Republic. The trio of growth, public services, and participation inspired the Gaullists as well as the Socialists throughout the Fifth Republic. Both were influenced by the same current, the same "reformist" ideology whose history remains to be written. The leading figures are known: the intellectual guide Pierre Laroque, François Bloch-Lainé, René Lenoir, etc.

It was a question here less of an articulated current of thought than of a network of intellectual influence, strongly marked by the Christian origins of its members, whose position of strength was in certain sectors of the administration such as the General Planning Commission, the social section of the Council of State, and certain directorates of the Ministry of Social Affairs. The affinity of this group was toward a union of Christian origins, the CFDT, although it did not belong quite to the same network. Thus when in this period Jacques Delors was praising Swedish-style dialogue and offering it as an example, the CFDT was still resonating with the myth of self-management. It should be noted, moreover, that a good number of the high civil servants belonging to this movement later rallied to the Socialist party. Jacques Delors, for example, became the minister of finance in the first Socialist government in 1981. It is no doubt here that one must look for a certain continuity in political practices: in the last analysis it is the same political-administrative personnel (sometimes more administrative, sometimes more political) who have defined the central lines of social policy.

V. PUBLIC SERVICES AND BENEFITS: DYNAMIC GROWTH MARKED BY SPECIAL ARRANGEMENTS FOR OCCUPATIONAL GROUPS

Of all of the elements of the new model of social development, it is the expansion of services and social benefits that seems to have been implemented most systematically. Yet the form taken by this expansion highlights the richness of occupational particularism in French society.

Benefits: The Formation of a Baroque and Ungovernable System

In the field of insurance, the extension of benefits was accompanied by a multiplication of institutions. The progressive expansion of Social Security coverage took place through the adjunction of specific funds for self-employed workers. Unemployment insurance, supplementary retirement funds, job retraining funds form a like number of new sediments in the institutional apparatus. The 1967 Social Security reforms further accentuated the complexity of this system by establishing a rigorous separation among risks relating to old age, health, and the family. Complexity soon became confusion when local governments and the State in turn developed more active social action policies. In the opinion of the majority of experts, this baroque system has proven to be particularly difficult to regulate because the institutions and agents in authority are so numerous and the centers of expertise capable of taking an overall view of the system are so weak (*Revue Française d'Administration Publique* 1987).

The prime movers of 1945 saw in the institutions of Social Security the premises of an original form of social democracy, one that seemed capable of opening the way to a solid dialogue, at least in the social domain. In reality, in the interest of guaranteeing financial responsibility, the State involved itself throughout the management, fostering its bureaucratization, centralizing its functioning, and at least limiting the weight of social representation.

The double process of increasing complexity and bureaucratization hence resulted in the formation of a baroque system, resistant to any overall policy of regulation. Throughout the Fifth Republic, the State has never known how to create the conditions for a systematic public debate on the major directions of policy in the field of social protection. Neither parliament nor the commissions of the plan have really known how to deal with this problem. The concentration of technical expertise on this subject in the Ministry of Finance has tended to favor an accounting approach to the problem. The very marginal proposals for action that emerged from the States General of Social Security in 1987 underline again the extreme difficulty of the problem: a system whose only organized reference center is held by financial experts is better suited to installing bureaucratic rationing than to instigating innovative forms of redistribution.

In the very domain where an active dialogue between social partners developed, beginning with the Fourth Republic, the combined action of sectoral corporatism and of a bureaucratizing administration has severely limited the reality of social participation.

Public Services and Corporatism

The same factors have marked the development of the large public services. Their growth was realized according to the forms and priorities of the dominant elites in each sector. Hence the health policy of the Fifth Republic was dominated by the overwhelming weight of the university hospital elite over this sector. Of course, the emergence of this elite did not occur without political support. Jamous has demonstrated how it took the joint action of the prime minister and of an elite of research-oriented physicians to produce the hospital law of 1958 and its principal result, full-time hospital employment (Jamous 1969). But once established, this elite was to exercise a lasting influence over the whole system.

By forcing the medical elite to devote itself full time to public hospitals, the State succeeded in disassociating a highly influential fraction of the medical corps from their colleagues. Henceforth the university hospital elite will act on its own in its negotiations with the State. By subsequently favoring an unprecedented expansion of public hospitals, it put its mark on the French system of care, which became hospital centered. By supporting the expansion of the system of medical education, which is at the base of its power, it contributed to the production of a large mass of physicians who are now upsetting the medical services market. Medical associations, despite their pretension of representing the whole profession, in reality represent only private practitioners, and their leaders meet with some animosity as a result (Steffen 1987).

It is in fact over this weakest segment of the medical profession that the State can most easily impose the burden of its demands for cost controls. A coherent policy of conventional rates was established for nonhospital medicine in 1960; it was not until 1985 that, through a global budget procedure, the State provided itself with the means to contain the irresistible pressure of hospital expenses.

Faced with the large public services, the Gaullist state presented itself as the heir of the great scientistic consensus that marks the French state. According to this view, a problem cannot be better treated than by the autonomous action of the great professions endowed with scientific knowledge. This scientistic consensus found its primary application in the great industrial, energy, and technological programs that marked the public policies of the Fifth Republic. But this Republic certainly was not absent from the social domain. The almost complete closure of public debate over health policy demonstrates well, for example, the weight of this alliance between science and the State in this sector.

VI. THE NEOCORPORATIST MYTH

Of all of the themes advanced by the reformists of the 1960s, it was that of a contractual social policy that had the greatest difficulty in taking root. The stakes were high: it was a question of recognizing wage earners as a collective actor in the conduct of economic and social policy.

The Institutionalization of Social Actors

This contractual policy was intended to find support in a vigorous policy of institutionalization of social actors. In French administrative language two terms with contrasting connotations are used to designate the social actors involved in policy. One speaks of "private interests" when it is a question of glorifying the role of the State as a guarantor of the general interest in the face of the insatiable egotism of the small and the great. One speaks of "social partners" in referring to dialogue with organizations that have been recognized as respectable.

We have elsewhere traced the stages of this initiatory journey, at the end of which the miserable special interest is elevated to the rank of social partner (Jobert and Muller 1987). Recognition constitutes the first stage, permitting the association to participate in various dialogues and eventually to receive office space and subsidies. This recognition can take a more formal turn when political authorities decide to accord the label of representativeness to a limited number of organizations. This label is not only a mark of prestige; it assures access to more important resources, including larger subsidies, participation in elections of representatives of occupational groups, seats on the Social and Economic Council, detachment of civil servants to work for the association, etc. It opens the way to a still tighter interaction with the public sphere when the partner is granted comanagement of important sectors of public policy.

The more the social organization is institutionalized, the more important becomes the contribution of the State as a proportion of its total resources. According to Frank Baumgartner (1985), in 1983 more than two thousand civil servants were loaned to the staffs of unions and associations affiliated with education. With regard to trade unions, income from membership dues was generally comparable to subsidies received for the support of training and advancement of the group (Catala 1983). For farm organizations, subsidies surpassed dues from members, particularly with respect to the National Center of Young Farmers (CNJA) (Keeler 1985).

Hence the large organizations with which the State organizes social dialogues are very largely dependent on the latter. While these organizations are not thereby transformed into creatures of the State, institutionalization contributes strongly to channeling and slowing changes in the organization of social mobilization. Public resources in fact loosen the dependence of leaders on their members. These resources also allow leaders to expand services, thereby reinforcing the loyalty of the membership. As a result it is a long and difficult process for a new and rival organization to attract members, even when they no longer truly feel represented by the existing organization. The State may attempt to accelerate change by rapidly recognizing the newcomer, but it then risks drawing the thunder of the old organizations, which often react violently to this type of effort. The National Federation of Farmers (FNSEA) never forgave Edith Cresson for attempting to establish and to consolidate rival farm organizations after the Socialist victory of 1981. The Federation launched a war of attrition against the Socialist minister, organizing numerous demonstrations and protests until the worried Socialist leadership replaced Cresson with Michel Rocard. Rocard then devoted himself to calming and reassuring the Federation (Jobert and Muller 1987). Institutionalization thus becomes a strategic resource for a recipient organization, which then attempts to assure itself a monopoly position against its rivals.

Paradoxically, the strategy adopted by the governments of the Fifth Republic consisted of inaugurating contractual policies at the most general level —the formation of a global social compromise on incomes policy—before attacking more specific problems such as the national agreements of the 1970s and the definition of the role of unions and wage earners within the firm, a problem finally treated in depth by the Auroux Laws of 1982. It appeared that the strategy of participation was seeking to skirt as long as possible the sensitive problem of power relationships within the firm.

In attempting to construct a house by beginning with the roof, one risks making grave miscalculations. The most patent failure concerned incomes policy, which appeared as the keystone of the strategy designed by the reformers. In order to achieve simultaneously the objectives of growth and reorientation of consumption toward public facilities, it seemed necessary to gain control over the movement of nominal incomes.

Encouraged by the success of "the wise men" in ending the great miners' strike of 1963, the Gaullist state attempted to launch an ambitious incomes policy. This attempt rapidly ended in failure. The unions denounced this policy as a simple device for regulating wages in that it largely ignored nonwage incomes, which were very poorly known and difficult to control. Moreover, rivalry between unions, the weakness of their active memberships, and the fragility of their organizations at the confederal level prevented them from conducting negotiations that were necessarily centralized. Had they attempted to do so, they no doubt would have been incapable of imposing the slightest discipline on their troops. The situation was little different on the side of employers, of whom we have elsewhere described the organizational weakness and the strong refusal of the majority to agree to even a minimum of openness and discipline in the conduct of their own businesses (Jobert and Muller 1987).

The myth of a grand neocorporatist agreement on incomes policy continued, however, to enrich the language of planners and politicians. It inspired the "great society" plan with which the government of Jacques Chaban-Delmas attempted to respond to the great social and cultural crisis of 1968. It inspired the social strategies of planners who later sought to link income to the distribution of work. The persistence of the myth was only equaled by its consistent practical ineffectiveness. At no time was the question of income distribution the subject of effective national negotiations. While the social democratic states have succeeded in obtaining collective agreements to limit increases in nominal salaries, in France increases in real salaries have been achieved at the price of strong inflation (Cameron 1984). The reduction of inflation since 1983 has not been the result of negotiations; it has coincided with a decline in the power of unions weakened by the economic crisis and by a loss of members. These facts confirm the results of comparative studies that show that only states endowed with a powerful, neocorporatist structure for central negotiations have been able to carry out sustained policies for the regulation of incomes (Marks 1986).

The new impetus given to contractual politics under the Chaban-Delmas government would no longer seek to achieve that utopia of global social compromise. The proposal established more pragmatic and limited objectives for interprofessional labor relations. After 1968 this dialogue was facilitated by a new attitude of employers toward unions. These were no longer perceived necessarily as troublemakers; they could be viewed as mediators who prevent little-noticed tensions from degenerating into spontaneous and uncontrollable social movements.

The Gaullist governments that succeeded each other after the social movements of 1968 (and particularly the government of Jacques Chaban-Delmas, in which Jacques Delors was the principal advisor) successfully placed systematic pressure on French employers to negotiate. An impressive amount of work was accomplished in a few years, particularly thanks to agreements that included most of the unions:

February 1968: agreement on partial unemployment
December 1968: agreement on reduction of the work week
December 1968: agreement on union organization within the firm
March 1969: agreement on job security
July 1970: agreement on monthly salaries for workers
March 1972: agreement on early retirement and on guaranteed income
December 1973: guarantees in cases of bankruptcy
1974: agreement on full compensation for unemployment
March 1975: framework agreement on working conditions

Several of these agreements were extended by further important actions, in particular the law of 16 July 1971 on job training, the law of July 13 1971 on collective agreements, and the law of 13 July 1973. Finally, a small beginning at a contractual incomes policy was attempted with the establishment of "progress contracts" in the public sector.

The dynamism of this policy was not linked exclusively to a man and his team. The departure of Jacques Chaban-Delmas did not put an end to innovation in labor and employment policy. Contractual politics continued to bear fruit, both with respect to the collective and individual rights of workers against dismissal (the law of 13 July 1973 on justification for individual dismissal; the general agreement of October 1974 on compensation at the rate of 90 percent of gross salary for layoffs due to economic causes; the law of December 1975 requiring administrative authorization for dismissals for economic reasons) and with respect to working conditions (creation of the National Agency for the Improvement of Working Conditions in 1973).

However, this contractual politics encountered increasing difficulties. The economic crisis, which little by little revealed its enduring character, increasingly limited the relevance of these broad agreements. Structural changes affect branches of the economy and individual firms in an unequal fashion, making it very difficult to define uniform standards for all. Economic conditions, as well as the issues treated in collective negotiations, such as improvement of working conditions, suggest that negotiations should be at the firm level. Yet it is at this level that employers are most reticent to engage in negotiations that might encroach on their power. Moreover, the incitement to negotiate diminished rapidly in accordance with the ebb of union membership and of union militancy during the crisis.

This fault in the system of industrial relations had been seen by the government leaders who commissioned a report from Pierre Sudreau (1975) on the reform of the governance of firms. However, the hostility of employers prevented any concrete results from being drawn from this daring report.

In reality it took the victory of the Left in 1981 in order for France to adopt, in the Auroux Laws of 1982, legislation that better guaranteed the expression of the voices of workers and unions within the firm. This set of four laws was initially the object of extremely violent attacks from employers and the conservative opposition. According to the latter, the disturbing intrusion of politicized unions into the firm gravely threatened the economic future of France. It opened the royal way for the implantation of Communists through the intermediary of the General Confederation of Labor (CGT). Listening to certain leaders, one would have thought that the nightmare of the communist soviet rotting away the whole of the country was not far off. In retrospect one can only be amazed at the excessive criticism that these laws aroused.

Denounced as a bogeyman at the time of its adoption by many employers, this body of legislation, in fact very modest in its ambitions, seems to have been implemented in a highly satisfactory manner. Agreements at the firm level continued to multiply, perhaps thus announcing the advent in France of a new culture of industrial relations. It is moreover significant that the rightist majority in the years 1986–1988 did not find it opportune to change these laws.

VII. THE RESTRUCTURING OF THE WELFARE STATE

The notion of crisis has never been as debased as in the case of the welfare state. To evoke crisis with respect to the Chilean state under Allende seems completely justified (Rayo 1987). What can be observed in France, as in the majority of European countries, is both the powerful overall resistance of systems of social intervention and some important modifications in their orientation. The latter are seen in the management of social modernization, the regulation of public expenditures, and the administrative decentralization of social policies.

The Management of Social Modernization: Delaying Action, Reconversion, and Exclusion

The End of Industrial Policies with Social Objectives. The way in which industrial relations have been built in France, as described above, has profoundly marked social management and the modernization of France. In effect all growth implies a sometimes painful redistribution of economic activities and of people. The more rapid the modernization, the more rapid the necessary pace of destruction of activities and redistribution of people. Faced with this problem, French social policy seems to have hesitated between a delaying action and the management of exclusion.

The hesitations of the "stretcher-bearer State" have been analysed by E. Cohen (1989). The delaying actions are those seen in the early 1970s, when sectoral plan after sectoral plan sought to save occupations and activities that modernization seemed to condemn. The case of the French steel industry offers a classic example of this type of situation. Despite repeated indications of crisis, one finds "the same congenital, systematic, institutionalized optimism" (Hayward 1986, 101). "For example, whereas the Sixth Plan had expected a fall in steel employment of four thousand from 1971–1975, the number actually increased by ten thousand" (Hayward 1986, 93).

In reality a large part of what was called industrial policy was social policy. This situation, moreover, was largely in accordance with the desires of French citizens with respect to publicly owned firms. A survey conducted by SOFRES/Fondation Nationale des Sciences Politiques at the beginning of the 1980s on the principal objectives of public firms showed clearly that the majority of the respondants assigned high priority to social functions (64 percent said to provide the maximum number of jobs) or consumer protection (56 percent). The idea that these firms should contribute to the growth of the nation came only next, with 48 percent, and, far behind with 17 percent, came the idea that they should promote new techniques. Hence there was a major gap between the industrialist conception of nationalization held by the Socialists and the value placed on this view by public opinion. It is not surprising, then, that the popularity of nationalization dropped very rapidly from the moment that the government authorized the nationalized firms to take off the fat of their surplus employees in order to face up to international competition. The same people who had been favorable to nationalization thus found themselves approving privatization.

This change in public firms illustrates one of the most striking turning points of social policy: the abandonment of industrial policies with social goals. It was with respect to such policies that the neoliberal rhetoric was most heavily used: it was no longer a question of aiding in the artificial survival of lame ducks, nor of delaying necessary cuts and restructuring in the name of social imperatives. Neoliberalism, with its Darwinian and war-like connotations, served as the legitimating rhetoric for the new captains of industry.

Between Reconversion and Exclusion. The management of the people who were thus pushed aside can be conceived either in terms of reconversion or in terms of exclusion. In practice the most common result was the exclusion of older workers from the job market (Guillemard 1988). The explosive development of systems of early retirement profoundly modified the nature of discontinuance of work, which became less the exercise of a right than a forced exclusion.

At the other end of the age chain, modernization increased the difficulty of finding employment for poorly qualified young people, particularly since firms tended to raise the required levels of formal education. Contrary experiments inspired by Bertrand Schwartz nonetheless showed that young people with limited formal education could hold skilled jobs in new techno-logical fields without going back to school (Wuhl 1988). Yet the efforts of the present government have concentrated on formal education, as if an increase in the number of officially approved degree holders offers a major way out of the difficulties presented by current economic changes.

Dualism of the Labor Market, Dualism of Systems of Training. The strong development of vocational training in France might have led one to hope for an approach to social modernization based less on exclusion. Indeed, the law of July 1971 on further education appears to have been the most lasting consequence of the "new society" plan recommended at that time by the Chaban-Delmas Government and by his principal advisor, Jacques Delors.

By imposing on all firms with more than ten employees a legal obligation to devote 1.2 percent of their payroll to training, this law allowed for a rapid growth of such activities, which in 1987 in fact represented 2.54 percent of total payroll. According to certain experts, the total of funds devoted to training places France among the most highly developed countries in this domain, comparable to Sweden (Bruhnes 1989).

In northern Europe, dismissals for economic reasons are difficult, necessarily giving firms a strong stimulus for internal flexibility and mobility. Elsewhere in Europe, and particularly in France, external flexibility is favored. What role can the strong development of vocational training play in this second context?

Social modernization implies a double requirement on the firm. It implies the marginalization, indeed the elimination of workers without skills or with obsolete skills. Each year some one hundred thousand semiskilled jobs disappear. But it also requires that firms hold and win the loyalty of personnel whose skills are not easily replaceable. It is a question of limiting the internal market of the firm and investing most heavily in that stabilized portion of employees.

The arrangements for further training clearly favor managers and skilled workers, promising sectors of the economy, and large firms (Dubar 1984). A quarter of the employees of firms subject to the 1.2 percent requirement go through a training period every year. This figure rises to 40 percent for training personnel, managers, and skilled white collar workers, but drops to 20 percent for employers and skilled blue collar workers (Coulon 1989).

The dualism of the labor market is thus extended by the dualism of training systems, since the task of providing training for the most vulnerable segments of the population has fallen to public authorities. A whole apparatus has been fabricated to prepare youth for the job market, an apparatus that now has been extended by the establishment of local training programs designed for recipients of the Minimum Insertion Income (RMI). The linkage of this second sector of training with the employment needs of firms remains very problematic. Training programs that are in fact holding operations do not seem to be on the way out. Is it by chance that recipients of the RMI are often the same young people who have already known the joy of training programs?

Decentralization of Social Policies. The consequence of this policy orientation is to leave large portions of the poorly qualified population in a situation of uncertainty regarding their social rights. The organizational model of Social Security built in 1945 rested on the linkage between access to social rights and stable paid employment. This link is increasingly difficult to maintain for groups that have been marginalized by modernization.

The extreme slowness with which the French state rediscovered poverty and vulnerability and put in place an apparatus to deal with it is revealing. Neither the unions nor the parties of the Left proposed the new policies. These actors were caught up with the administrative problems of dividing responsibility (What does insurance cover? Where does the State's task of assistance begin?). It took the active pressure of old and new charitable associations in order finally to bring to the public agenda the idea of a minimum income, an idea that however is in practice in various forms in most of the countries of Europe.

This fact itself raises a series of questions. The management style of the welfare state in France rests largely on a particular conception of social democracy according to which organizations representing workers and employers should play a pivotal role in its management. In practice, can the status of wage earners in general be considered to be sufficiently homogeneous and comprehensive to serve as a reference point for organizations charged with managing social affairs? Are we not witnessing a multifaceted differentiation among wage earners that makes any attempt at managing their needs through a single organization increasingly delicate? One can ask if this problem is not reflected in the increased development of territorial social policies: decentralization, job training policies associated with the Minimum Income, and social development of neighborhoods. While the core of regularly employed wage earners continues to be managed by the systems based on the insurance principle, the management of the poor and the vulnerable is being built on a more territorial basis, where the State and local governments become the principal actors.

The search for a better-coordinated, locally oriented social policy had been launched several years before by a modernizing coalition that criticized the sectoral and occupational model for social policies. This coalition was anchored in a network of high civil servants at the Directorate of Social Action and in the Planning Commission. A group of elite specialists on social questions coming out of the Council of State, apparently influenced by Pierre Laroque, Jacques Delors, and François Bloch-Lainé, occupied an eminent place in this network. This group produced a set of reports and decisions that laid out a new model of social policy aimed at supporting or rapidly reintegrating fragile groups by means of coordinated, preventative social activities backed by local government participation. This is in effect the same model that inspired the policies of keeping elderly people at home and psychiatric patients in their home districts, both begun in the 1960s; the law of 1975 on the handicapped; and the subsequent policies of redevelopment of deteriorated neighborhoods and of social integration of young people. All of these cases challenged the corporatist compartmentalization of the large social bureaucracies. They aimed at setting in motion local social policies coordinated around major problems that no single professional could resolve alone.

The diffuse influence of these new concepts was considerable, but an analysis of their implementation shows the formidable obstacles that are opposed to their blossoming (Jobert 1981). Extreme scattering of social institutions and rigid compartmentalization of occupations continue to mark the French social countryside.

On the other hand the reinforcement of local governments as a result of decentralization facilitated the development of contractual procedures between the central state and local governments for the purpose of promoting cross-cutting policies. The experience of the Commission for Social Development, renamed the Interministerial Delegation for the City, demonstrates the relative effectiveness of this line of action (Lévy 1988).

Neoliberal Ideology and Bureaucratic Rationing

The second modification in relations between professions and the state is the result of increasing pressure on public expenditures. During the period of rapid growth, a consensus easily could be reached between professions and the state on the development of policy in each sector. It was up to the occupational group to determine the needs and the methods to be used; it was up to the state to determine budgets and decide who would pay.

This division of tasks became difficult to maintain in a period of crisis. While the professions continued to think about problems of adapting to new situations in terms of adding on by sedimentation, the financiers demanded redeployment of resources. But whoever calls for redeployment calls also for evaluation of past programs and establishment of new priorities. The persistent misunderstanding between physicians and the State constitutes a particularly clear example of the difficulties of this exercise (Jobert and Steffen 1988). In the name of professional autonomy, physicians successfully opposed any close evaluation of their activities, whether from a technical, economic, or social perspective. This refusal subsequently worked against them, however. The most powerful centers of expertise and decision making in matters of health expenditures emerged in the Directorate of the Budget and the Ministry of Finance.

Having failed to take control of the economic and social aspects of their tasks, physicians now are more and more subjected to the procedures of bureaucratic rationing, the only kind that financial experts know how to handle. These procedures favor the consolidation of past gains more than the search for innovations necessary to adapt the health system to a new socioeconomic context. The repeated failure of policies seeking alternatives to hospitalization are evidence of this tendency (Steffen 1987).

It is in the context of rigidification of professionalized sectoral policies that recent controversies over corporatism must be seen. It is significant that the ideology of neoliberalism has found its spokesmen among the financial elite more than among the representatives of French employers. The successful essay of Alain Minc, "The Egalitarian Machine," thus draws a good part of its arguments from work done by the inspectorate of Finance on the evolution of public expenditures. Virulent criticism of the organization of public services and of the recognized professions attached to them reflects the powerlessness of the ruling elite to stimulate change and adaptation in the large public services. The recommended recourse to the market, to competition, thus appears to be the only lever for overcoming the resistance of these recalcitrant professions.

The doctrinaire neoliberalism held by conservative political leaders had a passing success as an intellectual basis of their opposition to the triumphant socialism of 1981. However, the profound attachment of the French to the social rights guaranteed by Social Security quickly led the parties of the Right to moderate their ambitions in this domain (Schnapper, Brody, and Kastoryano 1986; SOFRES 1982, 1983). In contrast, managerial neoliberalism, founded on a critique of the corporatist model of public management, seems to have gained increasing influence, extending far beyond the intellectual circles of the Right. Current French public opinion is marked by a profound ambiguity. It continues to view social rights as a major attribute of citizenship, while offering a triumphal welcome to anticorporatist efforts that challenge the traditional management principles of the large public services.

There remains the task of evaluating the effects of these increasing attempts at rationing on the evolution of social policies. The hypothesis developed here will be that rationing leads to the impoverishment of the public sector and that in the long term this can have two types of consequences. First, the impoverishment of the public sector generates *the blockage of innovation* in the public sector for fear of highlighting costly need—for example, alternatives to hospitalization—even when they are necessary. There follows from this a tendency to confer innovation, research, and the implementation of new solutions on the market, as in the case of management of dependent old people. This legitimizes the liberal rhetoric that presumes that the public sector is incapable of innovation and that management of social affairs should be conferred on new entrepreneurs.

Second, *the impoverishment of the public sector breaks up the social coalition favorable to the public.* As differentiation among wage earners progresses, there appears a new category of prosperous wage earners, willing to make personal contributions in order to obtain more and better services. A group of OECD experts alludes to the emergence of a new "well-to-do class," no longer making up 4-10 percent of the population but 40 percent. Its consumerist demands for quality services fit the aspirations of professional groups to put in place the most advanced techniques. In a period of economic growth, this coalition served as a fulcrum for the expansion of the public service, particularly hospital care. But were the public service to be impoverished, the same preoccupations could generate a powerful coalition in favor of privatization.

Rooted in democratic citizenship, social policies have proven their formidable capacity for resistance to change. But their mode of organization is suffering the backlash of structural changes that are going through French society: the growing differentiation of the world of wage earners and the increasing vulnerability of a large number of them place in doubt a model of social democracy that seems to have exhausted its dynamism. Is it by chance that the most promising experiments of French social policy have been carried out in the context of a more territorial conception of the protector state? But in the long term one cannot dismiss the hypothesis that bureaucratic rationing of social policies will lead to increased privatization of these services.

VIII. CONCLUSION

This journey through French social policy now allows for specification of some of the limits of neocorporatist approaches and suggests some complementary hypotheses concerning the linkages between public policies and social mediation.

The principal criterion used by neocorporatist approaches seems both relevant and limited. The existence of embracing social organizations, tending toward monopoly representation of interests and endowed with a centralized style of organization, seems to be a condition for the definition of concerted social strategies. Only powerful and centralized unions can limit demands for salary increases when they can reasonably expect that in return they will gain an active social policy as well as a guarantee of limited but real increases in income (Cameron 1984).

The French case confirms this hypothesis and at the same time shows the limits of political voluntarism in this field. All governments, all new political elites inherit a mode of organization of classes and professions over which they have very limited influence in the short term. The abundant resources given by politicians to the "social partners" and the institutionalization of a tripartite dialogue in certain instances were insufficient to overcome the segmentation and the organizational weakness of the major social actors. The global social democratic compromise remains a dream beyond reach even when Socialists are leading the country. The multiplication of partial compromises remains the rule and with them the maintenance of a dualist structure of mediation. Alongside the privileged sectors, in which an occupational group can obtain one of the partial agreements, remain large sections of the population that are excluded from social citizenship, if one understands that to mean participation in the definition of social policies through the medium of large organizations.

Hence the example of France demonstrates well that it would be incorrect to equate neocorporatism with the institutionalization of relations between the State and social organizations. If one attempted to construct a typology of political systems according to the State's share of resources available to social actors, it is not at all clear that the neocorporatist states would come out on top.

It would also be a serious error to equate the organizational weakness of the world of wage earners with a low level of social mobilization. If that were the case, it would be incomprehensible that France developed a set of social policies comparable in their breadth to those of neocorporatist states of the social democratic type. In this country the detour through political mobilization seems to have compensated for the anemia of large social organizations. The social state appears in France to be largely a dimension of democratic citizenship. This is what explains that the development of public services and benefits preceded by several decades the institutionalization of labor-management relations in the centers of economic power. This is also what explains the role of an elite issuing from the high civil service in the conduct of social policy.

The influence of the professions is the logical consequence of this weak overall organization of the major social actors and of the scientistic consensus that has had a lasting influence on French public activities. This influence varies, however, according to the political and institutional context. The strong party organizations of the Fifth Republic clearly limit the possibility of playing parties off against each other and thereby diminish the weight of the professions. Similarly, the reinforcement of the executive removes channels of access to the upper administration and weakens organizations that relied on the number of their members to impress Parliament.

Finally, it appears that public policy can even have a certain impact on the evolution of social structure. The organization of the survival of farmers and the old middle classes under the Third Republic is an example. The management of their accelerated decline under the Fifth Republic is a further example. Analyses of public policy have often favored the study of innovative policies, such as major technological programs and new urban policies. The problem of the social management of decline, whether it be a case of branches of the economy, regions, or social classes, has not received all of the attention that it deserves (for exceptions see Cohen 1989; Hayward 1986). It is here, no doubt, that some of the most significant differences between states would appear.

REFERENCES

Baumgartner, Frank. 1985. "French Interest Groups and the Pluralism-Corporatism Debate." Paper presented to the American Political Science Association, New Orleans, August–September 1985.
Berger, Suzanne. 1981. "Regime and Interest Representation: The French Traditional Middle Classes." In *Organizing Interests in Western Europe*, edited by S. Berger. Cambridge: Cambridge University Press.
Birnbaum, Pierre. 1977. *Les Sommets de l'etat: Essai sur l'élite du pouvoir en France*. Paris: Seuil.
Brunhes, Bernard. 1989. Interview in *Espace social européen* no. 20 (19 May): 10.
Cameron, David. 1984. "Social Democracy, Corporatism, Labour Quiescence and

the Representation of Economic Interests." In *Order and Conflict in Contemporary Capitalism*, edited by J. H. Goldthorpe. Oxford: Clarendon Press.

Catala, Nicole. 1983. "Les Moyens du pouvoir syndical." *Pouvoir* no. 16.

Cohen, Elie. 1989. *L'Etat brancardier*. Paris: Calman Levy.

Coulon, M. B. 1989. "Formation: Place aux professionnels." *Espace social européen* (19 May): 12.

Delorme, Robert, and Christine André. 1983. *Etat et l'économie*. Paris: Seuil.

Donzelot, Jacques. 1984. *L'Invention du social*. Paris: Fayard.

Dubar, Claude. 1984. *La Formation professionnelle continue*. Paris: Découverte.

Durkheim, Emile. 1964. *The Division of Labor in Society*. London: Macmillan/Free Press.

Ehrmann, Henry. 1957. *Organized Business in France*. Princeton: Princeton University Press.

Guillemard, Anne Marie. 1988. *Le Déclin du social*. Paris: PUF.

Hatzfeld, Henri. 1971. *Du paupérisme à la sécurité sociale*. Paris: Colin.

Hayward, Jack. 1986. *The State and the Market Economy*. New York: New York University Press.

Jamous, Haroun. 1969. *Sociologie de la décision, la réforme des études médicales et des structures hospitalières*. Paris: CNRS.

Jobert, Bruno. 1981. *Le Social en plan*. Paris: Éditions ouvrières.

Jobert, Bruno, and P. Muller. 1987. *L'Etat en action*. Paris: PUF.

Jobert, Bruno, and D. Renard. 1988. *Néolibéralisme doctrinaire et néolibéralisme de gestion: Les deux faces d'un phénomène français*. Grenoble: CERAT. Mimeo.

Jobert, Bruno, and M. Steffen. 1988. "Décisions et non-décisions en matière de politique de santé." Paper delivered to the Congrès de la Société française de santé publique, Lyon, 16 and 17 May.

Keeler, John. 1985. "Situating France on the Pluralism-Corporatism Continuum." *Comparative Politics* 17: 229–49.

Kuisel, Richard. 1981. *Capitalism and the State in Modern France*. Cambridge: Cambridge University Press.

Lehmbruch, Gerhard. 1984. "Concertation and the Structure of Corporatist Networks." In *Order and Conflict in Contemporary Capitalism*, edited by J. H. Goldthorpe. Oxford: Clarendon Press.

Lévy, F. 1988. *Bilan/perspective des contrats de plan de développement social des quartiers*. 2 vols. Paris: Commissariat Général du Plan.

Marks, Gary. 1986. "Neocorporatism and Income Policies in Western Europe and North America." *Comparative Politics* 18: 253–78.

Organization for Economic Cooperation and Development (OECD). 1985. *Social Expenditures, 1960–1990*. Paris: OECD.

Pisier-Kouchner, Evelyne. 1983. "Le Service public entre libéralisme et collectivisme." *Espirit* 12: 9–19.

Rayo, Gustavo. 1987. "La Politique sociale sous un régime autoritaire: le cas du Chili." Doctoral (third cycle) thesis in political science, University of Grenoble.

Revue Française d'Administration Publique. 1987. No. 43. Special issue entitled "La Santé est-elle sous administrée?"

Sartori, Giovanni. 1987. *The Theory of Democracy Revisited*. 2 vols. Chatham: Chatham House.

Schnapper, Dominique, Jeanne Brody, and Riva Kastoryano. 1986. "Les Finances et la sécurité sociale." *Vingtième Siècle* 10: 67–82.

Ségrestin, Denis. 1984. *Le Phénomene corporatiste*. Paris: Fayard.

Sellier, François. 1984. *La Confrontation sociale en France, 1936–1981*, Paris: PUF.

SOFRES. 1980. "Le Service public industriel et commercial." A survey conducted by Alain Lancelot for the Foundation Nationale des Sciences Politiques. Paris: SOFRES. Mimeo.

———. 1982. "Les Français et le progrès, 200 ans d'ère industrielle." A survey published in *L'Expansion*, 19 and 24 June.

———. 1983. "La France en 1983." A survey published in *L'Expansion*, 16–21 March.

Steffen, Monica. 1987. *Les Politiques alternatives dans le domaine de la santé: A report for the Ministry of Social Affairs and Social Solidarity*.

Wuhl, Simon. 1988. "L'Insertion des jeunes dit de bas niveau." *Pour no. 112.*

Zysman, John. 1983. *Governments, Markets and Growth*. Oxford: Martin Robertson.

ABBREVIATIONS

AGIRC   Association générale des institutions de retraite des cadres. Agency formed by mutual agreement between employers and employees in 1947 to coordinate diverse supplementary pension funds for *cadres*.

AL   Allocation logement familiale. Housing allowance based on family income, created in this form in 1987.

ALS   Allocation logement sociale. Housing subsidies to certain categories of individuals (handicapped, elderly, etc.).

ANPE   Agence national pour l'emploi. Agency formed in 1967 and primarily financed from unemployment insurance funds for retraining workers.

APL   Aide personnalisée au logement. Program created in 1977 to provide housing subsidies directly to individuals.

ARRCO   Association des régimes de retraites complémentaires. Agency formed by mutual agreement of employers and employees in 1961 to coordinate remaining suplementary pension plans for lower-level *cadres*.

AVTS   Allocation aux vieux travailleurs salariés. Minimum pension established in 1941 and kept as basic pension for all workers. Paid from the *régime générale*, or basic state pension fund.

BAPSA   Budget annexe des prestations sociales agricoles. Social security budget of all benefits provided through the Ministry of Agriculture for farmers and farmworkers since 1967.

CDC   Caisse des dépôts et consignations. A national bank that manages the financing of local governments.

CEL	Compte d'épargne logement. Subsidized and tax-exempt savings accounts for the purchase of a residence.
CES	Certificat d'études spécialisées. Degree awarded for largely theoretical education in medical specialities, replaced by residencies in 1982–1985 reforms.
CFDT	Confédération française démocratique du travail. The formerly Catholic trade union; generally sympathetic to the Socialist Party.
CFF	Crédit foncier de France. A semipublic bank created in 1950 to provide loans and subsidies for housing construction.
CFTC	Confédération française des travailleurs chrétiens. Catholic trade union that changed its name to the CFDT in 1964.
CGC	Confédération générale des cadres. Considered a labor union for the purpose of Social Security and represents *cadres* in all pension negotiations.
CGL	Confédération générale du logement. Tenants' association.
CGLS	Caisse de garantie du logement. Created in 1986 out of the old CPHLM to administer housing loans.
CGPME	Confédération générale des petites et moyennes enterprises. Principal association representing small businessmen.
CGT	Confédération générale du travail. The largest French trade union, with close links to the Communist Party. Frequently boycotts negotiations on pensions and other labor issues.
CGT–FO	Confédération génerale du travail–Force ouvrière. A trade union that broke away from the CGT over the latter's ties to the Communist Party; the least partisan of the major unions.
CHU	Centres hospitaliers universitaires. Research and teaching hospitals.
CIL	Comités interprofessionnels du logement. Administrative agencies that collect mandatory contributions from employers for the purpose of housing construction.
CNAF	Caisse nationale des allocations familiales. Fund providing family allowances, mother and child support; autonomously established since 1947.
CNAMTS	Caisse nationale de l'assurance maladie des travailleurs salariés. Principal fund for the administration of public health insurance, separated from general social security in 1967.

CNAV   Caisse nationale de l'assurance vieillesse. Fund that manages all state pensions and transfers contributions to other insurance funds for all retired benefits.

CNPF   Conseil national du patronat français. Main employer association, which conducts most national-level negotiations for social and unemployment insurance.

CPHLM   Caisse des prêts aux habitations à loyer modéré. A branch of the CDC charged from 1966 to 1986 with making loans for the construction of public housing.

CSMF   Confédération des syndicats médicaux français. Until 1960 the sole union representing physicians in private practice.

FO   Force ouvrière. A trade union that broke away from the CGT over the latter's ties to the Communist party; the least partisan of the major unions.

FMF   Fédération des médecins de France. Since 1960 the competing union to CSMF for the representation of physicians in private practice.

FNE   Fonds national de l'emploi. Fund financed from levy on employers to provide supplementary benefits to unemployment insurance benefits of low-paid workers.

FNS   Fonds national de solidarité. Fund provided from general tax revenues since 1956 to add supplementary benefits to low basic pensions.

FNSEA   Fédération nationale des syndicats d'exploitants agricoles. The dominant farmers' association.

HLM   Habitation à loyer modéré. Subsidized public housing, usually built and managed by public and semipublic corporations.

INED   Institut national d'études démographiques. Government research body that collects demographic data and advises on social policy.

MRP   Mouvement républicain populaire. French Christian Democratic party created after World War II.

MSA   Mutualité sociale agricole. Agency within the Ministry of Agriculture that collects social insurance contributions from the agricultural sector; now heavily dependent on transfers from the *régime générale* and state budget.

PAH   Prime à l'amélioration de l'habitat. Loans to low-income home owners for the rehabilitation of housing.

PALULOS   Primes à l'amélioration de logements à usage locatif et à occupation sociale. Loan program for the rehabilitation of HLM and other social housing.

PAP   Prêts d'accession à la propriété. Government program providing subsidized loans to low-income people for the purchase of housing.

PEL   Plan d'épargne logement. A subsidized and tax-exempt savings plan for the purchase of a residence.

PLA   Prêt locatif aidé. Loan program for construction of housing for low-income groups.

PLI   Prêts locatifs intermédiaires. Subsidized loans for construction of middle-income rental housing.

RMI   Revenue minimum d'insertion. Grants to individuals created in 1988 to support certain categories of disadvantaged, unemployed persons during job training.

RPF   Rassemblement du peuple français. The Gaullist party in the Fourth Republic.

SMH   Syndicat de la médecine hospitalière. Hospital physicians' association; politically affiliated with the Left.

SMIC   Salaire minimum interprofessionnel de croissance. Minimum wage automatically indexed to purchasing power of minimum income.

SNAM   Syndicat national des médecins, chirurgiens, spécialistes et biologistes des hôpitaux publics. Principal association of French hospital physicians.

SNCH   Syndicat national des cadres hospitaliers. Hospital directors' association.

UIMM   Union des industries métallurgiques et minières. Successor to prewar social research group of the Comité des forges, providing statistics and reports on social insurance to the private sector.

UNAF   Union nationale des associations familiales. Principal federation of family associations.

UNANIM   Union nationale autonome des nouveaux internes en médecine. Represents residents in general medicine.

UNCAF   Union nationale des caisses d'allocations familiales. Principal manager of family benefits.

UNEDIC	Union nationale pour l'emploi dans l'industrie et le commerce. Agency managing unemployment insurance under a mutual agreement of employers and employees since 1958.
UNIRS	Union nationale des institutions de retraites des salariés. Agency formed by mutual agreement in 1961, when supplementary pensions were generalized to most of the working population.
UNR	Union pour la Nouvelle République. The Gaullist party, 1958–1962; subsequently changed its name several times.

INDEX

Caisse nationale de l'assurance maladie des travailleurs salariés (CNAMTS), 43, 98–99, 130
Caisse nationale de l'assurance vieillesse (CNAV), 43
Caisse nationale des allocations familiales (CNAF), 36, 41, 43
Cameron, David, 1
Canada, 60, 62–63
Canlorbe, Pierre, 136
Catholic Church, 3, 107, 153
Catholic Left, 39
Catholics: and family policy, 145–46, 161, 166; and the welfare state, 9–11
Catholic schools, 8
Central Committee for Family Allowances, 149
Centre d'études des revenues et des coûts (CERC), 26
Centres hospitaliers universitaires (CHU). *See* University Hospital Centers
Certificat d'études spécialisées (CES), 113
Chaban-Delmas, Jacques, 45, 84, 170–72, 245–46, 249
Chefs de service, 118–22
Chevènement, Jean-Pierre, 20
Child care: for children of physicians, 104; expansion of, 164, 179, 181–82; partisan attitudes toward, 178–79; Planning Commission on, 154, 170
Child custody, 183
Children: aid to, 15; health care of, 123; legal categories of, 181; tax exemptions for, 164, 175
Christian Democratic parties, 9, 65–69
Christians: in planning and social administrations, 240
Chile, 247
Chirac Government: economic policy of, 187; health policy of, 111, 122, 126–33, 136–40; housing policy of, 222–25
Chirac, Jacques, 25, 184. *See also* Chirac Government
Citizenship: and social protection, 237, 254–56
Civil servants: and extension of social services, 98; and family policy, 155; in Fourth Republic, 236–37; housing of, 214; pensions of, 22; power of over social

policy, 256; prestige of, 21; and republican corporatism, 235; retirement of, 48; in social security agencies, 43, 53 n 13; training of, 19
Cohen, Elie, 248
College of Secondary Education (CES), 18
Collins, Doreen, 201
Comité de liaison et d'action des syndicats hospitaliers (CLASH), 120
Comités d'entreprise, 38
Comités interprofessionels du logement (CIL), 199
Commission de conciliation, 206, 220
Commission des comptes de la sécurité sociale, 131
Commission for Social Development, 252
Commission on Consumption and Social Modernization, 153
Commission on Manpower, 155
Common Program, 172
Communist Party (PCF): and family policy, 152–53, 156; and housing policy, 161; and mandatory social insurance, 9; and postwar social reforms, 38–39; in Socialist Government, 125, 201
Communist trade unions, 36
Compte d'épargne logement (CEL), 198
Confédération des syndicats médicaux français (CSMF), 99, 128–30. *See also* Physicians: associations of
Confédération française des travailleurs chrétiens (CFTC), 161
Confédération générale des cadres (CGC), 40
Confédération générale du logement (CGL), 213
Confédération générale du travail (CGT), 22, 38, 153, 155–57, 162, 247
Conseil national de la résistance, 97
Conseil national du patronat français (CNPF), 35, 36, 40, 44, 53 n 15
Conseil supérieur des hôpitaux, 109, 119–21
Conservative parties: and social expenditures, 65–67
Constitution of the Fourth Republic, 145
Corporatism, 223–24, 232–33, 235, 239–40, 242–47, 253–56
Council of State, 119

Crédit foncier de France (CFF), 189, 197–98, 201
Cresson, Edith, 244

Debré, Bernard, 120, 135–36
Debré, Michel: and education, 18; health policies of, 125–26, 136; on natalism, 165–66
Delors, Jacques: as advisor to Chaban-Delmas, 45, 246, 249; as Minister of Economy, 46; and neocorporatism, 240; as specialist on social policy, 170, 251
Delouvrier, Paul, 155
Democratic citizenship and social protection, 237, 254–56
Democracy: theories of, 232
Denmark, 60–64, 69, 70, 191
Deregulation of housing, 205–18
Derlin, Maurice, 130–31
De Swaan, Abram, 7–8
Devaquet, Alain, 128
Directorate of Social Action, 251
Directorate of the Treasury, 236
Disability insurance, 7
Divorce, 151, 158, 174, 182–83
Droit de dépassement, 100–101
Drug and alcohol treatment centers, 105, 107
Duclaud-Williams, Roger H., 189, 214
Dufoix, Georgina, 116, 120–21, 123, 179
Dupeyroux, Jean-Jacques, 170
Durkheim, Emile, 147–48, 235

Economic and Social Council, 183, 203
Economic growth and social policy, 68–70, 238
Education: expansion of, 21; higher, 18–19; and income distribution, 17–18; for parents, 183–84; pre-elementary, 24; secondary, 18, 24; and social equality, 17–19; and state-building, 21
Election: of 1951, 161; of 1965, 169; of 1962, 166; of 1978, 178; of 1981, 123, 127; of 1988, 140; to social security councils, 156–57
Employers: associations of, 235, 237–39, 245; housing contributions of, 198–99, 217; and social insurance, 7–8, 35, 47

Equality, 17–19, 232. *See also* Income distribution
European Community: economic effect of, 236–38; and French businessmen, 238–39; and French farmers, 238; and French housing, 229; and savings accounts, 217

Fabius, Laurent, 178, 181
Familialism, 10, 145–46, 159–60, 168
Familial vote, 152, 154
Families: changing conceptions of, 173, 182; legal definitions of, 158; traditional conception of, 158; types of, 148
Family allowances: administration of, 155–57; changing basis of, 168; expenditures for, 159–60; and income distribution, 16; origins of, 10; and poverty, 36; relative decline of, 174–75; socialist reform of, 23, 180–81; and wage levels, 156; for working mohers, 175–76
Family Code, 149–51, 154, 175
Family policy, 144–86; and housing, 161–63; origins of in France, 144–49; from 1918–1945, 149–52; in the Fourth Republic, 152–64; in the Fifth Republic, 165–85
Farmers: associations of, 238, 244; pension plans of, 23; and social security, 11, 46
Farm workers, 35
Faure, Maurice, 161–62, 164, 218, 220
Fédération des médecins de France (FMF), 129, 130, 137
Federation of Large Families, 149
Fédération nationale de solidarité (FNS), 41
Feminism, 154–55, 162, 169, 184
Fifth Republic: housing policy in, 165–85; social expenditure in, 74–83; social policies of, 1, 5, 237–38
Finland, 6, 60, 62–63
Fonds de solidarité pour l'emploi, 46
Fonds national de solidarité (FNS), 36
Fontanet, Joseph, 165
Fourth Republic: family policy under, 145, 152–64; ministerial stability in, 53; social expenditure in, 74–77, 81; social policies in, 10, 235–37
French Confederation of Christian Workers (CFTC), 161, 164

French Democratic Confederation of Labor (CFDT), 238
French Revolution, 97, 107
Front National, 28
Front Populaire, 11

Garbay, Michel, 121
Gaulle, Charles de: on birth rates, 153; on Europe, 166–67; on planning, 239; resignation of, 38–39; social expenditures of, 74–84; social policy of, 42–44
Gaullists: and interest groups, 237; and neo-corporatism, 240; and rights of women, 172; and social policy, 42; and solidarity, 97
General Confederation of Labor (CGT), 22, 38, 153, 162, 247
General Confederation of Labor-Force Ouvrière, 162
General Confederation of Small and Medium Firms (CGPME), 237–38
General Inspectorate of Social Affairs, 168
General Planning Commission. See Planning
Germany: development of social policy in, 5–7, 9; housing in, 191; postwar social policy in, 33–34, 37; social benefits in, 44; social expenditures of, 42, 60–64, 70
Gingembre, Léon, 238
Giroud, Françoise, 173
Giscard d'Estaing, Valéry: family policy of, 173–79; health policy of, 105, 123, 136–37; on rights of women, 172; social expenditures of, 23, 74–84; social reforms of, 44–45
Goodin, Robert E., 12
Grand bureau des pauvres de Paris, 3
Grandes écoles, 19
Grands corps, 98
Guesde, Jules, 9

Haby, René, 18
Hall, Peter, 21
Handicapped: aid to, 15, 97, 171, 193
Health care: for children, 163–64; complex organization of, 105; controlling costs of, 129–33; financing of, 124. See also Health policy
Health insurance: development of, 35, 43;

funding of, 98–99; and income distribution, 15; reimbursement levels of, 99. See also Health policy
Health policy, 94–143; of Chirac Government, 126–33; cost control in, 99–101, 105–11; growing consensus on, 140; origin and character of, 95–105; of Mitterrand governments, 123–28; and political parties, 136–40
Henri IV, 96
Hervé, Edmond, 119–21
High Commission on Population, 145, 149, 150, 178, 183
HLM. See Moderate Rent Housing
Home ownership, 188, 193, 194, 205, 222. See also Prêts aidés pour l'accession à la propriété (PAP)
Hospitals: administration of, 118–23; alternatives to, 254; beds in, 105, 107; cost controls over, 105–11; departmentalization of, 118–23, 139–40; private beds in, 125–27, 133, 135; in public sector, 96; staff of, 108. See also University Hospital Centers
Housing allowances, 193, 211
Housing policy, 187–231; in Britain, 188; in Chirac Government, 205–18; continuities in, 222–25, 228; and family policy, 161, 163, 177; financing of, 195–200; flexibility in, 228–29; history of, 189–91; in Mitterrand governments, 201–5, 218–22; redistributive effects of, 200–201; and tax subsidies, 193–95; in the U.S., 188. See also Rent control; Moderate Rent Housing; Housing subsidies
Housing rehabilitation, 193, 196, 209–11
Housing subsidies: for construction, 190–93, 195, 201, 205, 207–8; to individuals, 191–94, 204, 210–12, 216–17, 221–24, 226–27; for savings accounts, 190, 195–99, 201

Illegitimate children, 171–72
Immigrants, 26–28
Income distribution, 11–20, 26–27, 85–90
Incomes policy, 246, 255
Independent Republicans, 172
Industrialization and the welfare state, 2–5
Industrial policy, 248–49
Industrial workers, 234

INED. *See* National Institute of Demographic Studies
Inflation, 23
Inspection générale des affaires sociales (IGAS), 43
Institute of Childhood and the Family, 181
Insurance, private, 3
Interest rates, 203, 209–10, 217
Interministerial Delegation for the City, 252
Internat, 112–13, 141 n 5
Ireland, 60–64
Italy, 60–63

Jallade, Jean-Pierre, 12–14
Jamous, Haroun, 242
Japan, 5, 60, 62–63
Jaurès, Jean, 9
Jeanneney, J.-M., 43–44
Job training, 13, 27, 44, 241, 246, 249–50

Kervasdoué, Jean de, 106
King, Anthony, 2

Labor, 8–9. *See also* Trade unions
Labor management relations, 244, 246–47
Labor market, 249–50
Labour Party, 6, 43
Landlord associations, 202, 207
Landlords. *See* Rent control
Landry, Adolph, 149
Laroque, Pierre: as architect of welfare state, 21, 34; on centralization of social security, 38; as expert on social policy, 168, 236, 240, 251; on 1961 and 1967 reforms, 41–42
LeGrand, Julian, 12
Lembruch, Gerhard, 233
Lenoir, René, 170, 240
Le Pen, Jean-Marie, 26, 28, 140
Le Play, Fréderic, 9, 32
Liberalism, 3, 205–18, 234–35, 249, 252–54
Ligue de l'enseignement, 33
Ligue de prévoyance, 33
Livret A. *See* Housing subsidies, for savings accounts

Marchand, Jean, 130
Marriage law, 167, 171, 182–83

Mauroy, Pierre, 1, 178, 181
Mazey, Sonia, 201
Medical Charter, 95
Medical education, 101–3, 111–18, 128–29, 131, 139
Medicine. *See* Health insurance; Health policy; Hospitals; Physicians
Médecine libérale. See Physicians, in private practice
Méhaignerie, Pierre, 206–14, 218–19, 224
Mendès-France, Pierre, 162
Merchant marine, 35
Messmer, Pierre, 172
Millerand, Alexandre, 33
Minc, Alain, 253
Mine workers: health care of, 96; retirement age of, 48; social protection of, 7, 11, 22, 35, 234; strikes of, 246
Minimum Insertion Income (RMI), 13, 184, 250
Minimum wage, 52 n 8, 203
Ministry of Agriculture, 35, 44
Ministry of Education, 128
Ministry of the Family, 145
Ministry of Finance, 108, 241
Ministry of Health, 108, 115, 171
Ministry of Housing, 196
Ministry of Labor, 43, 149, 171
Ministry of the Rights of Women, 180, 184
Mitterrand, François, 1, 74–84, 105, 123–28
Moderate Rent Housing (HLM): and equality, 221; establishment of, 189; extent of, 163, 188, 190; funding of, 196–98, 214–16, 224, 228–29; organization of, 193; power of, 223; rehabilitation by, 209; sale of units by, 205, 207; tenant rights in, 200, 202
Montjoie, René, 170
Moore, Robert, 188
Morice, André, 157
Mothers: day of, 159; maternity benefits of, 157, 163, 177–78; rights of, 171–74
Mottin Report, 38
Mouvement républicain populaire (MRP). *See* Popular Republican Movement
Mutualité. See Mutual Societies
Mutualité sociale agricole (MSA), 35

Socialist Governments, French (*Cont.*)
179–85; and health policy, 123–28; and
housing policy, 201–5, 218–29; and minimum pensions, 16; and retirement policy,
35; social expenditures of, 54 n 21; social
policy of, 23–24; and unemployment compensation, 17; and the welfare state, 20
Socialist Party (PS): and education policy,
19–20; and family policy, 184; and health
policy, 105; and housing, 161, 219–20;
and neocorporatist model, 240; and social
policy, 23, 25–26, 39, 54 n 20
Socialist Party (SFIO), 152–53, 156
Social mobility, 17–19
Social policies: decentralization of, 250–52;
in the Fourth Republic, 235–37; in the
Fifth Republic, 237–38. *See also* Social
Security, Social welfare, and specific policy areas
Social protection. *See* Public insurance
Social Security: administration of, 22–23,
155; budget of, 165–66; expenditures for,
159–60; law of 1930 on, 10–11; taxes for,
12–13. *See also* Special welfare
Social structure and the family, 147
Social welfare: administration of, 43–44,
52 n 7; complexity of, 58–59; funding of,
46–50, 52 n 6; history of, 3, 32–51. *See
also* Social expenditure
Solidarity (*solidarité*), 10, 51, 97
Spain, 60–63
States General of Social Security, 132–33,
241
Steel industry, 248
Steel workers, 234
Stoffaes, Christian, 174
Stoléru, Louis, 174
Strikes of medical students, 115–16
Students, medical, 115–16
Study Commission on the Problems of the
Family, 165
Sullerot, Evelyne, 183
Surleau Report, 40
Sweden, 60–64, 69, 70
Switzerland, 5
Syndicat autonome des enseignants de méde-
cine (SAEM), 116, 136, 138–39
Syndicat national des cadres hospitaliers
(SNCH), 110–11, 138, 140

Syndicat national des médecins, chirurgiens,
spécialistes et biologistes des hôpitaux publics (SNAM), 116, 121

Tardieu, André, 11
Tax deductions for children, 16–17, 157–58
Tax subsidies for housing, 193–95, 207–8,
227
Teachers' unions, 235
Tenants. *See* Rent control
Tenant's associations, 202, 213
Terquem, Jean, 121
Thatcher, Margaret: housing policy of, 207,
225–27; market orientation of, 187, 205;
political strength of, 212; and the welfare
state, 24
Third Republic: housing policy in, 149–50;
resistance of to social legislation, 21; social
classes in, 234
Tiberi, Jean, 211
Trade unions: in administration of social se-
curity, 44; and social expenditures, 65–67;
and social insurance, 35–36, 233; on unemployment compensation, 43; weaknesses of, 245, 247; and the welfare state,
233. *See also* General Confederation of
Labor
Transfer payments, 87–88
Treaty of Rome, 238–39

UNAF. *See* National Union of Family Associations
UNCAF. *See* National Union of Family Allowance Funds
Unemployment, 27
Unemployment insurance: development of,
35–36, 43–44, 52 n 5, 241; and income
distribution, 17; in the 1970s and 1980s,
249–51; and pension funds, 49–50; socialist policy on, 46
Union des industries métallurgiques et minières (UIMM), 42
Union for the New Republic (UNR), 165
Union nationale autonome des nouveaux internes en médecine (UNANIM), 139
Union nationale des étudiants de France
(UNEF), 115

Union nationale des fédérations d'organismes d'HLM (UNFOHLM), 214
Union nationale interprofessionnelle pour l'emploi dans l'industrie et le commerce (UNEDIC), 35, 43, 52 n 5
United States: housing policy in, 188, 225–28; social expenditures of, 60, 62–63, 69; social policies of, 24–25, 41
University Hospital Centers (CHU), 105–6, 112, 126, 242

Veil, Simone, 45, 113, 175
Vichy regime: family policy of, 150–52, 158; and health policy, 124; social policy of, 36–37, 39
Vouchers. See Housing subsidies, to individuals

Welfare state: administration of, 36–41, 236; in Britain, 3, 6; causes of, 2–22; complexity of, 241–42; crisis of, 23–27; institutionalization of, 243–47; restructuring of, 247–54. See also Social welfare
Wilensky, Harold, 2, 3
Women: as physicians, 104; as a political issue, 169; rights of in marriage, 182–83; status of, 145–46, 151, 154–55, 158–62, 167, 169, 171–74, 180, 184; in the work force, 166–67
Workers' compensation, 96. See also Unemployment insurance
Workers' rights, 244–46
Wright, Gordon, 145

Zysman, John, 195